# how to open and operate a

# Restaurant

HOME–BASED BUSINESS SERIES

# how to open and operate a

# Restaurant

Arthur L. Meyer and Jon M. Vann

Guilford, Connecticut

Interior spot art licensed by Shutterstock.com

Editorial Director: Cynthia Hughes Cullen
Editor: Tracee Williams
Project Editor: Lauren Brancato
Text Design: Sheryl P. Kober
Layout: Justin Marciano
Diagrams: Lori Enik

Library of Congress Cataloging-in-Publication Data is available on file.

ISBN 978-0-7627-8189-8

Printed in the United States of America

10 9 8 7 6 5 4 3 2 1

This book is dedicated to those with the courage to follow their dreams of someday owning their own restaurants.

# Contents

# Acknowledgments

The authors wish to acknowledge our agent Rita Rosenkranz of the Rita Rosenkranz Literary Agency for her hard work in facilitating this project, Tracee Williams of Globe Pequot Press for her expert guidance in seeing the project through, and all of the editors at Globe Pequot Press for their talented input.

# Introduction

When considering opening a small business, you might think a restaurant is the perfect choice. Everyone has to eat several times every day. Statistics show that fewer and fewer meals are being cooked at home, and so the demand for prepared meals is immense. In addition to the required nutritional demands for eating, social gathering and celebrations bring people to restaurants all the time. Vacationing and traveling require every meal to be eaten out. Ethnic restaurants provide flavors that cannot be duplicated when meals are prepared at home and skilled chefs offer techniques that cannot be matched by the typical home cook. Restaurants offer the convenience of not having to shop and plan ahead; when you are hungry, you just go out and eat, and there is no messy cleanup afterward.

While this sounds perfect, the restaurant business can be quite a risky venture. There are so many skills needed to be a successful restaurateur that it is essential that you have extensive experience in the food service industry before setting out on your own. The less you know, the more you must rely on those who know more. This book can help in that regard. We have opened over twenty restaurants, all with excellent track records. Together we have drawn from over 80 years in the restaurant business, from busing tables and washing dishes to being executive chefs and owning our own restaurants and bakeries. We wrote this book because we wish we'd had a book like this when opening our first restaurant. There are quite a few books on opening and running a restaurant, but many of them focus on the business side of getting loans and writing business plans. There are specialized books on designing a restaurant, but few offer the practical knowledge of having worked for years in one, seeing firsthand what happens when you do not get the flow right, or when you arrange the equipment in an order that makes it difficult to get the food out quickly. Few who write these books understand the complexity of running a safe, sanitary facility where one can clean around heavy equipment and in corners. We are certified food managers and have taught safe food handling practices to restaurant employees and understand federal HACCP (Hazard Analysis Critical Control Points) guidelines. The public relies on you to serve wholesome, uncontaminated food and the government requires it. Food-borne illness and improperly handled food lead to lawsuits, food waste, and a bad reputation that will not be tolerated by the public.

Our experience comes in particularly handy with regard to equipment. You will need an ice machine, and you probably didn't need someone tell you this. But did you know that there are more than eight different forms and shapes of ice, and each has its own advantages and disadvantages? Do you know the best place to locate an ice machine? Should you lease it or buy it? While filtering the water to an ice machine is important, did you know to not use reverse osmosis (RO) filtering, even though it makes some of the purest water? How much ice will you need in a day? What size ice bin will you need? We answer these and many other questions you probably would not know to ask or even imagine are factors to consider, for every piece of equipment in a commercial kitchen.

There are so many types and sizes of restaurants that we cannot give specific guidelines for each. To that end, when amounts are needed for example and illustration, we use a virtual "3,000-square-foot restaurant that seats 100 guests (about 25 tables) serving lunch and dinner with different menus." We use this virtual restaurant when discussing fixed costs, such as leases; scheduling of labor for each shift; size of kitchen versus front of house; bar size; amounts of tableware, barware, and glassware to order; and services required to maintain this size facility.

Regardless of the size and type of restaurant you want to open, there is an order of tasks to follow to be sure you are always ready for the next stage or step. This book is structured chronologically for that reason. Each chapter should be studied and followed before proceeding to the next. Appendix A distills the information in each chapter to a chronological checklist for you to follow. Occasionally there can be tasks that make it difficult to decide which comes first, and often it really does not matter as long as they are accomplished before proceeding. You may have two locations that satisfy your criteria (with slightly different costs and advantages), and you may want to get financing before signing the lease with one of them, but your bank may want the location for the application to proceed.

The first chapters of this book relate the planning phase of your project. They include selecting a location, creating a concept, deciding on new construction or leasing, remodeling an existing restaurant or a space that has never been one. You will be told how to construct a business plan and be given ideas on how to finance your project. Along the way you will be alerted to licensing and permitting that can be initiated or is required in order to proceed. How to food cost your menu and how to construct a starting menu is discussed in detail. The second phase of your project involves creating architectural plans, the actual construction of the space, and ordering of equipment, supplies, tables and chairs, etc. to fill the space. Purveyors and suppliers of goods and services will be discussed. Finally it will be time to hire the entire crew and we give advice on how to conduct interviews, how to staff the various positions (whose duties are described in detail), how to write personnel manuals, and how to create a daily schedule of employees. Most importantly, you will be given advice on how to train the "front of house" (FOH) and the "back of house" (BOH), which train separately and learn the menu and how it is to be cooked, as well as the basic recipes needing to be prepared. The FOH and BOH are then brought together for final training, and you will be guided as to techniques of practicing "live fire" on friends and guests, readying for opening. Marketing strategies will be given to bring in clientele, maintain the clientele base, and bring in new guests on a regular basis.

Good luck in your quest for a rewarding and profitable business venture in the exciting and challenging world of food service and restaurant ownership.

# So You Want to Open a Restaurant?

You've heard that the failure rate for restaurants is very high. Studies have shown that between 25 and 30 percent close their doors after one year and by year three the number is 60 percent closure. There are many reasons why. This is a tough business and it requires a broad skill set to succeed. There is considerable financial obligation that can be difficult to sustain. To put things in your favor you should analyze the aspects that are most essential to having your dream of a successful restaurant come to fruition.

## A Self-Evaluation

Do you have experience in the restaurant business? How do you know that this is the business you want to run if you have never worked in a food-service establishment? It does not matter how often you eat out or where you have eaten. It makes no difference if all your friends say you are a great cook or make the best fried chicken they have ever tasted and that you should go into the restaurant business. Unless you have experience working in a restaurant, you really have no idea how one operates or how difficult every position is and what skills are needed for each job. The more positions you've worked, the easier it is to hire for those positions and get better employees, and the more you can fill in for an absent employee, whether it be running the dish machine, tending bar, or busing tables.

You must be well financed. A rule of thumb is to have enough money available to operate at a loss for one year. That is not to say that you will operate at a loss for that much time, but you must be realistic and not anticipate that you will be profitable in 3 months and could then use those profits to operate the restaurant. You may not be able to pay yourself a salary for quite a while (and remember that you have expenses beyond the restaurant—mortgage and car payments, for example). Underfinancing is the number one reason for not succeeding in a restaurant endeavor.

You must be organized. There are "millions" of things to keep track of during any business day. You should be good at multitasking. Problems tend to pile up and several will need to be addressed and tracked simultaneously. If you are the chef/cook as well, you must be able to handle a variety of dishes that need to be cooked at the same time, each with different cooking times, going to different tables, being picked up by the servers at just the right time so that their guests do not feel they are waiting too long or are being rushed through their meal. All dishes for the same table/ticket must come out together, all properly cooked and at the correct temperature. As the manager you will have to deal with scheduling and supervising employees, ordering goods, managing the money flow, keeping up with maintenance of the space, ensuring the quality of the food being cooked, and being compliant with health department codes and alcoholic beverage regulations.

How do you deal with stress? This is a stressful job and you must be personable at all times, both to your guests and your employees. "Losing it" when a crisis develops helps no one and you will lose the respect of your employees and lose your customers. Crisis management is key to running a successful restaurant, as crises develop all the time. Power outages, broken toilets, key personnel not showing up for their shifts, and missing deliveries of key ingredients are just a few of the problems that arise on a continuous basis. Often there is a "domino effect" where one small glitch in an otherwise smoothly running operation causes a cascade of problems. Murphy's Law could have been written for the restaurant business. When do you think the dish machine breaks? On a Monday morning when it can be conveniently fixed with little impact on that night's business or during the rush on a Saturday night when a repairman cannot come until the following Monday and dirty dishes are building up and the bar has run out of glasses? Can you cope with this kind of stress and do you have the personality to fit into the role of restaurant owner? A successful restaurateur wants to please others and make them feel comfortable and welcome and can never let on that a major disruption has just occurred.

Do you have the enormous amount of time required to own and operate a restaurant? Expect to put in 12-hour days on a nonstop basis, and typically up to 90 hours per week for the first year. Restaurants do not run themselves and you must be hands-on with every aspect. No one cares like you do and you cannot pay someone to care as you would want; your supervisors need to be supervised! Do you have outside obligations that require a good deal of your time? If you have a family, can they accept your absence as you spend most of your waking hours dealing with the restaurant? You will need their support.

A successful restaurant requires talent with regard to food. Someone has to cook the food—will that be you? If not you, then who will do it? Where will you find this person or persons? Do you know what good food is? You should have a palate that can recognize good flavor and taste. Even if you cannot cook, you must know what tastes good in the broadest sense, as hundreds of people, all with differing expectations and experiences with regard to food need to be pleased by the cooking at your restaurant. What kind of food will you offer? Will you rely on the recipes of others or will you be writing them yourself? Knowing what appeals to your guests is a key to a successful menu and successful recipes.

## A Reality Check

There is a joke about boat ownership that can be modified to having the experience of owning a restaurant. Stand over your kitchen sink and throw hundred-dollar bills into the garbage disposer.

If this chapter has made you feel uneasy and question your decision to open a restaurant, that's good. Don't expect to sit back and have others run the restaurant for you while you sit at the bar smiling, greeting your friends and buying them drinks. You must go into the venture with open eyes and realistic expectations. Identify your weaknesses so that you can compensate for them. Be confident and have the proper financial backing. Bring in or gain experience in a restaurant before opening one. Expect to put in long hours and to have to solve problems on a continuous basis. That being said, owning and operating a successful restaurant is extremely rewarding *because* it is so difficult to do. Positive reviews by the media and your guests reinforce your accomplishments. It is satisfying to please others, especially with great food, service, and ambience. There is an electricity to each day's opening of the doors, knowing how much could go wrong, but won't with your hard work and effort. Having a restaurant is like being on Broadway. Each day is like opening night . . . you only have one chance to get it right. But when you do, there is nothing more satisfying than sitting down at the end of a long day and realizing that you did it. Everyone left pleased with the food and the overall experience, the servers made good tips, and the kitchen was proud of what they produced.

There are many reasons why a restaurant fails. A few of these include poor location, overspending (over borrowing on construction, equipment, and design), failure to advertise and promote the business, too-high food or labor costs, and, of course, bad service. One thing that may not contribute? Food quality! Making good food does not guarantee success in the restaurant business.

These and other pitfalls will be addressed in subsequent chapters, from recommending separate bank accounts to immediately depositing money for taxes, to details on how to cost your menu to avoid loss of income and bad cash flow. We give advice as to the number of employees required to operate efficiently, avoiding payroll issues. Hiring methods and qualifications for management positions are given, as are training issues to avoid bad service. Location is addressed early in the book as it is essential that you locate in a space offering convenience, visibility, and a likelihood of filling your tables.

Soon you will have to begin making important decisions about your location, menu, type of service, size of space needed, and whether that space will be new construction or a remodeling. In order to proceed you need a concept to guide you through those important decisions. Who are your customers? What kind of food will you be serving? How do you envision the atmosphere in the dining room? In order to pin down these details, some decisions need to be made in the broadest sense about the type of restaurant you will have. You need a concept. The restaurant you will operate will be mostly based on three ideas—the style of service, the type of restaurant, and the type of construction or structure itself.

## The Concept

Consider the **style of service**. It often defines who your customers are. Generally the categories are as follows:

- *Fine Dining*—Fine dining or "upscale" implies the best ingredients cooked by the most talented chefs available. The menu is usually creative and the dishes are assembled with particular care and skill with techniques that require highly experienced personnel. Service is impeccable and everything from the chairs to the water glasses to the utensils is of the highest quality. The atmosphere is the result of talented interior design. Menu pricing will be considered expensive.

- *Casual Dining*—Most "sit-down" restaurants with servers taking your order and delivering your food fall under this broad category. Expectations are lower than for fine dining. Tablecloths are optional, and the flatware may be more utilitarian than stylish. Menus are more familiar and ingredients are not particularly exotic or expensive. Interior designs are simple and can be quite modest. Menu pricing will be considered reasonable.

- *Self-Service*—In self-service restaurants the guest is expected to walk up to a counter to place the order. When the order is ready the food may be delivered to the table or the guest may have to pick up the order at a counter or along a line, as in a buffet or cafeteria. Usually a name is asked for or a number assigned to the order. Guests usually pay when they place the order and may be expected to dispose of their trash at meal's end. Disposable utensils, cups, and plates are common. Typically these restaurants have low menu pricing. Many of the restaurants in this category, but not all, are called "fast-food" establishments.

- *Drive-In/Drive-Through*—These restaurants, usually with a drive-up window, cater to guests in their vehicles, and the food is taken home to eat. Alternately a server may bring the order to the car ("car hop") and guests will eat in the vehicle. Drive-through windows are sometimes a part of self-service operations.

- *Trailers and Food Trucks*—Not considered in this book, but an up-and-coming way to open a restaurant with a much lower monetary investment and simplified menu, food trailers and food trucks offer flexibility in location, a low start-up cost, and provide opportunity for talented cooks and idea persons to own their own restaurant. Labor costs are low, inventory is kept to a minimum, and fixed costs are quite reasonable.

Excluding fine dining, your restaurant may offer delivery service, and in the case of a pizzeria, your business may be based on delivery service. As well, you may offer to-go service with special accommodation for this type of order, such as reserved parking for pick-up orders, a pick-up window, or separate pick-up counter, and by accepting orders by e-mail, website, or texting.

There is a variety of **types of restaurants** to consider that will both overlap with the above styles and possibly dictate the style. They include seafood restaurants, steakhouses, theme restaurants, cafes, bistros, diners, 24-hour restaurants, buffets and cafeterias, pizzerias, health food and vegetarian restaurants, family dining restaurants, breakfast places, coffee houses, salad bars, bars and grills, sports bars, brew pubs, delicatessens, burger joints, sandwich shops, ethnic restaurants, and franchises of all types, including "corporate" dining (chain casual dining establishments).

## Formulating Your Concept

What kind of food will you be serving? Some of the types of restaurants are self-explanatory, such as steak houses, burger joints, sandwich shops, delicatessens, pizzerias, and seafood restaurants. Diners, 24-hour places, and family dining usually serve typical and/or creative American fare, as do cafeterias. Breakfast items, also typically American, are offered in restaurants that are usually open only for breakfast and lunch. Bars and grills, brew pubs, and sports bars have a strong beer and liquor component, along with sandwiches, burgers, and simply prepared entrees. They often have extensive appetizer and snack menus to complement the bar. Ethnic restaurants feature the foods of countries other than America, and American food has its subcategories of the regions of the South, Southwest, Cajun and Creole, barbecue, soul food, Tex-Mex, "modern American," and fusion, among others. Typical ethnic food restaurants feature the cuisines of Afghanistan, Africa, Argentina, Belgium, Brazil, Cambodia, the Caribbean, Chile, China, Colombia, Cuba, El Salvador, Eastern Europe, Ethiopia, France, Germany, Greece,

Guatemala, Honduras, India, Indonesia, Italy, Japan, Korea, Lebanon, Malaysia, the Mediterranean, Mexico, Middle East, Morocco, Nepal, Persia (Iran), Peru, the Philippines, Puerto Rico, Russia, Scandinavia, Singapore, Spain, Thailand, Turkey, Venezuela, and Vietnam. Many of these restaurants are owned and run by families from these regions of the world, and provide an avenue for assimilation into the American economy and lifestyle.

## Expert Tip

In addition to this book we recommend that you obtain a book with restaurant forms, worksheets, and checklists to help you get organized. An excellent reference is *The Encyclopedia of Restaurant Forms* (Brown, 2004). The Internet has many free forms for downloading. An excellent site is www .allfoodbusiness.com/forms.php. Use a search engine, typing in "free restaurant forms," and many sites will be listed. Highly recommended is a pay site called www.restaurantowner.com. It addresses every aspect of opening and running a successful restaurant with features on food-cost control, spicing up your menu, plus high-quality downloadable forms. Their print magazine is worth the price alone. If you can afford it, hiring a restaurant consulting firm can be a savior. They can do as little or as much of the work in getting you open as you can budget. And www.restaurantandbakeryconsultants.com would be an excellent starting point in your search for the best help with your venture.

## Ask Yourself Questions

To formulate your concept, ask yourself the following questions. Where do you like to eat? What kind of restaurant makes you feel comfortable and want to return again and again? If you cook, what are your strengths and favorite dishes to prepare? What types of restaurants are already established in the location where you are thinking of opening? What price range do you envision for your restaurant? What hours of operation do you think fit best into your plans—dinner only, all three meals, breakfast only, breakfast and lunch, lunch and dinner, 24-hour? Are you planning to build new construction or is a strip-center rental more appealing (and affordable)? Do you want to take over an existing restaurant space or possibly remodel a retail space and adapt it as a restaurant? What size restaurant are you envisioning? (Small restaurants seat fewer than forty guests and very large restaurants have over 150 seats.) From a practical standpoint, it is difficult to make enough money with fewer than thirty seats, and it requires a lot of effort, labor, and finances to make a very large restaurant break even, based on fixed expenses and labor needs.

### Alcoholic Beverage Service

Finally, you must decide on alcoholic beverage service. Will you have it at all? If not, your liquor licensing bureau may allow your guests to bring in their own beer and wine, should you allow it. This may not be an option in some municipalities. You can charge a nominal "corkage fee" for opening the wine and providing wine glasses if you so desire. Some regions are "dry" and do not allow the sale of alcoholic beverages at all. If allowed, the regulations vary from state to state and city to city. Often there are two types of licenses—beer and wine only, or all alcoholic beverages, including mixed drinks. The former license is often much cheaper and has fewer regulations and requires less bookkeeping. In some states there are a fixed number of licenses available, based on population. The license will define the hours that alcoholic beverages may be served in your restaurant, especially at the end of the evening. For an additional fee, a "late hours" permit may extend the closing time by several hours, especially advantageous on the weekend and/or if you have a music scene. An "off site" permit could allow you to serve alcoholic beverages when catering at locations other than your restaurant. Check with your state alcoholic beverage commission or ask a restaurant or bar manager in the location you plan to operate as to how it all works. The paperwork to obtain a license can be quite a chore and you should start the process as soon as possible. Often a bond must be posted and criminal background check done on the licensee. The sale of alcoholic beverages in a restaurant is one of the most profitable parts of its operation, so consider this carefully (and promptly).

## Location

Where will you open your restaurant? You've heard the three rules of real estate (location, location, location), but what makes a good location for your restaurant? Not any restaurant, but *your* restaurant. Compromises will have to be made. Not everyone can afford the rent at an upscale strip center in a great neighborhood, and your menu and concept may not be appealing to that demographic anyway. Everything is interconnected—your menu, your finances, your experience and talent. Cities often have development zones where they try to bring in new ventures to revitalize a neighborhood and make it a destination that attracts consumers. There can be tax incentives, low rents, and leases that favor the lessee. Expect business to be slow at first, but often there are rewards for those who can weather the storm and survive the slow times. Look for a location that is already a destination, where there are motivations that draw people there. Other complementary restaurants (not another pizzeria, if that's what you intend on opening) in a particular location can be good for business in all of the restaurants, including yours. (Have you noticed that car dealerships, usually a mix of small cars, trucks, and SUVs, are all lined up next to each other on the highway?) Busy shopping areas, movie theaters, and music and other entertainment venues are all destinations that draw people to an area, and clean, vital neighborhoods are destinations as well. Be careful about a location where people are just passing through to a destination. Why would they stop when they will be stopping soon to take in a movie? However, "it's on the way" may be a good thing if the site is convenient and accessible. If your menu is focused on dinner, locating in the downtown district of a city may not be a good thing. Would you drive home, change clothes, and drive back to where you spent the entire day? On the other hand, if breakfast and lunch are your strengths, downtown may be a perfect location.

## Type of Construction

Location is dictated by the **type of construction** you will engage. If you are planning on a new building from the ground up, older and well-developed areas may not have an empty lot (or a demolition project), the lot may not be zoned appropriately or have the proper dimensions for your operation, or it may be just too expensive. Remodeling an existing restaurant space can save the most money. A "grandfathered" existing space allows a business to operate under old, out-of-date regulations. This may be good for you to avoid expensive updates to the newest codes. However, any updating or any changes made will trigger all sorts of new regulations or zoning changes. It is not easy to appeal zoning regulations so be sure that your location is zoned for your business. Another thing to keep in mind is the original footprint of a structure, should you be doing an extensive remodel. If you maintain the original footprint, it is a "remodel." If you change it, it is "new construction" and the codes are quite different for these two scenarios. New lease space is another way to go, but is more costly than a remodel. Often the lessor will provide an allotment to finish out the space, but it is usually much less than needed. It is the second most costly way to construct your restaurant, ground-up being the most costly. However, equity is built from ownership, should you have the finances.

## Parking and Accessibility

Locations must be easy to access and there should be adequate parking. The number of parking spaces required by ordinance is often linked to the number of seats in your restaurant. In neighborhoods that are in transition, which now allow restaurants, there may be resistance from those residents still living in that neighborhood who do not want the extra traffic and inconvenience of your customers parking in front of their houses. Valet parking can often get around parking constraints, where you contract with a church, bank building, or parking lot that does not operate during evenings and weekends for their clients. Accessibility to your restaurant is very important. It is not a good idea to be on a one-way street or on an access road to a highway, as there is usually no convenient way to turn around if they miss your driveway or entrance the first time approaching the restaurant. Be sure your location's zoning allows for adequate signage to make your business easily identifiable.

## Other Determining Factors

Cities and towns often have barriers that divide the city between more and less desirable neighborhoods. Highways and railroad tracks are the most common barriers. It may be that on the north side of the interstate there are many nice locations that have shopping, other restaurants, and entertainment venues, but just on the south side, on the same road, it is run-down and starting to decay. There may be opportunities for very reasonable rents here and staying close to the barrier may entice customers to cross the barrier. This is the process of gentrification and you may be able to join in on this trend in your city, the earlier the better. There are instances where your location will define your menu, its pricing, and seating capacity (see the section on menu considerations). Very small towns do not offer much in the way of a variety of locations from which to choose. Unlike cities, small towns tend to be more homogenous and you may have to adapt your plans to this reality. A town of two thousand people cannot support a large restaurant and the demographics of the town will probably affect your pricing and the type of dishes offered. If you are leasing space, realize the city or town you select may have very different lease costs (see section on construction/site development). As examples, in New York City expect to pay more than $100/square foot/year, which comes out to $25,000 per month for the lease on a 3,000-square-foot space. In Houston, Texas, it may be around $25/square foot/year, or $6,250 per month for the same space. In Billings, Montana, it could cost $12/square foot/year, which is $3,000 per month for the building lease. Upscale sections of all of the above areas could add $20 to $50 per square foot/year.

Keep in mind, though, that if you are offering something really special, unique, or of extremely high quality, location may be less important, as people will seek out a rare or inimitable meal ("If you build it, they will come"). An example is a restaurant that was owned by an extremely talented and locally known chef whose dining room sat only about thirty guests. His restaurant was about a 1-hour drive from the nearest city with a population of over 500,000, in the middle of "nowhere." His restaurant was booked full every night and it was difficult to get a reservation within a 3-week window. Another example is a catfish restaurant, about 20 miles from a large city that was packed every night because they had a catfish pond by the restaurant and went out with a net to catch your fish when you ordered it. It wasn't a fancy place; they used paper plates and napkins, and you sat at picnic tables. Their menu was limited to just a few items, mostly fried. They sold over three hundred dinners every night, and you had to wait for a table if you didn't get there early.

Location can be seen on a macro scale that is in the broadest sense the state and city or town to locate your restaurant, as well as on a micro scale, regarding where within a specific city or town to locate. Considerations made on the macro scale must include such important things as proximity to where you live, talent pool, and availability of raw materials. Whether or not you are the head chef or cook, are there sufficient experienced cooks living in your location to support your kitchen and menu? Will there be a pool of servers from which to select qualified waitpersons and bartenders? Will there be surcharges for delivery of basic goods because you are not near a big city or a large highway? Are specialized purveyors available to keep your ethnic restaurant supplied (a Mexican restaurant in North Dakota, for example)?

Climate can affect location choices as well. In cold climates, are the roads often impassable due to storms? People tend to stay at home when it's cold and driving is difficult. If in a cold climate are there winter-based resorts nearby that attract visitors? Locations that are warm year-round often attract vacationers from cold climates and allow residents to get out more to shop, engage in sports, and generally focus on being out of the house more (which means dining out more often).

Location and utilities are interconnected. Does your municipality offer natural gas for your range and sauté station? Will you need to have propane for your gas needs? In cold climates propane is difficult to deal with as pressure becomes insufficient to use in the equipment. All-electric kitchens can be very expensive to operate and many chefs do not like cooking on electric ranges. Will you be connected to a municipal sewer/wastewater system? If not you will have to deal with septic systems and all of the problems associated with them. In very remote locations you will have to pay for power lines to be run to your site. Climate, location, and utilities are linked together. In hot climates a large electricity demand for air-conditioning is a reality. In cold climates heating a large space can be quite expensive.

### Remember That Location . . .

1. Affects the menu, both in the amount you can charge for a dish as well as what style of food you can serve.
2. Can dictate the size of the restaurant and whether alcoholic beverages can be served (and what types).
3. Often affects the operating hours of the restaurant.
4. Contributes a large percentage of your fixed costs through lease and construction costs.
5. Affects and dictates utility service.

Once you select your location, drive to it from several areas of town to see how accessible it really is. A famous chain serving gourmet hamburgers made a serious mistake with regard to location. In spite of constant national advertising the restaurant had to close due to difficult access to the business. Although adjoining a thriving shopping center, its parking lot was not connected to it, forcing diners to leave the shopping center and take a one-way access road along a major highway. There was no way to turn around if you missed the driveway and when traveling from the opposite direction you were on a one-way access road separated by six lanes of busy highway. You would have to U-turn at a major intersection that was always backed up. The moral is that there was no amount of money spent in advertising that could bring in the number of guests to make this famous-named restaurant successful.

## Naming Your Restaurant

As Juliet said to Romeo, "What's in a name? That which we call a rose by any other name would smell as sweet." The most important thing about naming your restaurant is that it has a name! Documents and forms will require one, so it's best to choose one earlier rather than later. There really are no guidelines, but common sense dictates a few things. It should be easy to pronounce and spell, and easy to remember. It may suggest the style of cuisine being served such as "Bob's Steakhouse" or "Johnnie's Delicatessen," or the ethnicity of the cuisine like "China Palace" or "Trattoria Romano." Naming a restaurant after a relative can give a comforting feeling to your clientele, such as "Nona's Table" or be trendy by naming it after the former business that occupied the space you are now in, such as "The Bicycle Shop." Addresses and zip codes make interesting names ("Twelfth Street Bistro"). Regions of town ("Southside Grill") work well. Single names are effective and can be stylish and upscale, such as "Tony's" or "Olivia's." Avoid trademarked restaurant names, even if your name is Wendy or McDonald.

## Logos

For many companies a logo is quite important. While not absolutely necessary for a restaurant, an attractive logo can be an efficient advertising method for brand recognition and can be placed on exterior signage, the menu, uniforms, meal tickets, and paper goods. Often a nice typeface or font for the restaurant name is sufficient. Logos can be expensive to have designed and embroidered on clothing and incorporated into your tableware. It adds to printing expenses as well. You may want to wait until you have good cash flow to incorporate a logo into all of these objects.

Fill in the blanks below before proceeding to the next chapter.

Type of restaurant (diner, sports bar, etc.)_____

Style of service (fine dining, casual, etc.)_____

Type of food (seafood, sandwiches, etc.)_____

Price range (expensive, moderate, reasonable, cheap)_____

Location (what city/town?)_____

Hours of operation (dinner only, 24 hours, etc.)_____

Size of restaurant (small < 40; medium < 90, etc.)_____

Alcoholic beverage service (beer/wine, full, etc.)_____

Construction (new/ground-up, remodel, etc.)_____

Restaurant name _____

Logo selected?_____

Having filled in the above, you are ready to make the important decisions that will be set out for you to make in chapter 3.

Your menu is the heart of your restaurant. What you offer and the prices you charge will define it. Writing the menu should be a carefully thought out process involving such things as what people want to eat and how much they expect to pay as opposed to how much you have to charge. A fixed menu should have easily obtainable ingredients that do not vary much in price with seasons; a seasonal menu varies with what is most plentiful and reasonably priced at the time. A fixed menu can take advantage of seasonal goods by offering "specials" not listed on the menu. Your menu defines the equipment needs and the space required to produce the food, as well as the type and amount of storage needed.

### Restaurant Needs and Design

It may surprise you as to how early in the planning process a menu needs to be formulated. It does not have to be the actual opening menu, but should be close to what it will be. The menu will define the type of cooking equipment you will need. If you are opening a diner-style restaurant featuring breakfast, you will need a lot of griddle (flat top) space for eggs, pancakes, breakfast meats, and omelets. These items require a lot of refrigeration for raw materials, handy to the cooking space. A steak house, on the other hand, will require a lot of broiler space and very little griddle area, and possibly a lot of walk-in space to age and store bulk meats. If you will be doing a lot of sautéing you will need quite a few burners.

Regardless, all equipment requires specific gas, electrical, water connection, venting, and drainage needs, and the total utility demand must be available to the construction engineer prior to breaking ground, or knocking down the first wall in a remodel. Outlets, breakers, and gas fittings need to be on the architect's plans and you need to know what equipment you will need and where it will go. Architect plans must be submitted before any permits are issued, so all of this must be decided very early on. The HVAC people need to know the specific equipment to calculate the length of vent hood required and to accommodate for "make-up air," the air needed to replace the large amount being drawn from the kitchen by the vent hood, and to do air-conditioning and heating capacities for the entire restaurant.

Having a menu means that you know what goods need to be purchased and how and where it will all be stored. A pizza parlor needs a lot of dry storage space for 100-pound sacks of flour, cases of #10 cans of tomato products, and paper and cardboard goods. A seafood restaurant, on the other hand, needs a large amount of quality refrigeration that is easily accessible and separate from other refrigeration needs. Walk-in refrigerators take up a lot of space and have important parts that may be remotely installed. If your restaurant will be serving alcohol, most states require separate storage that is secure and lockable. If beer is served from taps, the large kegs take up a lot of walk-in space.

Obviously you cannot do a start-up cost analysis without knowing the equipment expense, and the equipment is defined by the menu. Some equipment is better leased than purchased and these things must be decided early in the planning stage. You will have to qualify financially for a lease, so this involves your business plan and financials. Some specialized equipment may have a long lead time from ordering to delivery, as will fabrication of counters, shelving, and equipment stands. Your menu impacts the location of these counters and stands, which may not necessarily be of standard measure.

The menu also highlights any special foodstuffs that must be allocated and a reliable and steady source for them is essential. A seafood house in Kansas will have a more difficult time obtaining black cod than will a similar restaurant in Seattle, and by seeking suppliers for the goods you will need for your menu, you may realize that it is not practical to offer such items on a regular basis. Purveyors, when brought into the project early, can help formulate a menu that is sustainable and offers only the highest quality ingredients. Some ingredients are better prepared by one technique rather than another, which can influence the amount and type of equipment needed. For really specialized items, your purveyor may need months to find a steady and reliable source. Imported ingredients are such items. Ingredients vary from manufacturer to manufacturer, so if you have used and want to continue to use a specific brand of San Marzano tomatoes from Italy in your upscale Italian trattoria, your local purveyor will need time to find an outlet that their company can deal with on a regular basis. You may be required to order large quantities in order to make it worth their effort, and this may have an influence on the allocation of storage space. It is not unusual for a restaurant to be required to purchase their imported cheeses in complete wheels, which may weigh 75 to 100 pounds each.

Before starting your menu, pick a food purveyor that you can work with. Call several of the national and regional companies (see chapter 8 and refer to your local Yellow Pages) and speak with a sales representative who seems interested in having your business. An attentive sales representative is indispensable in providing suggestions, giving prices, and offering samples.

Who is going to cook your menu? If you are in a large, food-oriented city, there are cooks and chefs at all levels of ability to cook whatever you want to have. In other areas this is not usually the case, however, so keep this in mind when you decide on the dishes offered. What skill levels are required to consistently produce that menu item? You can train almost anyone to make a sub sandwich, but to cook a swordfish fillet perfectly, every time, regardless of how busy they are, requires a high level of skill sets, especially if complicated sauces are also required. Turnover is very high in the restaurant business and no one can work 7 days a week, so more than one person needs to be able to cook the menu you write. Keep the menu items simple and easy to prepare, so that your workforce can easily be trained to provide consistency and quality.

### Pricing Your Menu

You will need to decide the price range of your menu, which depends on your location, guests' expectations, style and type of food, and the competition. The number of items you offer has an impact on operational costs. A menu with a lot of items requires larger inventory, additional storage space, both dry and refrigerated, more skillful employees, and allows for more potential waste and spoilage. Recipes that require many ingredients and careful preparation with many steps also impact operational costs. Keep things as simple as possible! A good way to start would be to determine your "PPA" or price per person average, which is the average amount, in dollars, that each guest will spend. You can then consider how that total will be divided up by the way you offer your menu. Will you have appetizers? Does the salad come with the entree? What about side dishes? Do fries come with the burger or are they a separate menu item? Generally you can sell fries separately for more than when included in a basket, and the burger price seems lower as well when offered on its own, often encouraging the guest to order fries on the side. On the other hand, including a small dinner salad with a dinner entree can make your guests feel as though they are getting a lot for their money.

If you're the future owner of a small, neighborhood Italian restaurant in a middle-class neighborhood, you may decide that a PPA of $20 for dinner, less alcohol, seems reasonable. Try to keep the price of entrees between 50 and 75 percent of this average and your entrees will range between $10 and $15. Appetizers, soups, and desserts should then be about 25 percent or around $5. Most diners will not order something from every category, and they do not have to in order to meet your PPA. Remember this is an average, so one guest spending $14 (for an entree with salad and iced tea) is countered by another guest spending $26 (for an appetizer, entree with salad, and dessert with coffee).

As an example of costing a menu item, let's assume you want to open a casual hamburger-based restaurant with a fixed menu. Beef prices do not vary much with the seasons and this is a good place to start. Patties can be pre-formed and frozen or delivered pre-formed and fresh; bulk freshly ground beef can be hand-formed, or you can hand-trim, grind, and form your meat from large cuts of beef. Labor is low and spoilage not an issue with frozen patties, but quality is often low as well. Grinding your own meat will produce the highest quality, but involves high labor cost. What size patties will you use? What ratio of meat to fat will be used? All of these decisions lead to the selling price on your menu and what your menu will say to the public about your restaurant. If quality is most important then the selling price is dictated by this. As selling price becomes more important, it will dictate the quality and portion size of your product. Guests intuitively use a combination of quality and price as "perceived value." A 6-ounce burger made from hand-ground sirloin with premium toppings and a house-baked bun might be perceived at $8.95 a better value than a 4-ounce frozen burger on a standard bun for $4.95.

If price is most important, then find a way to make the $4.95 burger as good as it can be within the parameters of food cost (developing a unique seasoning mix to shake on a cooking hamburger patty can enhance flavor without incurring much food cost). When you allow the quality to dictate price, decide on the particular ingredients that you want to have and make the hamburger exactly as you want it to look and taste. Then calculate the food cost. For the 6-ounce hand-ground sirloin burger, you cost the product at $2.70. Assuming a 30 percent food cost, you would have to sell it for about $9. For the hamburger that has to sell for $4.95, first apply the 30 percent food cost and compute $1.50. You have a total of $1.50 to work with in order to fit into that price, and you can discuss with your purveyor the options you have to meet that cost. One national purveyor has options ranging from $0.49 to $0.80 per 4-ounce patty, depending on several factors, including packaging, quantity, and percentage of meat to fat (usually 75/25 to 90/10).

So many things are interrelated that you may want to do some rough calculations to see where you are at with respect to menu pricing. There are many formulas out there to use but to simplify things, try these two rules of thumb.

- First multiply your total square footage by $225 and this should approximate the sales required per year to break even. This multiplier assumes you are not in the one of the highest-end markets, opening an upscale restaurant, but an average restaurant in an average city. Assume you have a restaurant that seats 100 with 3,000 square feet of total space. You will need $675,000 in annual sales or about $56,250 per month to break even. If your PPA is $20 then about 100 guests or "covers" per day are needed, based on 28 days per month.

- A second calculation involves your monthly fixed costs (see "Estimating Monthly Fixed Costs") and the net percent profit. If your fixed costs are $8,000 per month (a low figure) and you have a 15 percent net profit (a high number) of total sales, the calculation yields a monthly sales of $53,000 to cover these fixed expenses, which comes to ninety-five covers per day. In either case you need to almost fill your restaurant every day to break even. Every restaurant has slow days, and if you are half full on a Monday night, you will need to compensate for this with an additional forty to fifty covers on another night. On a positive note, many successful restaurants fill all of their tables twice and sometimes three times on a weekend evening. Realize that for this example the restaurant is only open for dinner. Adding lunch to a restaurant is an excellent way to boost profits, as fixed costs are just that, regardless of the hours of operation. A less optimistic scenario would be about $10,000 in fixed cost and 10 percent net profit, which comes to $100,000 in sales per month. The industry guideline is that fixed costs should fall between 6 percent to 10 percent of gross sales.

Location and clientele also dictate menu prices and offerings. Consider the difference between a hamburger restaurant across from a high school or college compared to one in an upscale shopping center. Expect higher volume, faster turnover, and having more affordable prices when students are your primary customers. For the casual shopper in an upscale neighborhood, more sophisticated, higher quality, and healthier ingredients are expected, along with a more leisurely pace while dining. Your location also impacts the menu by the monthly lease or mortgage cost. Greater sales are needed to overcome additional fixed costs, all other things being equal.

## Estimating Monthly Fixed Costs

_____Rent/lease

_____Loan payments

_____Equipment leases

_____Fixed salaries + taxes

_____Bookkeeping services

_____Legal/professional fees

_____Utilities (gas, electric, water, wastewater)

_____Insurance

_____Website, phone, Internet

_____Office supplies, postage, shipping

_____Janitorial/maintenance

_____

_____Total fixed costs

## Writing Your Menu

When constructing your menu, which may include appetizers, soups, salads, entrees, and/or desserts, be sure to survey the market by visiting similarly priced restaurants in your area. If everyone is offering cheesecake for dessert, you may want to consider an alternative. There are many high-quality products offered by your food purveyor if you do not want to (or cannot) bake, but there are only so many distributors that service an area and you don't want to serve the same product as your competitors.

Make sure your menu is balanced and has broad appeal to a wide range of tastes. Unless it's "calamari" with marinara sauce, offering "squid" is probably not a good idea. Liver, and organ meat in general, has limited appeal as well. In addition to balancing the ingredients of your menu, also balance the method of preparation. Too many fried foods limit healthy choices for the public and overloads one of your cooking stations in the kitchen. Foods can be steamed, sautéed, poached, grilled, roasted/baked, braised or broiled as well as fried. Regardless of ingredients or cooking method, portion size is significant in encouraging guests to order several categories from your menu. If you have very filling appetizers in generous proportion, you are encouraging guests to skip the entree and possibly just order a salad to accompany. Likewise if entrees are overly large, they will skip ordering an appetizer or dessert. Don't be skimpy on your portions, but consider a reasonable amount that is nourishing and has perceived value, but is not overly large so as to discourage ordering from other parts of your menu.

When writing your menu, make the descriptions appealing and enticing and try to include as much information as to ingredients and method of preparation. The guest will then be able to decide without having to ask a server much in the way of how it is prepared and what is in the dish. If you are serving red snapper in the style of Veracruz, Mexico, then "Red Snapper Veracruz" does not provide enough information and assumes the guest knows what that means. In addition there are always variations to a dish like this. You can keep the "Veracruz" and explain how it's prepared: "Red Snapper Veracruz—sautéed fresh Gulf red snapper topped with a spicy mixture of olives, chiles, tomatoes, and onions" or just: "Sautéed Red Snapper with a Spicy Tomato Sauce of Olives, Chiles, and Onions." Don't get too carried away by trying to state every ingredient in the recipe. Eight to ten entrees should be enough to start your menu.

Having variety in preparation methods and in ingredients goes for appetizers as well. This category can be particularly profitable, as the portions are small (but flavor should be big) and this is a good place to be creative in utilizing leftovers and low inventory. You may not have enough shrimp on hand for tonight's entree or you need to use them up before expiration. Here is a perfect place to use them. Add a unique dipping sauce, or top them in a casserole with sauce and melted cheese. Adding some crabmeat and sherry to a prepared artichoke dip from a purveyor is simple and can increase your PPA and make the dip special and unique to your menu. To start, try offering four appetizers, keeping it simple. By the way, appetizers are a good way to stimulate drink sales, as a properly trained server will recommend an appetizer with a cocktail order.

Consider a soup category for your menu. One or two offerings should be enough and this category is another way to utilize leftovers and small inventory. If two soups seem right, have one of them a fixed offering and the other a "soup du jour." Leftover rice can be added to chicken stock and a few vegetables. Too much broccoli in the walk-in? Make cream of broccoli soup. Soups can be made in bulk with low labor cost and big flavor. Adding some spices and herbs to a leftover soup can turn it into a "Southwestern Chowder." Again, your purveyor may have excellent prepared soups that you can tailor to your menu with some simple additions and seasonings.

Many diners have a sweet tooth and dessert can boost PPA. Your purveyor carries several levels of quality of prepared and frozen desserts, so consider this source as a low labor option to baking your own. However, "homemade" is an appealing addition to a menu description, should you have the ability, space, and/or the time. Adding a homemade sauce, fresh fruit, a scoop of ice cream, or a dollop of real whipped cream can customize and elevate a purveyor-supplied product. Two desserts, one being chocolate of some form, should be enough to start.

If you are open for lunch and dinner, will you have the same menu for both? Typically sandwich shops, burger joints, delicatessens, ethnic restaurants, and such have the same menu throughout the day. Restaurants that have dinner PPAs over $15 will probably need a separate lunch menu with a more moderate PPA. Instead of a separate lunch menu, consider having "lunch specials" as an insert or table tent to accompany the dinner menu (which can be ordered from during lunch). Restaurants that are open all day can have a breakfast menu, with a separate menu that combines lunch and dinner. Some will serve breakfast all day, and often have just one menu for the entire day, as many diners do. To have one menu and limit the service of breakfast a simple statement of "Breakfast served until ____" can suffice.

The menu that you hand your guests does not have to be fancy. Using your laser printer and a clear plastic sleeve keeps printing cost down and allows you to change prices or add/delete items on a daily basis if you wish. There are plenty of attractive fonts and quality papers to use. Keep in mind that the menu should be readable, and black type on white paper offers excellent contrast and simple fonts are most readable. For (daily) specials, consider adding an insert to the menu or a tabletop tent. A "specials board" is often hard to read, poorly lit, angled so few guests have line of sight, and often handwritten and illegible. Avoid having your server recite the specials, as most people do not remember the first item after hearing the description of the third one.

### Recipes and How to Write Them

Food is what it's all about in the restaurant business and the food you serve should be tasty with a lot of flavor. Having recipes that are delicious and reasonably easy to prepare are the heart of your business. Since you have already come up with a concept and a rough idea of your menu, you will need recipes for each item on your menu. If you've been a professional cook, you probably have a file from which to draw ideas. If you are hiring a chef, he or she will have files, but not necessarily on the specific recipes you will need. Regardless of the source, recipes will need to be adjusted, modified, cooked over and over, and checked for flavor before being incorporated into your kitchen. Recipes from home (your mom makes the best meat loaf) need to be expanded to serve many more than her recipe intended and simple multiplication does not always work, especially with salt, herbs, and spices. The book *Professional Cooking, Trade Version* is an industry standard and has hundreds of basic recipes written in volumes appropriate for restaurant kitchens. The Internet is an excellent source and there are websites for professional chefs that also have recipes scaled for professional kitchens. An excellent start is at Starchefs.com. Trade journals, such as *Food Arts*, are also a good resource for professional recipes.

When writing recipes for a restaurant, it is a good idea to have the yields in convenient multiples of eight servings and usually not more than twenty-four. This is because many measures and ingredients are also in these multiples and most tables seat an even number, four being a common table size. One pound is 16 ounces, one cup is 8 fluid ounces, and one cup is 16 tablespoons, as examples.

Recipes always list ingredients in the order in which they are used and you should try to use ingredients in their packaged amount. When making a marinara sauce, write the recipe using #10 cans of tomato sauce, so that there is no leftover sauce to place in a container in the walk-in, only to occupy valuable space and then be tossed out later in the week. If you think an expanded recipe needs 14 ounces of butter, try it with a pound and make adjustments elsewhere, if needed. Since 1 tablespoon equals 3 teaspoons, avoid 2 1/2 teaspoons of a commodity and try 1 tablespoon, which saves labor and improves accuracy in having one measurement rather than three just to add that ingredient. Five tablespoons is almost 1/3 cup (which can be written as a "scant" 1/3 cup in the recipe and 6 tablespoons can be written as a "generous" 1/3 cup).

There are three types of recipes in the commercial kitchen:

- Basics
- Sub-recipes
- Finished dishes

Basics include stocks and broths and basic sauces, and other prepared ingredients that are to be used in other recipes. To make a beef barley soup, you will need beef broth; to make a cheese filling for manicotti you will need a béchamel sauce. In the final recipe you will specify all of the sub-recipe ingredients and any others to produce the final menu item. Let's say you have meat loaf with gravy and mashed potatoes on your menu. You will need a basic recipe for beef stock to make the (sub-recipe) gravy. You will need sub-recipes for meat loaf and for mashed potatoes for referral in the final recipe of meat loaf with mashed potatoes. The final recipe will stipulate the weight of meat loaf, potatoes, and gravy for one serving (8 ounces meat loaf, 1 cup mashed potatoes, 4 ounces gravy, 1 teaspoon chopped parsley, for example). By writing recipes in these categories, they will easily fit into your food-costing scheme. Basic recipes and sub-recipes can go into your "Prep Master" file. The final recipe that produces one finished serving will go into "Menu Cost." You may want to use all three categories in your food-costing scheme and have a "Basics Master" for the most fundamental recipes that are used in multiple sub-recipes, a "Prep Master" for sub-recipes and "Menu Cost."

As stated, when writing recipes always list the ingredients in the order in which they are being used in the instructions. This allows for efficient assembly of ingredients prior to preparation and avoids leaving out a critical ingredient while preparing the recipe. Measured quantities of a specific ingredient can be ambiguous if not cited in a specific way. "2 cups garlic, chopped" is an example. Do you first measure the garlic and then chop it or do you chop the garlic first? The difference is significant.

Chopped garlic packs much more densely than whole cloves, almost 50 percent more! For volume ingredient of prepared ingredients (sliced, chopped, minced, etc.) the preparation method should precede the ingredient. "2 cups chopped garlic" is preferred and unambiguous. For individual units, the method follows the ingredient such as "4 medium tomatoes, roasted, peeled, seeded, and chopped." In professional recipes as much preparation of the ingredient as possible is written into the ingredient list, and not in the instructions. For the previous example, avoid "4 medium tomatoes" in the ingredient list, with "Roast, peel, seed, and chop the tomatoes" appearing later in step 1. To be consistent, specifying weight is preferred over a numerical quantity. How big are "medium" tomatoes? "Two pounds" of tomatoes works regardless of their size.

Your recipe may be written for a specific amount or number of servings or you may want to have the recipes written in such a way as to indicate the amounts in multiples, in a chart-like fashion, rather than a single yield. The recipe calling for garlic and tomatoes above may be written as follows:

| Ingredient | Instruction | 8 servings | 16 servings | 24 servings |
|---|---|---|---|---|
| chopped garlic | peeled | 1 cup | 2 cups | 3 cups |
| medium tomatoes | roasted, peeled, seeded, chopped | 2 pounds | 4 pounds | 6 pounds |

It is important to have accurate yields in convenient units. If a sub-recipe calls for three quarts of beef stock (and if most other recipes require "quarts"), that is the way to indicate the yield. You may want to use multiple units for convenience, such as "yield: 10 quarts = 40 cups = 2 1/2 gallons." For sub-recipes, such as meat loaf, indicate the yield in number of servings rather than a total amount. If the recipe yields twelve pounds of cooked meat loaf, state the yield as "24 8-ounce servings" as well as the total weight.

Encourage the prep cooks to always follow the recipe regardless of how many times he or she has cooked this item. Consistency and accuracy are important to the overall quality of the restaurant. Have the recipes in files that are convenient for them to utilize. The kitchen is a messy place, especially when prepping the basics for the cooking line. Consider laminating recipes and placing them alphabetically in vinyl-clad binders. Have them on shelves accessible to the prep cooks. It is not a good idea to allow the cooks to make copies from a computer to use, as this may lead to having the recipes carried out and then made available to competitors. Consider a computer monitor in the kitchen dedicated to recipes called up from the kitchen computer. There are monitors and keyboards made for "hostile" environments prone to dirt, water, and grease.

## Food Costing and Creating Master Lists

It is critical to keep control over the cost of food. Restaurants work under a very narrow profit margin. Menu prices, and the cost of making the items, must be checked regularly. The first thing to do is to create an "Inventory Master List," containing every item purchased for the entire menu. Before you can create an Inventory Master, you must have a complete menu, final recipes for all menu items, and purveyors to supply these items with purchase prices. For each recipe copy the ingredients and make a list, combining items that repeat in recipes. This will give you every ingredient needed for your menu. Divide this list into categories such as "produce," "meats," "pantry items," etc. so that the proper purveyor can be found easily for each of these ingredients.

### Typical Categories of Ingredients/Purveyors

- *Grocery*—canned goods, spices, frozen foods, cheeses, flours, oils, pastas, sugars, rice, sauces, etc.
- *Meat*—beef, pork, lamb, prime and dry-aged
- *Poultry*—fresh chickens and parts, turkeys, quail, pheasant, specialty eggs
- *Fish/seafood*—shellfish, regionally caught fresh fish, frozen fish, exotic fish
- *Dairy*—milk, cream, butter, sour cream, ricotta, yogurt, etc.
- *Produce*—all manner of fresh vegetables, fruits, herbs
- *Specialty/Internet*—hard to get items such as rare imported cheeses and canned goods, exotic spices, top-line chocolate, etc.

To create the Inventory Master List the purchase price of every ingredient is calculated down to the "unit measure" used in the recipe. For example, tomato sauce can be bought in cases of six #10 cans. If recipes using tomato sauce require #10 cans, then that is the "unit" that is costed. If recipes require cups of tomato sauce, then the calculation is based on cups. Let's say a case of six #10 cans (the "pack/size") of tomato sauce costs $23.74. Dividing by 6 gives the cost per #10 can (the "unit measure"). Keep track of things using the following guide, which will work nicely in Excel.

| Description | Pack/Size Form | Current Price | Unit Measure | Units/Pack | Yield | Unit Cost |
|---|---|---|---|---|---|---|
| Tomato sauce (Hunt's) | 6 #10 cans/case | $23.74 | #10 can | 6 | 100 percent | $3.96 |

If the recipe requires cups, then the entry would be:

| Description | Pack/Size Form | Current Price | Unit Measure | Units/Pack | Yield | Unit Cost |
|---|---|---|---|---|---|---|
| Tomato sauce (Hunt's) | 6 #10 cans/case | $23.74 | cup | 72 | 100 percent | $0.33 |

A #10 can yields 96 fluid ounces, multiplied by 6 cans per case, divided by 8 ounces per cup = 72 units/pack (72 cups per case of 6 #10 cans). Often both entries are required.

The "yield" column accounts for certain items with trimming or preparation loss. For example a can of whole tomatoes, when drained, trimmed and seeded loses about 30 percent of its volume. This should be figured into the cost for accuracy. To calculate, divide cost as done above and then divide by 0.70 to compensate for loss.

| Description | Pack/Size Form | Current Price | Unit Measure | Units/Pack | Yield | Unit Cost |
|---|---|---|---|---|---|---|
| Canned tomatoes | 6 #10 cans/case | $28.50 | cup | 72 | 70 percent | $0.57 |

Note: If you did not compensate for loss, the cost would be calculated as $0.40, leading to a significant error in calculating recipe costs.

You will have to do experiments to determine the percent yield of trimmed and prepared items, or look up the information in reference books or on the Internet. For example, whole chickens yield about 67 percent meat after trimming, so a whole chicken at $0.89/pound would calculate to boneless chicken meat at $1.33/pound ($0.89/0.67). Many fresh vegetables require experimentation to figure accurate yields.

## Creating an Inventory Master Form

Use the examples on previous page when creating your form. The headings are:

**Description**—what the ingredient is (may include the brand name)

**Pack/Size**—how the ingredient is packaged for sale; how you receive the goods from the purveyor

**Form**—container the ingredient comes in, such as cases of cans or bags (be specific as to quantity)

**Current Price**—the price you pay for the entire pack/size (all six #10 cans in the case, for example)

**Unit Measure**—how the ingredient is measured in the recipes in which this ingredient will be used

**Units/Pack**—how many of these measured units (cans, pounds, fluid ounces, etc.) are in the pack

**Yield**—amount of ingredient in prepared recipe (compensate for any waste, trimming, bones, etc.; if the entire form is used, that is 100 percent)

**Unit Cost**—obtained by dividing the current price by the units/pack

For the Hunt's tomato sauce, it comes shipped to you in cases of six #10 cans (pack/size). The form is #10 cans. The cost of the case is $23.74 (current price). Your recipes call for measuring out cups of tomato sauce, so "cups" are your unit measure. There are 72 cups in a case of six #10 cans (units/form). You use the entire contents of every can so the yield is 100 percent. Each cup costs 33 cents (unit cost), calculated by dividing the "current price" by the "units/pack."

After you have created a complete Inventory Master List, you are ready to make a "Prep Master List." This file calculates costs of basic recipes used in final menu recipes. For example, to do a food cost calculation of spaghetti with meatballs, the Prep Master List prices the marinara sauce and then that value is used in calculation of the "Menu Cost." Using the tomato sauce example above, we create an entry to the Prep Master List for marinara sauce (see Example Prep Master List). The recipe calls for five #10 cans of tomato sauce and the recipe makes 6 gallons (768 fluid ounces) of marinara sauce.

## Marinara Sauce

| Ingredient | Unit Measure | #Recipe Units | Unit Cost | Recipe Cost |
|---|---|---|---|---|
| Tomato sauce | #10 can | 5 | $3.96 | $19.80 |

*All other ingredients filled in as above...........................* $36.38

Cost: $56.18
Yield: 768 fluid ounces
Cost per Yield: $0.073 per fluid ounce

To do a Menu Cost entry, fill in the recipe costs:

## Spaghetti with Meatballs

| Ingredient | Cost | Recipe Amount | Menu Item Cost |
|---|---|---|---|
| Cooked spaghetti | $0.028/ounce | 10 ounces | $0.28 |
| Marinara sauce | $0.073/fluid ounce | 6 fluid ounces | $0.44 |
| Meatballs | $0.40/meatball | 3 | $1.20 |
| Parmesan cheese | $0.53/ounce | 1/2 ounce | $0.27 |

| **Menu Cost** | | | **$2.19** |
|---|---|---|---|

The cost of the cooked spaghetti, marinara sauce, and meatballs come from your Prep Master List and the Parmesan from your Inventory Master List.

To calculate food cost, divide the menu cost by the selling price and multiply by 100:

*If the selling price on the menu is $9.95,*
*then your food cost is $2.19/$9.95 x 100 = 22 percent*

**A "rule of thumb" is to keep food cost below 30 percent to be profitable.**

Don't forget to add in any "freebies" (which are really not free). Do you place bread and butter on the table for all guests? If so, this must be figured into your food cost. If your dinners come with a side vegetable, be sure to cost this in as well.

The final word on food cost will come from the numbers at the end of the week or month after a detailed inventory of the kitchen has been performed and compared to sales figures. This is most important to get right and is based on a thorough and proper inventory.

## Taking Inventory and Food Costing

To get an accurate measure of your food cost, you must do a proper inventory of the BOH. Everything must be accounted for, from the amount of salad dressing in the walk-in to the number of servings of lasagna in the reach-in, to the number of cans of tomato sauce, to the amount of oregano in the spice jar. From the Inventory Master and Prep Master lists you will calculate the value of all of the food and ingredients on hand and compare this to the previous inventory and purchases for the time period you set. It is recommended that you do this weekly, so that adjustments can be made before you get into trouble with a food cost that is out of line.

Two persons should do this inventory—one to call out the item and the other to write it down. Start at the back of the kitchen and work your way to the line. Dry storage is straightforward. Record every unopened case, can, bottle, bag, etc. For opened packages (stored rice or flour in a plastic container) estimate the amount from your knowledge of how full a 50-pound bag fills the container (mark this with a permanent marker on the container when first filling it.) Clear plastic containers are best when storing items as they allow you to see the amount inside without opening.

The walk-in will contain a lot of items that will need to be estimated, and clear containers with graduations marked will make this task much easier. Start in the back, on the top shelf, and work your way down the shelves and to the front of the walk-in. With appropriate containers it should be easy to call out "2 quarts of house dressing, 1 1/2 gallons of marinara sauce" and the like. Having a battery-operated digital scale can deal with wedges of cheese, trout fillets, and such. After the walk-in is done, continue with all of the reach-in refrigerators (also known as "refers") and freezers and finish with the under-counter refers on line and pantry refers. Check all shelving on the walls for spices and other small items stored in the prep area and on line. Don't forget the wait station for table service items (excluding beverages and beverage prep items).

With the inventory done, a total value of all items on hand can be calculated from the Master Lists either by hand or by computer, depending on the sophistication of your programming (Microsoft Excel is good for doing this). To calculate food cost, fill in the "Food Cost Worksheet" for the time period done.

## Food Cost Worksheet

| | |
|---|---|
| Beginning inventory (from previous period) | 1. _____ |
| All purchases | 2. _____ |
| Add line items 1 and 2 | 3. _____ |
| Present inventory | 4. _____ |

**Cost of food:**

| | |
|---|---|
| Subtract line item 4 from 3 | 5. _____ |
| Food sales (from POS or bookkeeper) | 6. _____ |

**Percentage of food cost:**

| | |
|---|---|
| Divide line item 5 by 6 and multiply by 100 | 7. _____ percent |

For example, you had a beginning inventory of $2,650 from last week. Purchases from all invoices came to $6,450 for the present week and today's inventory came to $1,930. The POS reported food sales (no beverages or alcohol) as $26, 600.

| | |
|---|---|
| Beginning inventory (from previous period) | 1. $2,650 |
| All purchases | 2. $6,450 |
| Add line items 1 and 2 | 3. $9,100 |
| Present inventory | 4. $1,930 |

**Cost of food:**

| | |
|---|---|
| Subtract line item 4 from 3 | 5. $7,170 |
| Food sales (from POS or bookkeeper) | 6. $26,600 |

**Percentage of food cost:**

| | |
|---|---|
| Divide line item 5 by 6 and multiply by 100 | 7.  27 percent |

27 percent should be an acceptable amount, based on the guidelines set out in this book.

## Labor Cost

Labor costs, calculated separately when evaluating a successfully run restaurant, are a function of the menu and vice versa. The previous example for meatballs and spaghetti shows a 22 percent food cost, but you must consider the labor that went into producing it. The pasta needed to be portioned and cooked; the meatballs prepared, cooked, and held; the marinara sauce made and stored; and the cheese grated. A steak might have a 50 percent food cost, but there is no labor other than the grillman cooking it and putting it on a plate. The more ingredients, and the more steps to produce a final plate, the lower the food cost should be. On the other hand, cooking time can slow down the time for serving the item, which may increase labor costs. If you are serving a large steak, the time to cook it can slow down the entire order for the table. As a rule of thumb, kitchen labor should be kept below 15 percent of food sales. You will probably need to track kitchen labor carefully and often, and make adjustments as necessary. Compare your food cost guidelines with labor cost to see if you have a problem.

# 04

# Financial Planning

The experts say that the primary reason for restaurant failure rates being so high is a lack of realistic financial planning. Careful planning and reasonable expectations are critical to your success. Planning for the worst-case scenario is often passed by for more optimistic and usually unrealistic goals. Do not expect to show a profit for quite a while. Take your time and make sure you are prepared to give your financial institution accurate and reasonable profit and loss statements with sales figures that reflect the reality of this highly competitive business. You will be expected to contribute up to 40 percent of the estimated cost of the entire project, so be sure that you have additional funds on hand before expecting a financial institution to offer you a loan.

## Start-Up

Opening a restaurant is an expensive and risky endeavor. The number one reason for the high restaurant failure rate is lack of funds. Underestimating the amount of money it will take to open is a common mistake. Securing the right amount is essential before signing a lease or construction contract, and estimating this amount accurately is critical. Accurate evaluation of costs is also paramount to obtaining financing, as financial institutions expect realistic figures and carefully planned proposals. You will need a Federal Employer Identification Number (EIN), sometimes called a tax ID number, on a variety of forms, so apply for one now. Depending on your location you may need a separate state or county ID number as well. You will also need a state sales and use tax license/permit from your state comptroller.

## Paying Your Taxes on Time

One of the most common ways that a restaurant fails is by not paying its taxes, and we recommend that you set up a separate tax bank account to deposit funds weekly for sales tax, alcohol taxes, and payroll taxes. It is a good idea to have a separate account for the BOH as they will need to write checks for COD deliveries and emergency purchases. Federal taxes include income taxes withheld from employees, Social Security/Medicare taxes withheld and matching amounts you must contribute, and unemployment taxes based on your gross payroll. As of January 1, 2011, all federal taxes must be paid online at www.eftps.gov/eftps. For the first year in business, you must deposit these taxes monthly. After a year it will depend on your total payroll taxes from the previous year. If more than $50,000 you must pay semiweekly, otherwise payments are due monthly. Check with your state alcohol commission for when and how to pay these taxes, as well as with the state comptroller for sales tax payments.

## Construction Expense Estimates

Before you can do the financials and submit applications for loans, you will need a rough estimate of the cost of opening your doors to the public. How much money will you need to borrow? This depends on the way you will acquire your restaurant.

- *Turn-Key*—Taking over an existing restaurant that is in good repair with little to do except change the sign and polish up the decor.
- *Restaurant Remodel*—Taking over an existing restaurant that has lapsed in its maintenance and needs some structural repairs, equipment updates, and refurbishing.

- *Retail Remodel/Strip Center*—Taking a space not built for a restaurant, a new space, or any non-restaurant retail space.
- *Ground-up Construction*—All new construction, including site development, parking, etc.

### Common Expenses

Regardless of the way you will be creating your restaurant, they all have common expenses and fixed costs. You will need to completely stock the kitchen with food and basics, enough for the first week. The full-service bar, should you have one, needs to be stocked with beer, wine, and alcohol, along with garnishes, juices, and so forth. Utility deposits and licensing fees must be paid before opening and you will need appropriate signage for your named restaurant. Janitorial and cleaning supplies, paper goods, bookkeeping and record-keeping supplies must be on hand. You should figure at least $25,000 for this. If your restaurant is more upscale, the inventory to stock the kitchen and bar will cost more, so keep this in mind. Regardless of the style and type of restaurant and the costs incurred to get it open, you must have a reserve of funds to operate at a loss for several months or up to a year. Consider your fixed costs to operate per month (lease, loans, utilities, etc.) and have a minimum of 3 months held in reserve (more is better). Fixed costs can run from a modest $5,000/month to more than $15,000/month depending on the size of the restaurant, location, and quality level (see chapter 3). For a 3,000-square-foot restaurant seating one hundred with reasonable utility bills, $8,000 to $10,000 may be a modest estimate of monthly fixed costs. Plans must be submitted for your health department permit and construction and building permits and licenses and a licensed architect will have to produce them. This cost will vary based on the extent of remodel or new construction. An attorney should be brought in to look over all leases, loans, contracts, and agreements before signing. Have contingency funds available for the unexpected. The walk-in condenser/compressor may have checked out fine at the time of inspection prior to signing the lease, but if it breaks in 3 months you will need to replace it, at a cost of more than $3,000. A reserve of $10,000 would be a safe amount to overcome any "surprises" while the restaurant is operating for the first 6 months. For everything mentioned above, $40,000 to $50,000 should be added to the costs outlined next.

## Turn-Key

For a turn-key operation, the space should need a thorough cleaning and some touch-up and minor repair work only. All equipment should be in good working condition and the building structurally sound with no plumbing, electrical, or HVAC issues and should be ADA compliant. You may need to add specialized plates and dinnerware, glasses, and tableware, and replace or add to the stock of these items. A conservative estimate would be $10,000.

## Restaurant Remodel

A restaurant remodel can be costly, especially if there have been maintenance issues (restaurants that have to close due to financial difficulty often let maintenance slide to pay for important and urgent bills at hand). The entry, dining room, bar, and bathrooms are the FOH (front of house) and may need considerable attention to make a good first impression on your guests. Expect to do a complete paint job after any structural repairs or changes. Some of the tabletops may be damaged and new fabric for all of the chairs and stools is probably in order. The carpeting may need replacement or removal for a hard floor. The bathrooms may need plumbing and fixture attention and some updating, design, and paint. Check the HVAC system for efficient operation and needed repairs. If there is a full-service bar, plumbing and refrigeration issues and any updating or modifications should be considered. The POS system often requires updating or reprogramming.

The back of house (BOH) includes the kitchen, storage areas, and office. It will need a professional cleaning/degreasing as will the vent hoods. There will be appliances to repair or replace. Some new equipment may need to be added for your particular menu. All refrigeration should be checked, repaired, lubricated, and properly filled with refrigerant. The walk-in should be thoroughly cleaned, shelving replaced as required, and the compressor and mechanicals serviced or replaced. There will be plumbing repairs and modifications, and electrical updates and service to meet your current needs. The floor may have to be patched and recoated/sealed. Walls will need epoxy paint and/or stainless steel as required. The grease trap should be pumped and checked for leaks and repaired or replaced as necessary. Office equipment, such as computers and printers may need upgrading, and the office should have a new coat of paint and may require some new furniture. Budget a minimum of $50,000 for a relatively nice space and up to $100,000 for a neglected restaurant that is fairly run down.

### Non-Restaurant Remodel

When remodeling a space never intended to be a restaurant, such as a former residential building or a retail space in a strip mall, a large sum of money will have to be spent to convert it to a restaurant. Drains will need to be installed for sinks in the bar, kitchen and wait station, kitchen equipment, and new bathrooms, often requiring breaking into a poured concrete foundation. A grease trap may be needed. Gas lines and heavy electrical lines must be run. Ventilation will need to be upgraded, and the floor plan altered to meet the needs of a restaurant. For a 3,000-square-foot space allow at least $100/square foot or $300,000. The FOH will need tables, chairs, dishes and flatware, glasses, bar glasses and smallwares, bar stools and small tables, a POS system, and music. Some interior design elements must be added. For one hundred seats in the dining room figure at least $40,000 to finish the space out modestly. For quality chairs and tables, with upgraded table service and more upscale decor, this figure could easily reach $100,000. Add in the kitchen equipment and smallwares, vent hood, walk-in, refrigeration, tables and counters, small appliances, and bar equipment and refrigeration, assuming all new equipment, which can cost around $80,000 for a reasonably equipped kitchen and bar. Adding specialized equipment, such as a blast chiller to cool down hot foods or a wood-burning pizza oven, can bring the figure to $150,000. Overall, a remodel of an existing structure or retail space of 3,000 square feet to a one-hundred-seat restaurant can cost between $400,000 and $600,000. This figure assumes all new furniture and equipment. Carefully scouring the used restaurant equipment market could save you $50,000, but be sure the equipment is reliable and working properly and the furniture will hold up to abuse for several years.

### Ground-Up Construction

For ground-up construction the "sky is the limit." You can take the figures above for the retail or residence remodel and add the cost of land to build upon, the exterior structure, parking, and site development, and come up with an estimate that will vary based on the size and price of the lot and the quality of materials used in exterior construction. Adding an additional $400,000 to $600,000 to the estimate for remodeling a space that was never a restaurant brings a newly constructed restaurant of 3,000 square feet with one hundred seats to approximately $800,000 to $1.2 million.

## Securing Finances

Unless you are quite financially secure you will have to borrow money to open your restaurant. Realize that all institutions, including government-secured loans, require you to put up a certain amount of your own money for the venture. No one will lend you 100 percent of what you need, so be prepared to show funds equal to 15 to 40 percent of the total necessary to open. Small Business Administration–guaranteed loans may require as little as 15 percent (but can be up to 25 percent), and most commercial institutions will only lend about 60 percent of what you need for a restaurant. Restaurant loans are considered very high risk in the banking industry and can be difficult to obtain. The more you bring to the table, the easier it will be. As to timing it is best to have the total amount required for the venture secured about 6 months before you need it.

Here are the avenues of securing finances. Some of these sources can be used to meet the requirement of a percentage of the total you will need to bring into the venture.

1. Financial institutions such as banks can offer an unsecured business loan or a line of credit. A line of credit gives a maximum amount the bank will loan, but rather than offering it in one lump sum, as in a straight business loan, you only use what you need when you need it. This saves in interest as the inter-

est amount is calculated only on what you are borrowing at the time. If you are given a $100,000 line of credit, but you only need $40,000 right now, you will only be charged interest on $40,000 and a payment will be based on this figure. At any time you can draw additional funds, up to $100,000, and only be charged interest on the amount you have drawn with a proportional payment. A $100,000 loan has payments with interest figured on the full $100,000. Also you will be expected to put up 30 to 40 percent of the total required for the venture. A line of credit is preferable to a full loan most of the time.

A personal or business equity loan is based on equity you provide to the bank to secure the note. If you have owned your home for a while (or the land on which you will be building your restaurant) you may have built up a considerable amount of equity. You may borrow against this equity, typically up to 80 percent of the amount. A lien will be placed on the property until the loan is paid. Often one can make just interest payments for a predetermined period to get started.

An SBA loan is a government program that guarantees the note to a bank, but does not actually lend the money. Interest rates are lower and your contributing share of the total needed for the venture is lower as well, typically 15 percent. While long delays in getting the loan can be common, you can save time by going through a Preferred Lender, a bank that has arranged with the SBA to be in the PLP (Preferred Lender Program). Check into minority, women in business, and veterans' loan programs offered by the government, should they apply to your situation.

2. Personal savings are usually not enough to finance the entire project, but can be important to meet your obligation to a financial institution to provide a certain percent of the total cost of the project. The same is true for any personal lines of credit you may already have. High limit credit cards can be dangerous to use as they often have exorbitant interest rates, so be careful here.

3. Venture capital is money invested in exchange for an equity stake in the business, rather than a loan with interest to pay off. With billions of dollars in food sales in the United States alone, food venture capital firms and restaurant venture capital firms are popping up to take advantage of this type of business venture. Venture capitalists' return is based on the success and profitability of the restaurant and so they are often very selective as to whom they choose to fund. It is said that, on average, one in four hundred proposals is accepted for funding.

4. Consider selling "shares" to friends, relatives, and people who are familiar with your restaurant idea. For a modest return on their investment, postponed until the restaurant gets off the ground and makes money, there are those willing to invest $5,000 to $10,000 to be part of a restaurant, to call it their own, and to entertain others in the establishment (which is good for business). Invite prospective investors to a gathering to sample the food you will be serving and have a packet prepared that describes your idea, a sample menu, a business plan, and helpful information about their return on investment. Consider several gatherings, one for relatives, one for friends, and another for word-of-mouth interested. Entice them with discounts off their bill, exclusive invitations to wine tastings, and food roll outs of new menus. Offer them preferential reservations, last-minute seating, and other perquisites to make them feel special.

5. Take advantage of leasing companies. By leasing as much equipment as possible, you will need to borrow less to open your restaurant, a savings up front allowing you to use available cash for other things. The leasing company purchases the equipment that you specify and then formulates a monthly fee over the term of the lease. At lease end you may have the option of purchasing the equipment at an agreed-upon price at signing (lease-purchase), which is usually a very low figure as the company has gotten all of its expense back at lease end. A straight lease where you return the equipment after a certain period allows for updating equipment as technology improves. Since the equipment itself is equity, your financials need not be as strong as when you obtain a loan for the purchase amount from a bank. Long-term savings by straight leasing comes from a tax advantage, as leased equipment cost is fully deductible. If you were to purchase the equipment, the IRS places equipment into depreciation categories of 5-year, 7-year, etc., where you must spread out the cost over the time period allotted. The paperwork alone is quite complicated.

6. Bring in a full partner to share in the financials and the work. This can reduce stress on you and make it much easier to obtain financing as there may be two homes that can have equity to borrow against, two savings accounts to come up with matching funds, and so on. Partnerships can experience many pitfalls, so be sure you can work closely with this person, accept criticism, and share in both the good and bad times. Having complementary skills

would be a good starting point in selecting the right person. Ideally you have a cooking talent and he or she is good with people (or vice versa). The partner may want to be silent and uninvolved in daily activities but provide significant financing while you will supply "sweat equity" and run the business.

7. Borrow money from relatives and/or friends. This is usually not a good idea from the standpoint of harmony, and should be considered a last-resort option. The pitfalls that can break up a friendship or sour relationships with relatives can be avoided by treating the loan just as you would one from a financial institution. Write everything down. Agree to terms and payoff schedule and adhere to them. Don't think you will be allowed to "slide" just because they are close to you. Agree to when it is appropriate to discuss the loan or you may get an earful every time you see them.

8. Raise money by opening a "pop-up" restaurant. A pop-up restaurant, or supper club, is a temporary restaurant that occupies unused space. The space can be a private home, an existing restaurant's off-hours of operation, or a rented or vacant space. Locations for pop-ups can move from one event to another. A pop-up can exist for one service, or remain open for a given amount of time. It can operate on a temporary or catering permit and sometimes the opening is a "guerrilla" operation, operating briefly outside the laws, with no permits or taxes being paid (not recommended by the authors). Various social media are the usual means of advertising or it can be strictly word of mouth. As well, this is an excellent way to try out an idea, concept, or menu prior to opening to the public at your fixed location.

## Organizing Your Business

There are three ways to organize your business and each will influence how you get a loan and the protection you will receive from lenders. A sole proprietorship means that you alone are the owner and are fully responsible for all debts incurred. There is no distinction between the business and the owner. To use the name of the restaurant in business dealings, you will file a "DBA" (doing business as) with local authorities. This is required when opening a bank account and allows you to write, deposit, and cash checks made out in or to the name of the restaurant.

A partnership is an agreement between two or more people to operate and finance a business. Unlike a proprietorship the partnership is an individual entity legally separate from the individuals. Each partner has equal rights to make decisions, and can make them without consulting the other partner(s). Partners should share the work associated with operating a restaurant and should have complementary skills to augment each other. A strong partnership agreement should be drawn by an attorney spelling out who will do what for the restaurant, how the restaurant will be financed, how the partnership will and can be dissolved, and what happens in the event of the death of a partner. Partnerships require the flexibility to negotiate and compromise and everyone shares in the liability, regardless of who might have been at fault.

Corporations are a separate legal entity from the investors and therefore provide protection through limited liability. A shareholder in a corporation can only lose as much as he or she has invested in the corporation should it fail (bankruptcy) or be sued. Shareholders are not liable for the debts of the corporation. If shares in the corporation are not traded publicly, it is known as a "close corporation" and is owned and managed by a small group. When publicly traded, the corporation is subject to more regulations and disclosures to the general populace.

When starting a restaurant many think that by immediately forming a corporation, their personal lives will be protected from their debts, should they fail. Unfortunately, unless your corporation has assets, financial institutions and leasing companies will not do business with a corporation without equity. Often the rule of thumb is to incorporate when your business is on its feet, stable, and beginning to earn steady profits.

### Insurance

Restaurant insurance falls into the general categories of financial and life, covering bank loans and mortgage, property insurance for liability and injury, and employee insurance, which includes worker's compensation and unemployment insurance.

> **Most Common Employee Accidents in a Restaurant**
>
> 1. Being struck by an object—knives and moving equipment most common
> 2. Falls on the same level—due to slippery surfaces or tripping/rough surfaces
> 3. Burns and scalds—contact with hot food or hot grease, hot pans
> 4. Overexertion—muscle strains from lifting boxes and cartons, heat exhaustion

You were probably required to obtain some insurance when applying for a loan or line of credit. General liability is often covered under an umbrella policy that includes accidental injury, food-borne illness, allergic reaction, and the like. Many states require that restaurants with alcoholic beverage licenses obtain liquor liability insurance for protection against customers who overindulge and then cause injury to themselves or others. If a restaurant has a company vehicle, then it should be covered under the restaurant's policy, as should valet parking damages or theft. Some umbrella policies cover criminal damage, such as employee theft, forgery and alteration, money and securities, coat check and check room theft, counterfeit currency, and such. EPLI (Employer Practices Liability Insurance) protects business, management, and employees from sexual harassment and wrongful termination suits, as well as some other civil cases.

There are special categories of restaurant insurance that are available at extra cost, often at a premium price. Loss of business insurance covers the restaurant for lost sales due to specific causes, and premiums and deductibles are usually quite high. Food contamination insurance covers the restaurant for food spoilage due to loss of power. Specific peril insurance covers loss from a natural disaster that falls outside the boundary of standard coverage, such as an earthquake or flood; it would also cover loss incurred by power interruption during such an event. Lastly, a restaurant might get specific coverage for works of art that are part of the decor, with an appraisal to establish intrinsic value. There are many insurance agencies that can provide coverage for your restaurant. Use a trusted agent or company with whom you are familiar and/or from whom you get positive reviews and referrals.

### Point of Sale (POS) System

Think of a POS system as a computer joined to a cash register and you get the general idea of what they can do. Powerful software allows for a great deal of information to be gleaned and shared. You and your provider will work together to program the software for your specific report needs and your menu. The input device is usually a touch screen where the server can tap in the order for a table or call up the bill for a check out register. The system is able to print guest checks, send orders to the appropriate station in the kitchen or bar, process credit cards, and run reports. The POS system can be as simple as one register at check out or multiple screen inputs at wait station, bar, and host station. There can be printers at each kitchen station or "bump screens" where the dish ordered appears on a screen by the cooking station and can be tapped when complete, sending that information to the server and expediter. When the server enters the table's order, the appropriate station is notified of each dish to be cooked. The server can control the timing and have only the appetizers started and the system will wait for the server to indicate when the entrees should be fired. Software can be programmed to know the different cooking times for entrees and control when each station is notified to begin cooking so that the entire table's food comes out at the same time.

The POS can produce all kinds of reports and analyses, such as the number of each item ordered and send an ordering list to the kitchen manager, cross referencing the inventory, to maintain par levels set when programmed. For example, the system knows that inventory had forty sirloin steaks on hand, twenty-six were ordered that night, and fourteen should be left in the walk-in. Having set the par level for sirloin steaks at a minimum of thirty-six, a report is sent that twenty-two steaks should be ordered from the meat purveyor for next day delivery. The system can keep track of every ingredient linked to each recipe and to the inventory par levels required. It can generate every report imaginable, close out each server, reconcile the credit card charges, track sales of each server, be the time clock for all employees, and alert management of potential overtime.

The host's terminal can have the dining room seating plan programmed into it and can keep track of each table's status. A bus person can enter when he has cleaned the table, indicating it is now ready for seating. He can be alerted by the server or FOH manager that a table needs cleaning or attention. Reservation information can be stored and tracked throughout the night and every seat and table can be tracked by time of occupation.

Very modest systems can run about $5,000 and can easily climb to over $50,000, depending on your needs. Even small systems are powerful and can help control inventory, monitor profitability, issue important reports, track liquor sales, keep track of employee hours and payroll, and resolve credit card charges and tips. Be sure that your credit card processor works with the POS system you are considering.

## The Business Plan

In order to obtain funding from financial institutions or persons, you must have a detailed business plan. It should be comprised of the following components.

1. Overview or Summary
2. Market Analysis
3. Description of the Company
4. Management and Organization
5. Marketing and Sales
6. Funding Needs
7. Financials

### Overview or Summary

This is the opening statement that should grab the attention of those reading it and make an immediate good impression about your business proposal. It should offer a statement as to why your business will be successful. Focus on your experience, background, and decisions you've made in entering this business. Convince the person reading the proposal that you are filling a need, creating a niche and/or providing a service that solves problems associated with others in the restaurant business.

### Market Analysis

Demonstrate your knowledge of the restaurant business, especially as it pertains to the type, size, and location of the restaurant you have proposed. Describe the state of the restaurant industry and any trends, growth rates, and characteristics, demonstrating your knowledge and research into the business you have chosen. Identify your target market and how you will fill its needs. Provide estimates as to the number of guests you will be serving, the PPA, pricing strategy and gross profits, and how you arrived at these figures. Identify your competitors in your market location and their strengths and weaknesses. Be sure to mention any regulatory requirements that you are aware of and will meet, such as health department and alcoholic beverage commission.

### Description of the Company

Describe the type of restaurant you are opening and to whom it should appeal. Include factors you will put into place that will make it a successful restaurant. How will it satisfy the needs of your clientele?

## Management and Organization

Provide the ownership organization scheme you are following—proprietorship, partnership, or corporation—and the qualifications of all who are part of the owner- ship organization. Include a working organization layout of who will be doing what, accounting for every aspect of running the restaurant and who will be responsible for each critical function. For each owner provide his or her name, percentage of ownership, unique skills, prior experience in the business, track record, and primary responsibilities to the restaurant.

## Marketing and Sales

In this section describe how you will be bringing customers into your restaurant initially and continuously. Address the ways in which you can make your restaurant grow in sales, size, and offerings. Discuss your ongoing plans to sustain business throughout its life. For restaurants "social media" have become an important method that you should address, such as Facebook, Twitter, food-oriented websites, and your Internet presence.

## Funding Needs

This is where you will state the amount of money you will need to start the restau- rant, and estimated future funding needs, the amount you need to borrow as well as the amount you will be bringing into the business. Provide the specific details as to how you will be using the requested funds, including equipment purchases, construction costs, start-up costs such as licenses, etc. Creditors are also interested in the future. Are you planning to expand or franchise? After a period do you want to sell to a prospective restaurant group? Be sure to include a time frame so they may know the reality of paying off your loans.

## Financials

Provide all prospective financial data in this section for a 5-year period, going year by year. Include estimated sales figures, income statements, cash flow, balance sheets, and budgets for expenditures. Make these projections monthly for the first year and quarterly for the remaining 4 years. Be sure that all of this data matches your fund- ing requests in the previous section.

There are many templates available for you to download or purchase to aid you in writing your business plan. They will provide structure and advice along the way. Look for those that are specific to restaurants and their unique needs. Have a table of contents to help the creditor find information quickly. There should be an appendix that is offered only on a by-request basis. It should have letters of reference, résumés, copies of licenses and permits, copies of leases, building permits, contracts, bid lists for equipment and furniture, names of consultants, accountants and attorneys, and details of your research into the viability of your idea.

# 05

# Equipment FOH and BOH

There are many decisions to be made when selecting the equipment for your restaurant, from the type of fuel or power to run the equipment to which side the hinges should be on for opening doors. Some equipment will require ventilation and automatic fire suppression while others may only need excess heat exhaust. The specifications of the basic equipment you will need are dictated by the menu and its complexity of preparation, as well as the anticipated volume of sales and number of seats in the dining room. Some equipment can save on labor costs and are nonessential, while other units are a necessity of every kitchen. Start with the basic equipment of every kitchen and then allow your sales and labor pool to dictate adding additional time-saving or large-batch equipment as needed. As an example let's assume a Mexican restaurant serves a house-made cooked salsa for each table. It can certainly be produced with a cutting board, a knife, and a stock pot on a cooktop burner. But if you serve two hundred guests per meal, you may need more than six gallons of salsa for a shift. That could take a prep cook several hours by hand and occupy a valuable cooktop burner. Purchasing a "Buffalo chopper" and a ten-gallon jacketed kettle will reduce prep time to 15 minutes and allow the sauce to simmer unattended, off the cooktop or range, saving more than enough to justify the additional expense of this equipment. Properly maintained equipment is reliable and always ready to work "24/7." Employees may not be.

## Equipment Basics

All restaurant equipment should be National Sanitation Foundation–certified to assure that it can be properly cleaned and sanitized. Noncompliant equipment may not pass local health department codes. All heated cooking equipment will have a stated minimum distance requirement away from flammable materials, located in the specifications sheet. Designers, architects, electricians, plumbers, and HVAC contractors will want specification sheets (usually in PDF format) on all major equipment used in the restaurant, to assure that their services satisfy the requirements of the equipment. If casters are used on equipment to allow for easier cleaning under and behind the unit, flexible gas hoses will be required for gas-fired equipment. See chapter 6 and "Scale Drawing for a Restaurant Kitchen" on page 108 for more details on equipment placement.

### What Your Architect and Contractor Need to Know About Equipment

- Dimensions—length, width, and height, including legs, casters/wheels for proper height

- Door clearances—front opening, right/left

- Door hinge side—right or left; are they reversible on site or do they need to be specified when ordering?

- Electrical—voltage, phase (single or three), amperage, GFCI circuit required?; plug type

- Gas—inlet diameter, minimum psi; does the equipment require a flexible connect?

- Spacing of equipment—minimum distance from flammable materials/walls

- Vent—required?; what type (I or II)?

- Water—required?; hot and cold?; inlet/outlet diameters; position and size of drains

- Filtered water—required?

- PDF files on each piece of equipment can be downloaded from the manufacturer's website or a restaurant equipment supply company's website.

There is a wide range of manufacturers of kitchen equipment and you must carefully examine and specify all parameters of equipment before making purchase decisions. Equipment is sold by dealers, distributors, jobbers, manufacturer's agents, or directly by the manufacturer, depending on the size of the order. In many cases local or regional restaurant and hotel supply companies are best equipped to serve local restaurants, but there is a wide range in pricing by equipment dealers, and comparative shopping is essential.

## Utilities Sources—Gas versus Electricity

Your choice is determined by personal preference, what is available in the area, and the cost of the utilities. Most chefs prefer gas since it responds faster to adjustments in temperature. One exception is a preference for electrical heat for baking ovens, as it is a more even heat and less prone to hot spots. With electrically powered kitchen equipment, a higher voltage source is often more economical to operate than a lower voltage source (220V versus 110V). In many areas natural gas is more economical overall than electricity. If you operate in an area that does not have natural gas utility lines, your gas cooking equipment will have to be purchased as, or converted to, propane or LPG-fueled (liquefied petroleum gas). Propane uses a different regulator and smaller burner openings as it operates at roughly twice the pressure of natural gas, and therefore a conventional natural gas range would have to be converted in order to burn propane. New equipment can be specified to use propane, usually at no extra cost. Tanks should never be stored inside due to risk of explosion should they leak, as propane is heavier than air and collects near the ground. During the winter, more of the gas condenses in the tank, resulting in low pressure. For this reason, you should keep your propane tanks topped-off during the frigid months, or use an approved, safe method of keeping your tanks warmed.

## Obtaining Equipment—Lease versus Purchase

There are two pieces of equipment that warrant close examination between purchasing and leasing. These are the dishwasher and the ice machine, since they are the two pieces of equipment that require regular maintenance, cleaning, and fine-tuning to keep them problem-free. When you lease equipment, regular service is part of the package, and should the equipment break down, you should expect priority repair. With dishwashers, your lease obligates you to use the soaps and chemicals of the company leasing the machine, normally with a minimum purchase amount per month. If the dishwasher is purchased, it is possible to purchase chemicals and soaps from wholesale grocers or janitorial suppliers cheaper than from the leasing company. Buying the machines and doing your own maintenance is often less expensive, but those tasks often get overlooked, resulting in breakdowns or poor performance. To do a cost analysis, consider that lease expenses are fully tax deductible, and compare that deduction to the tax amortization schedule given by the IRS. Other than comparing the purchase price versus lease price, do not neglect utility ratings and projected costs. Leases often have provisions for equipment upgrades over time, while used dishwashers and ice machines are difficult to sell and do not get top dollar when they do. Entire equipment packages can be leased from companies that specialize in restaurant equipment leases, but equipment lease packages for restaurants are much more difficult to qualify for now than in years past.

### New Equipment Sources

The most typical source for new restaurant equipment is the local or subregional restaurant equipment dealer, who will be charging list price, or slightly lower. If the equipment is needed immediately, and they have it in stock, it is the best bet. Some buyers might prefer local vendors out of a desire to "keep the money in town," or to shop from a hands-on source where they can see and touch the equipment, or compare products side-by-side. If the local vendor doesn't have the product in stock, the wiser bet might be to consider other sources with better pricing. Another source is the consolidated regional restaurant equipment dealer, who can offer better pricing due to higher sales volume. Be wary of distance; the farther away you purchase, the higher the freight costs. Be sure to consider the national broadline or regional food suppliers, such as Sysco, US Foodservice, PFG, Ben E. Keith, or Labatt. Many of them sell equipment as well as food, often at competitive prices.

Cost-wise, an option to consider is an online source, such as Bigtray.com, Centralrestaurant.com, Webrestaurantstore.com, or Katom.com. All have online catalogs, with complete lines of equipment, appliances, tableware, and smallwares (see Appendix E). PDF spec sheets are available with the click of a mouse, and all offer toll-free phone numbers for detailed equipment consulting or questions. Their prices often run 50 to 60 percent of list, with free shipping when the order is over a nominal amount; freight costs on heavy items like equipment, glassware, or dishware can be very expensive. Many do not add tax to the order, but you may be responsible for the sales tax to your state.

### Used Equipment Sources

One strategy to lower restaurant equipment costs is to purchase used equipment. Used restaurant equipment costs about 40 to 60 percent of the new retail price, is often cosmetically substandard, and may or may not perform as new. Always test the equipment before purchasing, and avoid purchasing any equipment "as is." Never buy used refrigeration unless you plan on replacing the compressor and gaskets; often, by the time you get through paying these expenses, you could have purchased a new piece for the same amount.

Refurbished or factory-reconditioned equipment generally sells for about 60 percent of list, and comes with the same warranty as "new" equipment. It usually looks and works like brand-new. One advantage is the assurance that a technician adjusted the equipment and restored it to factory specs. Local new equipment retailers often have used trade-ins or repossessions that are for sale, and these pieces are generally given the once-over by their staff technicians and are in relatively decent working order. There are numerous used restaurant equipment dealers who repair or restore used equipment for resale. Restaurant equipment auctions offer equipment that is sold "as is" for cash, with no guarantee. Attending these auctions is time consuming, with travel costs involved, and no guarantee that what is needed can be purchased for a fair price. The crowd is often sprinkled with knowledgeable "shark" buyers who outbid the rookies at the last minute, or bid-up prices unnecessarily to benefit the auction house. Genuine distressed or out-of-business restaurant equipment auctions might be the best option if trying to buy cheap, but there is no guarantee any of it actually works. With any auction, expect to pay cash, or with a check accompanied by a bank letter of credit, and have the ability to haul off your purchases at the end of the auction.

## Equipment Selection

There is an old adage for selecting equipment: "Get the right piece for the job and the quality level required to perform the task." Aside from that adage, there must be adequate utility service and capacity to satisfy the demands of the equipment. You do not want equipment that demands more than your utilities can provide, unless you have the capacity in the budget to upgrade your utility service.

The first step in equipment selection is coming up with a list of the equipment required to prepare and store all of the items on the menu, with thought given to future needs. Purchase efficient Energy Star–compliant equipment whenever possible, since restaurants use about two and half times more energy per square foot than other commercial buildings. Reduced energy and water use directly translates to increased profits over time, and is more socially responsible.

Once the equipment list is formulated, consider the expected volume of sales and the mix of items on the menu, which will help determine what size or capacity of equipment is required. For example, if the menu offers several options for pancakes at breakfast, or you expect to sell many hamburgers at lunch or dinner, a 48-inch or 60-inch-wide griddle might be preferable to a 36-inch griddle.

Consider any desired options when selecting and pricing the equipment; available options will be listed on the specifications sheet. Are legs or casters preferred? Are extra shelves needed, or do hinges need to open in a certain direction for proper worker access? Is a remote compressor preferred, or an upgraded surface needed? All selected options will affect the final price and perhaps availability of the equipment.

Match work surface heights when selecting countertop and under-counter equipment to ensure a seamless work surface, paying particular attention to the finished height of the equipment and whether the height of the legs or casters have been included in that calculation. For some areas a backsplash might be preferred on countertop equipment, and in other arrangements a backsplash could prove to be detrimental.

When considering refrigeration, think about the sizes of items that will need to be stored, as well as the total volume of supplies required, considering the delivery schedules of your vendors. For example, if the business can get daily delivery of items, less refrigerated storage will be needed. If the restaurant requires storage of cases of meats or vegetables, which are large and bulky, a walk-in cooler will be required. If the restaurant requires cases of frozen goods on hand, a walk-in freezer might be required (and is often part of the "walk-in"). For the cooking line, consider how much refrigerated space is needed for the cooking and pantry staff. It is essential to have foods within easy reach and accessible.

Dealers do not include uncrating or installation with purchases. Both transportation and installation have to be arranged by the buyer, or may be arranged by the dealer for an additional charge. All newly delivered equipment should be immediately uncrated or unboxed to look for shipping damage. Any damage should be reported immediately and the shipment refused. If accepted the equipment should be checked as soon as possible make sure that it works properly. If kitchen equipment is ordered from or purchased abroad, it is important to check specifications and standards to ensure that they comply with local rules and regulations. Electrical equipment not from the United States is almost always 220V.

All equipment should be checked, adjusted, and calibrated by a local equipment technician after it is installed and before you start testing recipes and certainly before the restaurant opens for business. Refrigeration needs adjustment and thermostats should be checked for accuracy. All burners and ovens need to be calibrated to ensure that they are operating at peak performance and proper temperature.

## Major Kitchen Equipment

The pieces of equipment below are the workhorses of the kitchen. They allow you to broil, sauté, grill, melt, brown, reheat, steam, simmer, bake, and roast. They are found on the line to serve the food from the menu and to prepare the basic sauces, stocks, and other bulk items headed for the line.

### Charbroilers

A charbroiler is the best piece of equipment to deliver true char-grilled taste, and is used for grilling meats, fish, and vegetables. Most charbroilers, also known as underfired broilers, are countertop-installed and usually require a separate equipment stand, although freestanding models are available. Gas-fired charbroilers are the most commonly used. Electric charbroilers are available, but not very popular.

Charbroilers come in widths of from 2 to 6 feet (mostly specified in inches), in 1-foot increments. There are several options of flame diffusers—ceramic briquettes and lava rocks, which sit in gridded cast-iron trays, and steel radiants with grease covers. Steel radiants are the most efficient, but the best flavor is produced by ceramic briquettes and lava rocks, which catch dripping juices and produce smoke, with lava rocks being the most absorbent and thus contributing the most flavor. Both briquettes and lava rocks have to be replenished over time, but replacement cost is minimal.

There are different styles and materials of grate, which is the cooking surface. The style of grate affects the aesthetic "marks" on grilled items. Narrower grates with closer spacing are generally better for fish and seafood grilling, as they produce less sticking during the cooking process. The height of the grate above the heat source and the grate angle are generally not adjustable, except on larger crank-type horizontal grates. Easily removable catch trays and grease collection wells are preferred, with adequate holding capacity to get through the shift. Heavier gauge metals, especially stainless steel, are desirable when used for the construction of the frame and sides. Every charbroiler should be have a wall behind it with stainless steel covering, as the grill produces quite a mess on the wall and needs to be scrubbed daily. A conveyor broiler, or "clamshell" broiler, has radiant broiler elements on the top and bottom, which cook the food as it moves through the heated area on a metal grate conveyor belt. Conveyor broilers are normally used in fast-food restaurants.

Wood-burning broilers usually require a separate exhaust hood and frequent careful cleaning of the ductwork and exhaust fan, due to embers and increased fire danger from accumulated creosote and grease. They also require a secure, covered wood storage area and a supplier who delivers and stacks the wood. Skill is required to maintain even cooking heat with burning wood and coals throughout the shift. There are numerous styles of wood-burning charbroilers on the market, in a variety of sizes.

### Overhead Broiler, Finishing Oven, or Hotel Broiler

Overhead broilers are used to melt cheese or toppings, slowly bake dishes or keep dishes warm, create or finish glazes or sauces, brown or reheat foods, or caramelize desserts. They are often used in cooking steaks because overhead heat has the advantage of allowing high-fat foods to be grilled without the risk of flare-ups from below. They are most often positioned over the range, and are wall-mounted, but in steakhouses they can be stacked and freestanding. Overhead broilers can be gas or electrically heated, with gas being preferred, and come in lengths ranging between 3 and 6 feet (usually measured in inches), with 36 inches being the norm. The longer the length, the more heat zones and controls there will be. Gas infrared burners are more efficient than open-flame broilers, and burners can be thermostatically controlled on the more expensive models.

There are two types of overhead broilers—the cheese melter and the salamander. A cheese melter has a nonadjustable shelf positioned a fixed distance from the burners. They cost less and are simpler to use. A salamander has a locking mechanical "pistol grip" or slotted device to move the shelf away from the burners. Salamanders cost more and take a little more effort to use, but offer much more versatility in cooking or browning. Units with removable drip trays are preferred. When wall-mounted, overhead broilers use extra-heavy-duty mounting hardware and anchors, as the cabinets are very heavy. Pay special attention to ergonomics when positioning the broiler, so that height and reach are comfortable for the users.

## Griddles

Griddles are superb for cooking pancakes, flatbreads, eggs, omelets, steaks, chops, burgers, and other foods prepared in batches and that require very even heat. Flat-top griddles come in lengths between 1 and 6 feet in length (usually measured in inches). Griddles can be countertop units or freestanding, with a countertop unit sitting on an equipment stand as standard. They can be heated with gas or electricity, and the longer the width, the more heating zones they will have. Steam or infrared-heated griddles are newer to the market, and are gaining acceptance. Generally gas griddles are preferred, because they produce more even heat and offer quicker response, but electric griddles are considered more efficient. Thermostatically controlled heat zones are preferred. Griddle tops, or "plates," are made from cast iron, steel (cold-rolled or polished), or aluminum.

Cast-iron tops are preferred by many chefs for their heat retention and ability to quickly recover temperature, but are harder to find. "Antique" units with cast-iron plates are desirable, *if* they are not warped. The thicker the plate, the better and more evenly it cooks, the better it retains heat and reheats, the more resistant it is to warping, and the longer it lasts. Chrome-plated tops are easier to clean and radiate less ambient heat into the kitchen. Look for adequate grease collection wells that are easy to remove, with a removable drip tray underneath. Above all, a griddle should be easy to clean. The goal of cleaning and maintaining the cooking surface is to keep a seasoned, nonstick surface. Never use cold or cool water to clean a griddle; it can cause the plate to warp.

## Ranges and Cooktops (Hot Plates)

For many restaurants, the bulk of the cooking can be done with a range, which is a cooktop with oven(s) below. Ranges can be fueled by either gas or electricity, with gas being more responsive, a critical element for professional chefs. All ranges should be AGA-certified for gas equipment and UL-listed for electric equipment, which assures their inherent safety. Ventilator hood systems with fire protection are required over all gas and electric ranges, with local fire codes setting the specific requirements. The higher the backsplash you have in the back of the stove, the easier cleanup will be, and removable grates on open burners and pull-out crumb pans beneath range tops make cleaning simpler. There should be a smooth, level transition between burner grates, so that it is easy to slide pots and pans between burners. Optional over-shelves are useful for storing sauté or other pans. Ranges are available in many configurations, from four burners to ten burners, single and double oven, in 2-foot length increments (a standard six-burner is 36 inches wide, while a ten-burner is 60 inches wide).

Commercial range gas burners heat at much higher BTU ratings than a home stove, with commercial burners peaking at 35,000 BTU. The number, size, and type of burners desired depend on the diameter of pan or pot being used and its purpose. For example, if predominately sautéing with 10-inch skillets, you might select six high-heat burners on a 36-inch cooktop, while cooking more with large pots or saucepans might dictate selecting four wider diameter burners that cook with lower, more even heat.

Conventional range ovens are sized as full, which hold full-sized sheet pans (16 x 24 inches) or half, which hold 12 x 16-inch sheet pans. The width of the range will determine the possible size of the oven or ovens underneath.

Ranges are also available as "dual fuel," which indicates gas burners and electric oven or ovens. This is an ideal setup, since it allows for high-heat cooking on the cooktop and uniform electrical heat baking in the oven. Gas or electric ovens can also be ordered as convection units, which use a fan system to circulate the air inside. This speeds up cooking time by as much as 25 percent and reduces cooking temperatures by as much as 30 percent while baking or roasting more evenly, ending up more cost effective and time efficient. Convection oven ranges are deeper to allow for a fan system in the back, and require a 120V outlet.

Hot plates are countertop units, require an equipment stand, and do not have ovens. Gas pilots can be conventional or automatic electric lit. Separate convection ovens are often installed when using hot plates. Buying a freestanding range with an oven underneath is less expensive than buying a hot plate with an equipment stand and separate ovens.

## Door Openings

When ordering any piece of equipment with doors, be sure the doors clear everything around. Check to see how many inches a front opening door intrudes into the workspace—you should be able to stand in front of the equipment and comfortably open it. Doors that swing right or left must be checked this way as well as to see whether the hinges should be placed on the left or right, considering other swinging doors and obstacles.

Electric ranges are available in either the solid French hot plate or high-speed, open-coil styles. The open coils heat faster, while the French plate cooks more evenly. Commercial electric ranges are often more expensive than gas ranges and require 220V service. Electric induction burners are becoming more popular, and are available as freestanding ranges or as countertop units. Electric induction cooks by using alternating current (AC) through a copper coil, producing an oscillating magnetic field, which produces resistive heating inside the vessel to cook the food. The current is large, but produced by low voltage. Electric induction heats rapidly and efficiently, keeps cool on the surface of the cooktop, reduces kitchen cooling needs, and shuts off automatically when the cooking vessel is removed. Electric induction burners require using cookware that is ferromagnetic (steel or cast iron—if a magnet sticks to the side of the vessel, it can be used). Ranges with electric induction cooktops are still very expensive, but individual electric induction cooking plates are affordable and useful.

### Fryers (Deep Fryers)

Fryers are available as gas or electrically heated models. Gas is considered more desirable since it is more responsive and recovers temperature faster. Countertop and drop-in models are almost always electric, while freestanding models are usually gas. A single-tank, double-basket, freestanding fryer is a minimum of 15 inches wide, holding anywhere between 35 and 80 pounds of frying oil (fryer capacity is measured in pounds of oil). Single- and double-tank units are available, and stainless steel tanks are preferred. Double tanks are often required when frying fish along with other foods that could pick up unwanted "fishy" flavors and smells. The thicker the gauge of metal used in the tanks, the less prone the tank is to warping and the longer it lasts. Many fryers feature a "cool zone" that allows breading and debris to fall down below so that it does not scorch or burn, prolonging the life of the frying oil and helping to keep the flavor fresh. More expensive models feature an automatic top-off system, which draws oil from a reservoir to keep the oil at a certain level. The newest trend is low-volume, high-efficiency fryers that eliminate the cool zone, resulting in using less oil while speeding up recovery time (using less energy). These new models require more frequent filtering, but save money in the long run. Smaller countertop or drop-in fryers are available, which feature shallower tanks with less oil capacity and smaller baskets. They work well for smaller restaurants that fry infrequently (and for frying specialty items, such as fried pies). Countertop fryers usually have a lift-out fry pot that is easily handled when pouring the oil through a filter cone.

The fryer area needs a place for a breading station, on which containers hold a liquid batter and breading trays. On the opposite side of the fryer is a "dump station," an electrical infrared warmer with a holding pan and grate to hold the fried food from the basket. The fryer needs to be 16 to 18 inches from any open flame (depending on local code), and conveniently, the narrowest work table available is 18 inches wide. This allows for plenty of room on either side to set up the breading and dump stations.

Fryers need a method to filter the oil daily (or more frequently, depending on fryer type and sales volume). The most basic method is to have a filter holder with a paper cone filter suspended over a metal pot large enough to safely hold the capacity of the fryer tank. There are aftermarket filtering pumps, which use gravity feed or an electric pump to send the oil through a filter, as well as fryers with built-in filtering systems (the most desirable and easiest to use). There are wheeled grease disposal carts with manual pumps that make it easier to transport used fryer oil (called "yellow grease") from the kitchen to the oil waste disposal barrel outside, which is periodically collected by a waste oil or rendering company.

## Steam Tables

Steam tables are designed to safely hold cooked (prepared) foods until service. The national requirement is to hold food at 140°F or more, but local ordinances may exceed that temperature. They can be freestanding or countertop, and heated by gas or electricity. Gas is more responsive, with a faster recovery time, while electricity is more efficient, with more even heat. Steam tables can be "wet," where hot water is poured into the body of the unit to better conduct heat to the bottom of pan inserts. Wet tables need an easily accessible, large diameter drain for clean out, and are positioned so that it's easy to get a large pot or bucket underneath when draining. "Dry" tables indicate that no water is placed inside the unit, heating the bottom of insert pans by heating the air contained inside the unit. Dry tables produce less steam and humidity in the kitchen, but are less effective at heating the insert pans. Some units can be used as wet or dry tables. It is best if the steam table has a stainless well liner so it will not rust, and heavier gauge metal construction is preferred. A shelf or cutting board attached to the front edge is beneficial to use as a work surface and to hold plates, pots, and pans.

Steam tables are available with one to five individually controlled wells, each holding a full-size hotel pan. Adapters can be used to change the configuration of each well to utilize different-size pan inserts in combination, for example, a single well might hold a half pan, a quarter pan, and two eighth pans. Adapters allow for round inserts as well. Lids in all sizes are available and hinged lids are convenient for full-size pans. Smaller-size electric countertop units are available in full- and half-size options, as are soup warmers. Drop-in units in all sizes and configurations are available for built-in applications.

### Deck Ovens

Deck ovens are the workhorse of any kitchen that bakes almost anything, from breads and cakes to pizzas, casseroles, and food preparations of all kinds. They can be gas or electric, with electric providing more even heating while gas is quicker responding. Most baking ovens are electric, while pizza ovens need the fast response time that gas provides. The surrounding kitchen space benefits from having a basic Type II heat exhaust fan and hood for electric ovens, although it is not generally required. Gas ovens require a Type I exhaust hood. See "Exhaust or Vent Hood" on page 64 for more information. Deck ovens are expensive, large, and bulky, but for the most part are reliable and trouble-free. Their main benefit is that they allow baking and cooking on a large scale. They come in widths of 42 and 60 inches, and in a variety of oven heights from 6 to 16 inches, depending on the manufacturer. Units are stackable and offered in many different configurations. Popular options include adding plumbing for steam injection, ceramic decks, interior lights, and high-temperature thermostats (usually 650°F). It is advisable to have pan (bun) racks nearby as many baked products are placed on sheet pans before being inserted into the ovens.

### Pizza Ovens

Pizza ovens use higher heat than a normal deck oven, and because the door is opened and closed almost constantly, they require rapid temperature recovery. They are usually shorter in height (7 or 8 inches), and have heating elements on top and bottom. They are usually wider, so a larger space is required, and they can be stacked. The fuel source can be electric, gas, gas and wood combo, wood-fired, or coal; the fuel source determines the highest temperature possible, with coal being the hottest. Wood adds an appealing smoky element to cooked products but skill is required to maintain even temperatures when cooking with wood over extended periods of time. Wood fuel also requires a wood source and a dry, secure storage area. Pizza ovens can also be used for conventional baking and roasting, but these are not the most economical uses for a pizza oven, which is relatively expensive to purchase. The deck, or bottom, should be very thick steel or lined with thick ceramic to retain high heat and produce a crispy crust.

### Convection Ovens

Convection ovens are used for baking and roasting, heating casseroles, etc. An electric fan keeps air inside the oven circulating so that it cooks more efficiently. It speeds up cooking time by up to 25 percent and reduces the required cooking temperature by as much as 30 percent. Since cooking times and temperatures are shortened, there is a learning curve required over using a standard oven. Convection ovens can be gas or electric, countertop or freestanding, half size or full size, or extra deep, which hold rectangular pans in either direction. Installation will require extra depth for the rear-mounted fan motor, and a 120V outlet for gas models. Electrically heated models will require 220V outlets.

### Cook and Hold Ovens

Cook and hold ovens are used for slow-roasting meats and then holding them at serving temperature, such as for prime rib or other roasts. They are almost always electric, and can be freestanding or countertop/under counter. Their size is determined by the number of pans they can hold, usually seven to sixteen. Double-stacked units are available and there are smoker options. If holding prime ribs and roasts, be sure to allow a convenient spot nearby for meat slicing and portioning.

### "Combi" Ovens

The combi oven combines multiple cooking modes of heat, steam, and hot-air convection, in any combination, all in a much smaller footprint than having separate units. The steam mode is ideal for vegetables and shellfish. The hot-air mode operates as a regular convection oven for baking. The combination mode is used to reheat foods and to roast or bake. Additionally, with the combi mode, cooking time and shrinkage are reduced, with no flavor transfer. Options include a smoking mode, a microwave mode, and the ability to poach, reheat, and defrost. Countertop and floor models are available, and specifying a boiler-less unit will virtually eliminate scale and lime problems. These units require a filtered water source and a drain, and the optional rinse-out sprayer on a hose is well worth the extra cost. The downside of a combi oven is the relatively high cost.

## Smokers

Large-volume barbecue operations use pit-style smokers made of steel or masonry. These pits can hold hundreds of pounds of meat on grates covered by heavy lids, which are raised and lowered by a pulley system (or hinged doors providing front access). A flue system controls airflow, the temperature and speed that the fire burns, and the amount of smoke concentration. Steel ash cans are necessary for safely holding ash and coals during the cleanout; many dumpster fires are caused by disposing of ash that was thought to be "cool enough." Another type of smoker is a low-temperature oven fitted with a small, electrically heated woodchip box and a sealable door. These vary from small countertop units capable of holding 30 to 50 pounds to larger freestanding models that can hold up to 300 pounds. They use electric heat and small amounts of chips to smoke meats 8 to 10 hours. They can also be used for cold-smoking cheeses and seafood by using only smoke to cure the product. Asian equipment suppliers also produce cabinets for barbecuing or smoking poultry and meats, using hanging hooks or wire shelves. With these, the heat source is either gas or electric, with a water pan to reduce shrinkage, and a woodchip box to provide smoke if desired.

## Holding or Heated Cabinets and Proofers

Holding cabinets are used to keep prepared food at a safe temperature (140°F) until ready to be served. Cabinets are normally on casters, and can be insulated or uninsulated, humidified or dry, and heated by thermostatically controlled electricity or by petroleum gel canisters. Heights can be under counter (32 1/4 inches), half (44 3/4 inches), three-quarter (62 3/4 inches), or full height (69 inches plus). Doors can be single or Dutch (two doors, upper and lower), clear glass or solid stainless steel, and the cabinets usually come fitted for full (18 x 26-inch) sheet pans, or they can be configured for hotel pans (to hold bulk food for a serving line), or for other options. Pass-through units are used when cabinets are not placed against a wall, and feature doors on both the front and back, allowing easy access from both sides. These units are often placed in areas where one person can place products in the cabinet and another person can remove it from the other side. A roll-in cabinet is designed for a pan/bun rack to be rolled into and enclosed within the cabinet, while a roll-through cabinet is designed for a rack to be rolled in from one side, held at temperature, and then removed from the opposite side. Insulated banquet carts are designed to hold large quantities of covered plates or hotel pans, where they can be plated in the kitchen and then rolled out to the banquet floor for service. These carts can be heated electrically or with chafing fuel. They are normally used for catering, banquet service, and hotels. Restaurants might use a heated cabinet for holding products such as casseroles at the proper temperature during service. Choose units with magnetic door gaskets, and self-closing doors if possible.

Proofing is the final dough-rise step before baking. A dough proofing cabinet provides warm temperatures and controlled humidity ideal for yeast growth and dough rising, usually 80 to 135°F. Proofers can be insulated or not and should be humidified for best results.

### Exhaust or Vent Hood, with Fire Suppression System

In the restaurant design and building trade, this is known as "CKV," or Commercial Kitchen Ventilation. This system is required to be installed over all gas equipment sources with flames and almost all cooking equipment. The purpose of the exhaust hood system is to evacuate air contaminated with heat, steam, smoke, grease, fumes, and particulates. It requires an integrated fire suppression system that dumps chemical fire-control foam on the cooking equipment while shutting off the gas supply to all equipment in the event of a fire. Fire suppression systems are inspected by the local fire department and must get periodic inspections and occasional recharging over time by companies that specialize in fire suppression equipment. If you use an equipment-specific nozzle pattern (the spray is directed to a specific area or zone), you will have to modify it if you change equipment position. If you use a full-flood nozzle pattern (overlapping), equipment changes seldom require a change of nozzles.

There are legal, zoning, and permit concerns with an exhaust hood system. The local health department is concerned with sanitation issues, while the local fire department has concerns about whether the hood presents a fire hazard and if it can abate a sudden flare-up. The insurance company looks at it from a hazard risk to the property, while the local environmental department (and the restaurant's neighborhood) has possible concerns about smoke emissions. Generally, the hood must overhang 6 to 8 inches on each side of the cooking line, and 12 inches in the front. If the ceiling height is less than 8 feet 6 inches, a low ceiling–style hood system is required. The bottom front edge of the hood must be a minimum of 78 inches from the finished floor. Some local codes may dictate that wood-burning equipment, charbroilers, or other equipment have their own separate hoods, divided from the main hood.

Most hoods must be fully welded (not riveted) to pass inspection. The hood system requires coordination between the HVAC contractor and a sheet-metal fabricator (and occasionally a mechanical engineer), to construct a hood that is sized properly for the cooking equipment and the BTUs involved, the size and layout of the cooking line, the UL listing of the fan equipment, and the dynamics of the building's HVAC system. Typically, 50 to 75 percent of a restaurant's heating and cooling costs can be drawn out by the exhaust hood, which is why it is important to achieve a balanced system that exhausts the bad air while keeping in the good air.

It is desirable to have a make-up air (MUA) system, a separate source of air to replace the large volumes that the vent hood draws. Fine-tuning by the HVAC contractor after installation to adjust variable-speed exhaust fan motors is needed to achieve balance. Options to standard hood systems include make-up air, side curtains, variable-speed fan controls with thermostats and smoke sensors to automatically reduce exhaust fan speed when not needed, automatic filter and hood water-wash systems (requires hot water and drain), and filters that preheat water from the cooking line before it enters the water heater. There are several kinds of removable grease filters available, including the channel or baffle, or the metal mesh styles. These are the lower-end types and are quite acceptable. The high-end offers centrifugal fixed baffles and scrubbing systems, which are labor saving.

There are two types of exhaust hoods, Type I and Type II. Type I is the typical restaurant exhaust hood with fire suppression and grease filters as previously described. Type II is designed to evacuate only nominal heat and water vapor, and does not have either fire suppression or grease filters. Type II filters are used over dishwashing machines and electric ovens, and anywhere excessive moisture or heat is produced without a flame.

## Refrigeration

Twenty percent of total energy consumption in a commercial kitchen is from refrigeration. You should determine your needs based on menu, volume required (measured in cubic feet), and the location and available space where refrigeration is needed, such as bulk storage, in the prep area, on the cooking line, and in the pantry. Refrigeration with remote compressors that are used in extremely cold environments will require a winter kit.

### Reach-in Refrigerators

These are upright models, like home-consumer refrigerators, and come in widths of 20 to 32 inches per door section, with either a full-height door, or stacked half doors. The doors are available in glass or metal. Upright or full-height refrigerators usually come in one-, two-, or three-door models. It's always more cost-efficient to use a multiple-door unit than to use several single-door or two-door models. A three-door model is cheaper than a two-door and a single, or three singles, but three-door units are difficult to fit through many openings. Multiple-door units provide more usable space than combining single-door units. To get an accurate comparison, figure out the cost of the units and the total cubic feet of each unit and then compare. Most standard reach-in refrigerators are furnished with adjustable wire shelves in each compartment. You may need to order extra shelves. If you use a lot of sheet pans or hotel pans, you will want to opt for pan slides instead of shelves. A sheet pan on slides can function as a shelf when both are needed.

Reach-in refrigerators are available with either bottom-mount or top-mount compressors, with bottom-mount being considerably less expensive, but they add heat to the workplace. Refrigerators can be outfitted with a remote compressor, where the refrigeration unit is roof-mounted. This removes noise and heat from the kitchen. New options are hitting the market: coilless evaporators (easier to clean and they run cooler), removable magnetic door gaskets, quick-leveling legs, front-serviceable compressors, high-efficiency motors, and environmentally friendly refrigerants. You may want an Energy Star compliant unit if available.

### Under-Counter and Worktop Refrigerators

Under-counter models are designed to fit under a table or counter, while a worktop refrigerator is designed to have the refrigerator top function as the work surface. Both units can be ordered with doors or with sliding drawers, or a combination of the two. Drawers work best at holding quickly accessible foods for a cooking station on the line. There are also refrigerated equipment bases with drawers, designed to hold countertop cooking equipment. Worktop units can be ordered with a raised lip at the back of the top, or with a smooth edge. Models with drawers can be option-ally ordered as "deep" models, which hold two hotel pans per drawer instead of one. Under-counter and worktop refrigerators will have their compressors on the right or left side; make sure that your design and placement allow them to vent properly. Reach-in, under-counter, and worktop refrigerators are available as freezer units as well. There are also dual-temp coolers, which have refrigerator and freezer combined in one unit. Another consideration with freezers is the chest freezer, which is better for long-term storage.

Another option in worktop refrigeration is the sandwich prep box and the pizza prep table. A sandwich box has the shelving or drawers of the regular worktop cooler, except that the top has a section along the length of the back which holds third-sized insert pans so that they stay refrigerated and accessible to the user; a closable lid seals them off when not being used. These are available in lengths that hold between 6 and 16 third-sized pans (one-third of a full hotel pan). With adapters, these units can hold a multitude of ingredients to suit your needs. There is usually a cutting board rail along the front edge. Similar to a sandwich prep box is the pizza prep table, which gives the user a larger, deeper work surface on the top for building pizzas.

### Walk-in Refrigerator

The walk-in is used for the bulk of your refrigeration needs as a central cold storage unit. A walk-in is constructed of interlocking panels and is assembled on site. To determine the size walk-in needed, you should determine your peak cold storage needs based on your menu and your purveyor's delivery schedules. As a rough guide, 1 cubic foot of walk-in space will contain about 28 pounds of solid food. If you are not sure how much space you need, visit a restaurant of similar size and menu and ask a staffer what size they have, and if it is ideal.

The walk-in cooler can be either inside your kitchen, or outside and adjacent to the kitchen (preferably with an interior entrance). Hopefully it can be located in the coolest part of the building. It must be easily accessible to kitchen staff and near to the delivery area. Outdoor units need an insulated floor, a winter kit, and a sealed rain roof. It should also be enclosed by security fencing. You will need to decide if a portion of the walk-in refrigerator needs a walk-in freezer. Common sizes available combine widths from 4 to 12 feet, depth from 4 to 20 feet and usually run 7 1/2 to 9 1/2 feet in height. The floor of the walk-in can be your poured concrete kitchen floor if installing indoors; otherwise it will need to be insulated. All freezer floors should be insulated. Insulated floors are desirable and more energy efficient and thermal breaks should be installed under all wall sections.

A remote compressor can be mounted up to 50 feet away from the walk-in unit, removing noise and heat from the work environment. A remote compressor will raise installation costs, but save money over time by reducing cooling needs in the kitchen. Evaporator coils can take up large amounts of space inside the walk-in and the new "penthouse" evaporators solve this problem by combining coils with the condensing unit on top of the walk-in.

The outer material of a walk-in is referred to as a "skin." Metal skins of stainless steel are the best, or should be painted G90 galvanized steel or aluminum. Doors come in several widths and can be hinged left or right. Options include reinforced hinges and frame, deadbolt locking option, and inside safety release. A plastic air curtain is a necessity, and if using insulated floors, a ramp could be required by local or federal codes.

## Ice Machine

The ice machine can be the most problematic piece of equipment in the restaurant.

Many are of the opinion that ice machines should always be leased instead of purchased. Ice machines are expensive to purchase, and expensive to maintain, unless regular periodic maintenance and cleaning are done in-house. When you lease an ice machine you get regular servicing, sanitizing, and maintenance, and quick, priority response when there is a problem. When your purchased ice machine needs repair after 5 p.m. or on weekends, you pay a premium for a technician, and parts are often unavailable until the next day or later. Lease contracts can also include provisions for regular upgrades to keep you abreast of new technology. Ice machine problems are amplified when you live in an area with less-than-ideal water, accelerating problems with bacteria build-up, scale, liming and mineralization, and failing seals and gaskets.

Every ice machine needs a waterline and a drain, and power requirements vary with maker and model. The most common type of ice machine makes cubes. The shape of the cube depends on the machine's manufacturer, with varieties ranging from elliptical to cylindrical with a hole in the middle to actual cubes. Cube size affects the beverage. A larger cube (full dice) cools liquid slower, but lasts longer and dilutes the beverage the least. A smaller cube (half dice) chills the beverage quicker, but dilutes it more. This is an issue particularly if you serve liquor, when dilution of a spirit might be considered a negative. Generally, cube ice results in less ice consumption by the patrons.

A second form of ice is compressed flake ice formed into little nuggets. Nugget ice cools drinks quickly without foaming (great for sodas) and melts slowly (faster than cubes and slower than flake ice, described on the following page). Nugget machines use less water and energy than cube, are more compact, and require less maintenance. Flaked ice machines make soft flakes that rapidly chill beverages, but melt faster than nuggets or cubes. Flake ice is commonly paired with soda dispensers, and is ideal for molding around salad bar containers and seafood displays, storing refrigerated seafood, and using in blended drinks and cocktails. Flake machines are the most affordable. Restaurants that require both cubed and crushed ice can add an in-line crusher to their head and have a split bin below to keep the cubes and crushed ice separate. A simpler and more economical solution is to get a stand-alone, adjustable ice crusher.

Once you've decided what kind of ice you prefer, you need to select the type of machine you need. Get a machine that has been treated with an antimicrobial agent, which will reduce bacteria, slime, and scale. Make sure your machine is Energy Star certified. Modular units are commonly available in widths of 22 inches, 30 inches, and 48 inches, depending on the volume you need, and designed to fit on top of an insulated ice bin, an ice machine dispenser, or a soda dispenser. Outputs range from 250 pounds per day to more than 1,400 pounds per day

### Ice Machine Needs

- Restaurant—1 1/2 pounds per customer

- Restaurant/cocktail bar—3 pounds per seat

- Salad bar or food-display bar—35 pounds per square foot (L x W x D: convert the depth to feet if less than 12 inches). Flake ice is preferred for a salad bar.

- Fast food—8 ounces per 12- to 16-ounce cup; 12 ounces per 18- to 24-ounce cup

Self-contained ice machines are great for small cafes or bars, or fast-food operations that don't need large quantities of ice. The ice machine head is combined with a storage bin, and they are designed to fit underneath a 40-inch counter. Productions peaks at around 350 pounds per day. Countertop ice dispensers or makers are compact units that dispense nugget ice for quick service settings and may also dispense chilled water. They have a small bin but can still produce up to 400 pounds of ice daily.

Next you will need to decide on an air-cooled, water-cooled, or remote condenser. Air-cooled machines are the most common and the most cost effective, since they do not involve any additional water costs for cooling. Water-cooled are not usually recommended unless specific installation limitations require one. If a remote condenser is used, refrigerant lines run between the condenser and the machine, with the condenser mounted up to 50 feet away, generally on a roof. This removes the majority of the noise and heat of the ice machine.

You will need to figure the ice capacity your business requires. An ice-machine head can make a certain quantity of ice, which is then stored in bins of varying sizes. Pay careful attention to ambient air temperatures and water temperature on the manufacturer's spec sheets. The warmer the air and the water source, the less ice will be produced in a given amount of time. Estimate your needs based on anticipated peak use, allowing for traffic to increase over time if you are a newer business. Most restaurants will add a 15 to 20 percent buffer to that number to account for growth and contingencies. An ice bin that's too large will result in a lot of wasted, melted ice. Too small an ice bin means you could run out. Remember the old restaurant adage: "It is cheaper to store ice than to make it." Simply put, a larger bin that leaves some leftover ice after the rush is far more efficient than one running constantly to keep up with needs.

All ice machines should have a filtering system installed on the water intake, preferably one recommended or approved by the manufacturer. Filters make the unit run more efficiently, prolonging the life of the machine and improving flavor and clarity of the ice. It is estimated that over 60 percent of all ice machine service calls are water-related. If your machine is not already treated with an antimicrobial agent, purchase antimicrobial sticks or pouches and add them to the machine. RO (reverse osmosis) filtration is generally not recommended with machines; there has to be minimum mineral content in the water for the electric water-level sensors to properly function.

## Small (Counter) Kitchen Equipment

Many home cooks are familiar with smaller versions of these handy pieces of equipment. They have been scaled up in capacity for restaurant use. They are used to chop, slice, blend, mix, juice, and weigh materials used in the prep kitchen.

### Food Processors

Criteria for selecting a food processor include matching the machine to the task, capacity and bowl size, power, and cost. For smaller restaurants a 10- to 14-cup processor with around 700 watts of power will be adequate. Additionally, having a smaller 3- to 4-cup processor is beneficial for handling small tasks. For larger or busier restaurants the next step up is a machine with a 1-horsepower motor and the option of using it as a 3-quart food processor, or using the provided continuous feed chute for prepping large quantities of vegetables. For bigger jobs like mincing large quantities of hamburger meat, cutting big batches of granola, or making batches of salsa, a bowl cutter (aka "Buffalo chopper") is the ideal machine. With a typical bowl cutter, the 14-inch bowl revolves at 24 rpm while twin blades make 3,500 cuts per minute. With care, any of these machines should last 7 to 10 years.

## Immersion Blender

For pureeing, emulsifying, blending, mixing batters, or whipping large batches of liquids, the immersion blender is ideal. It allows you to blend the batch in its large cooking vessel or storage container, avoiding the need to process small batches. For light duty, a 200-watt machine will handle most jobs. For commercial tasks, look for a 10-inch shaft model, which will do batches of up to 6 gallons at a time, or a 14-inch shaft model, which can process batches of up to 12 1/2 gallons. For easy cleaning, the shaft and head should be removable and dishwasher-safe.

## Mixers

For light duty mixer use in the kitchen, a 5- to 7-quart model will handle most tasks. Recommended machines are generally in the 575- to 1,000-watt range, handling 4- to 6-pound batches of dough. For more production, the 20-quart countertop mixer is the tool of choice. For even larger batches, a 60-quart floor mixer is typical, able to mix up to 100 pounds of food. All of these mixers have optional attachments that can perform tasks like grinding meat, stuffing sausages, shredding vegetables, and grating hard cheeses and work off a power hub on the front of the machine (#12 hub for the 20-quart mixer).

## Slicers

Food slicers are designed for precisely slicing. Selection criteria are power, cutting blade size, carriage size, manual versus automatic, speed selection, safety, and ease of cleaning and sharpening. The more power, the denser the material it can handle. Blades of 9 to 10 inches are considered light duty, while 12- to 14-inch blades are for heavy-duty use; 12-inch is considered standard. Most 7 1/2-inch to 12-inch-long foods will fit on a standard carriage. A manual slicer is hand-operated, while an automatic slicer's carriage is motorized, cutting the food without an operator once it is set up. Ideally your machine is easy to break down for cleaning, and has a built-in sharpening system. It is best to have a permanent location for your slicer.

### Scales

Scales are needed to ensure portion control, check incoming bulk deliveries for accurate weight, aid in bulk food preparation, and ensure uniformity of results. Digital scales are recommended and those with rechargeable batteries are most useful in that the scale can be moved around without an awkward cord hanging or requiring an outlet close to where it's used. Their weighing range is from hundreds of pounds to less than an ounce.

### Juicers

Many restaurants with bars need fresh juices for a number of recipes. For citrus juicing, the least complicated option is an old-style hydraulic hand-operated citrus press. Depending on the volume of the operation and the juice needs, an electric centrifugal citrus juicer might be required. Vegetable juicers are handy to do vegetable juices for recipes or bar drinks.

## Dishwashing

The least glamorous job in a restaurant is dishwashing, yet it may be the most critical. How can a restaurant operate without clean plates, utensils, glasses, pots, and pans? If not done right, it won't take long for your guests to be turned off by greasy utensils or water glasses with food residue stuck to the rims. All food produced by your restaurant comes into contact with the items that come from the dish line, and it is essential that sanitary practices are observed at all times.

### Dish Machine

Dishwashing is one of the most critical elements of the restaurant business. If your pots and pans, plates, and glassware are not properly sanitized, you run the risk of making your customers ill. If your machine breaks down in the middle of a shift, with no clean plates or glasses, your restaurant can come to a grinding halt. The dishwashing line is the largest consumer of water and energy in the restaurant, so making smart decisions about your dish machine is important. When deciding if the restaurant needs a dish machine, consider that a skilled manual dishwasher will take more than twice as long as a dishwashing machine to wash the same number of dishes, and will use more water, chemicals, and utilities in the process. It will cost an average of $20,000 per year for a typical restaurant serving one hundred meals three times a day for hand washing. A dishwashing machine can accomplish the same task for about $6,000.

Dish machines are expensive to purchase. Many restaurants lease their dish machines from a local service company, which also provides required chemicals and regular (and emergency) service and repairs. These arrangements usually have a monthly fee plus a charge per rack, with chemicals and service included. Leasing a machine makes it easier and cheaper to upgrade to new technology. Some restaurants buy their machines outright and purchase chemicals and service from a local service company, paying a slightly lower monthly fee, and slightly increased rack fees. Other restaurants buy their machines and their own chemicals, do their own maintenance, and bring in a service company only for repairs. This last option is the least expensive, but can also be the most problematic when your machine breaks down during a weekend evening shift.

Low-temperature machines wash the dishes at a lower temperature than their hot-water counterparts, relying on a chemical bath to sanitize. They use less electricity but more water and chemicals. They are less expensive to purchase and operate than high-temperature machines. High-temperature machines sanitize by using an internal booster heater to heat the water temperature above the NSF standard of 180°F, and also have a flash dry cycle to help sanitize and dry the washed items. High-heat machines normally also use chemicals to aid removal of grease and improve sanitation. These machines use more energy, produce more steam, cost more, but are considered superior. A condensation hood (Type II) with exhaust fan is highly recommended to provide proper ventilation over your dishwasher, extracting humidity and heat. Check local codes to see if one is required. Humidity in the kitchen not only makes your HVAC work harder, it reduces the effectiveness of your machine's drying cycle, makes the work environment less comfortable, and can also contribute to tile floors "sweating," causing falls. A scale-inhibiting filter will remove minerals and sediment from your water source. It will reduce maintenance problems, will lengthen the life of the machine, and will help remove spots and streaks on glasses and flatware. These filters are highly recommended.

### Under-Counter Dish Machine

This is the commercial equivalent to residential models and can handle up to thirty-five standard racks per hour. They have a built-in booster heater to heat dishes and ware to 180°F for sanitization. Estimates range from seventy-five to one hundred customers per hour can be served by these machines; expect the lower end of the estimate to be accurate. Booster heaters are used to preheat water to the NSF-required 180°F for proper sanitization in freestanding machines. They operate independently of the dish machine and ensure that enough hot water is available for washing, especially on large machines with high output volumes.

## Freestanding Dish Machines

These sliding-door machines are larger than under-counter models and can handle up to 150 racks per hour. This is the most common type used in restaurants. They have a large, pass-through door on each side that opens and allows racks to easily slide in and out on rails. They are available as straight-line or corner models. These units should be able to handle up to three to four hundred meals per hour with two operators, but a single operator is the norm for most restaurants. Dish tables must match the openings and guiderails of the machine you select.

## Prerinse Sprayer

This will remove most of the food from dirty plates and will greatly speed up the dishwashing procedure while making the operator and machine work more efficiently. Some states have implemented controls on the GPM (gallons per minute) rates of prerinse nozzles in order to cut back on water usage without sacrificing efficiency.

### Garbage Disposals

These are units that finely grind organic matter after it is sprayed off of dishes in the racks. Some municipalities have outlawed their use, based on increased water usage, since they require a steady low volume stream of water to lubricate the grinding process. Garbage disposals lessen the amount of scraped garbage that has to go into your dish operator's trash cans, cuts back on the number of trips to the dumpster, and considerably reduces the total waste volume (and liquid waste) in your dumpster. Before planning on a disposal, check local requirements. If they are allowed, they will reduce labor and waste. Units are sized according to the restaurant's volume, and generally are hard-wired for 220V service. Disposals are not recommended for use with septic tanks.

## Hot-Water Heater

For a restaurant to be sanitary, it must have a constant supply of 140°F hot water. The health department will shut you down temporarily if you do not meet this basic requirement. From 20 to 25 percent of a restaurant's energy bill goes into heating water, and the vast majority of that water is used for washing dishes. The FDA has a website that succinctly outlines how to figure out your hot-water demands and how to match those demands with the appropriately sized water heater. Your hot-water heater needs to be on 6-inch legs and away from food prep or service areas. Make sure it is not in a drafty environment, does not present a fire danger, and that it is easily accessible for service.

A conventional or storage water heater can be fueled by gas or electricity. Gas offers a faster recovery time, with fan-assist being even faster. Electricity is more thermally efficient but gas is cheaper to generate hot water. Gas water heaters heat water faster than electric heaters, so they require smaller holding tank capacities. Electric heater tanks are roughly twice as big as a similarly rated gas heater tanks. Alternatives to traditional water heaters include solar water heaters that preheat the supply water going into your water heater; hybrid water heaters that function like a heat pump HVAC unit, preheating water by using the steady, warmer temperature of the earth deep underground; and tankless, on-demand heaters with no storage tank to keep full and hot.

## Wait Station Equipment

In addition to the kitchen, some foods and all beverages come from the wait station, relieving the pressure for this work from the line. Your waitstaff is responsible for a good-tasting cup of coffee, properly brewed tea, and the correct amount of ice in each beverage glass. Beverages are some of the most profitable items you will sell, so do not skimp on good, reliable equipment here.

### Coffee Brewing

With the popularity of high-quality coffee shops, the public expects a higher grade of coffee than in years past. There are several styles of brewers available, with the newer thermal airpot system being the most popular and best for preserving the flavor of coffee over a period of time. It is possible to lease your coffee service from a local supplier, but you have to use their beans, which are often substandard. Many restaurants buy their brewing equipment new or used, and buy their fresh-roasted beans wholesale either locally or online. For high-quality coffee, buy fresh-roasted beans and grind them in batches as needed. A commercial grinder is adjustable and grinds with low-friction burr grinders, which produce little heat during the grinding process. Typically these machines grind up to 1 pound at a time.

All water used for brewing coffee or tea should be filtered. A pour-over brewer drips heated water down over the grounds into empty decanters below. A three- to five-pot unit might cover the needs of a small cafe. It makes 3.8 gallons per hour, is the least expensive option, but is old-school technology. An automatic brewer is much like the pour-over, except the operator just pushes a button when coffee is to be brewed, as it is digitally controlled and has a plumbed water source. It is capable of 7.5 gallons per hour with a five-warmer machine; larger units have hot-water dispensers for making cups of hot tea. It requires a filtered water line and a 110V outlet.

An airpot brewer is an automatic brewing system where the machine is plumbed and requires a filtered water source and a 110V outlet. A twin airpot system makes up to 15 gallons per hour and includes a hot-water dispenser for making hot tea. It brews directly into 1.9- to 3-liter insulated airpots, which keep coffee hot and fresh for hours. Racks are available to hold multiple airpots for service or self-service.

## Tea Brewers

Customers really appreciate a well-brewed glass of iced tea, and the best way to produce this is with an infusion brewer that uses loose (unbagged) leaf tea. You can select high-quality tea leaves and also brew batches of mixed tea leaves for custom blends. The most basic infusion brewer brews directly into a 3- or 4-gallon dispenser, and can produce 16.3 to 26.7 gallons per hour. For conventional tea brewing using large commercial tea bags, there are many models available. All automatic tea brewers are plumbed, needing a filtered water line and a 110V outlet.

### Beverage Sales Mean High Profit

The most profitable items on your menu are nonalcoholic beverages, and your waitstaff should be encouraged to sell these items. A 16-ounce glass of iced tea has a food cost of around 4 cents per glass. A decent cup of coffee is about 10 cents. A 22-ounce soft drink (with ice) has a food cost of about 13 cents.

## Bar Equipment

Before you design or select bar equipment, you need to make a few decisions regarding bartending method and practice in your bar. Will you have draft beer or bottled beer, or a combination? Will you have a soda gun, bottled sodas, or a seltzer dispenser with soda syrups? Will you have an under-counter glass washer or an in-sink glass washer (if in-sink, will it be electric or manual?). Will you offer frozen drinks? Espresso? There are arguments for each, and each choice affects the equipment selected. Volume of sales and the number of selections offered also help determine the size or capacity of the equipment chosen. With all bar refrigeration, compressors are located on the right or left side, so make sure that the design and refrigeration placement allow the unit to breathe adequately. Pay attention to the height of the unit and whether or not it is to be used with no legs, with legs, or with casters (all will affect the finished height). It is beneficial if adjacent pieces of equipment are all at the same height, so the finished countertop is smooth and uniform. All doors and pour spouts behind the bar should be lockable.

### Backbar Cooler/Backbar Storage Unit

Backbar coolers have multiple functions. They store refrigerated mixers, provide for chilled spirits storage, and offer extra counter space for glass or bottle storage or a cash register. Doors can be solid or glass; glass is advantageous if you are merchandising certain items, such as imported bottled beers, but glass doors are more expensive. Depending on the length of the space available, you can have one, two, three, four, or six doors. Doors come in several styles—swinging doors, sliding doors, drawers, or in combination. If it is a tight space, sliding doors or drawers might be the best option. Exterior finish can be stainless steel, textured black vinyl (which is excellent at hiding wear and tear), or a combination of stainless and vinyl, stainless being more expensive. The wire shelving inside can be stainless or vinyl-covered and should accommodate additional shelving beyond that provided with the unit.

### Bottle Cooler

A bottle cooler is designed to hold bottles and/or cans. The spec sheet will give you the unit's capacity in both bottles and cans. They are available in varying length units with between one and four sliding horizontal doors, which access divided storage bins beneath. Most modern units chill the product on top very quickly.

Many units have adjustable dividers so that the interior can be customized. Exterior finish can be either stainless steel or laminated vinyl with stainless steel top.

### Draft Beer Cooler/Keg Cooler

Draft beer coolers come in a variety of sizes, from one to five kegs and one to two dispensing draft tab towers. Bars with more than five draft beer choices can store more kegs in a walk-in cooler, and then run remote lines to the draft unit. Kegs come in many different configurations working with a variety of sizes and shapes. Exterior finish can be stainless steel or laminated vinyl with stainless steel top. There is a specialty type of keg cooler called a "Club Top," which adds a horizontal sliding door on the left side where you can access chilled glasses, bottles, or cans. You will also need a connected $CO_2$ canister nearby. Keg coolers need to be connected to a drain for pouring overflow. Options include double-headed draft columns, three-way tapper manifolds, tap locking mechanisms, and remote cabinets.

### Glass Chiller/Mug Freezer

The units are designed to rapidly frost mugs or chill bar glasses and hold them at 0°F or lower. Available with one or two horizontal sliding doors on top, they normally have split shelves so that glassware can be easily rotated with additional shelves available for different interior configurations. Size is typically based on the number of 8-inch and 10-inch mugs the unit can hold. Exterior finish can be stainless steel or laminated vinyl with stainless steel top.

### Soda Gun

There are many points to consider when deciding on whether or not to have a soda gun. You have little flexibility as to the brands and flavors of syrups you can purchase. If you choose Coca-Cola, you get Sierra Mist instead of 7-Up. If you want 7-Up, you get Pepsi for your cola. You will need space underneath the bar for a carbonator, which needs a 110V plug in a GFCI outlet. You have to have space to store bag-in-box syrups or syrup canisters. If a carbonator is used you also need a place behind the bar for a $CO_2$ canister, as well as surplus tanks. The containers can leak syrup, which is hard to clean and attracts insects, and if the system isn't skillfully tuned by your route driver or service technician, the soda will not be blended correctly. Bottled sodas always taste exactly as the manufacturer intended, you can get the brands

e bottles do not leak. On the negative side, bottled
  sodas and take longer to serve, take up more space,
ed bottles, which go flat.

st bars and restaurants lease them from a local name-
eliver the syrups, repair your system, and do regular
e. Post-mix systems (most restaurants opt for this)
ter source. The gun will also need a drain connection.
 below your cocktail unit's ice bin. The soda gun can
; and provide a multitude of flavors, chilled water, and

irce and carbonates it to produce sparkling water. The
 iat there be a cold plate in the bottom of your ice bin
 ie liquid below 40°F. Carbonated water is most often
ck dispenser, mounted on the edge of the bar. It can
ups to produce Italian sodas or hand-mixed sodas, or

her

are usually purchased and can do up to one thousand
 noisy and release steam each time the door is opened
ure that you have ample room to store empty glass
d allow space to stage racks of clean and dirty glasses.
These units need hot and cold water sources and a 110V GFCI outlet. You should
consider having a triple sink as back-up.

### In-Sink Glass Washer

An in-sink glass washer is a sealed motor that drives a set of five matched rotating
brushes designed to thoroughly scrub a glass inside and out by inserting the glass onto
the center brush. It fits inside any bar sink, is manually operated, and can wash hundreds of glasses per hour. Upright models have the motor mounted on a shaft that sits
just above the water, and submersible models allow the motor to sit below the water's
surface. Most bars prefer the submersible unit because it tends to be a little quieter and
requires less space above the sink. The unit requires a 110V GFCI outlet.

### Blenders

There are many blenders available for bar use, and models made specifically for the bar with two speeds are ideal. They are very tough 600-watt units with all-metal drives that will blend ice with ease. Higher-powered units with 1- to 1 1/2-h.p. motors make fast work of frozen drinks, and commercial 2-h.p. blenders will make a frozen cocktail in just a few seconds.

### Wine Bottle Cooler

A wine cooler is a specialty refrigeration unit designed to hold chilled wine bottles at the proper serving temperature, higher than normal refrigeration units. Wine coolers can be under-counter half-size units or freestanding full-size units, and size is rated by the number of bottles it holds. Doors can be glass or solid stainless steel.

### Frozen Beverage Dispenser

When looking for a dependable margarita machine, research the brands that the party rental companies select. They can be purchased or leased and generally require 110V. You need to decide if you want a single-, double-, or triple-flavor freezer as there is a hopper for each flavor. A multiple-flavor machine uses less space and costs less than several single-flavor machines. Some people prefer clear plastic hoppers, as they create visual interest and boost sales. There are some desirable features to look for in a machine such as fast freezing of new batches, easy cleaning, and reliability. Some models have a mix reservoir that continually replenishes frozen product in the barrel and self-closing dispense valves to prevent waste. Lockable spouts and a "mix low" light that alerts the user when to refill the reservoir are desirable features.

### Espresso Machine

For most restaurant or bar applications, a semiautomatic Italian-made machine with a double boiler running on 220V power is the best choice. Semiautomatic machines feature an automated pump, automated temperature controls for the boiler, and activation switches to engage and disengage the pump. You decide when to turn the pump on and off, so you still have control over the quality of the brew. Double boilers allow you to brew and steam simultaneously. Machines are specified by the number of "group heads" (the unit that holds the filter and packed coffee grounds in place, channeling the pressurized, heated water through the coffee grounds and into the cup. A commercial machine should have at least two group heads, but can have more than four. To ensure quality, only the bartender or some other highly trained staff person should make espresso. Filtered water is an absolute must for the fewest operating problems. Regular cleaning and maintenance is critical. For the best taste, use fresh-roasted beans that are ground to order, or ground in small batches throughout the shift. Many experts agree that the grinder can be as important in making a great cup of espresso as the machine itself. A quality conical burr-type grinder is preferred. The grinder can be a doser type, which grinds a selected amount, or a doserless type, which has no preset amount to grind. Espresso machines can be leased from coffee suppliers in populous regions. Above all, do the homework before committing money to a commercial espresso program, for which there are many online resources.

### Stainless Steel and Shelving

Stainless steel is the preferred material for counters, tables, shelves, sinks, and such due to its impermeable nature and its ability to be thoroughly cleaned and disinfected. You will need a variety of products for your restaurant. The best quality is 14 gauge (thickest) and economy units are made from 18 gauge.

#### Sinks

You will need a variety of sinks throughout the restaurant. Hand-washing sinks are required by code to be accessible to workers who prepare or cook food. A three-compartment sink is also required by code for the kitchen for washing pots and pans, all dishes, and glassware. It comes in a variety of bowl sizes and depths. Drainboards can be specified for either or both sides of the sinks, in a variety of lengths. Four-compartment and two-compartment sinks are also available for additional duties such as salad washing. They are also there to serve as an emergency option if the dish machine goes out of service. The first sink compartment is used for presoaking and washing (minimum 110°F), the second is for rinsing (minimum 110°F), and the third for sanitizing solution (75 to 120°F water, plus 50 to 100 PPM chlorine solution for 7 seconds or longer). It is beneficial to have a flexible prerinse sprayer mounted over the sink, as well as an oversize debris basket in the first sink to prevent debris from clogging up the drain. Most restaurants that have a dish machine use the triple sink primarily for pot washing and bulky items. A separate mop sink is required for janitorial duties.

## Tables

Flat-top tables come with a front and back rolled rim edge and are standard height of 35 1/2 inches. Undershelves are of stainless or galvanized metal. Drawers can be ordered in a variety of widths. All tables have adjustable feet for irregular floors. Tables can be ordered with a backsplash panel from 1 1/2 inches to 10 inches. Tables come in 24-, 30-, and 36-inch depths and lengths of 2 feet to 12 feet. If you need to fit a piece of equipment under the table, then an "open base" table is specified and no shelf or center bar support will be added. There are corner tables and enclosed tables with drawers that slide or pull. Specialized tables can come with a poly top or butcher-block hardwood rather than stainless.

## Shelving

Pole-mounted shelving above the tables of the cooking line is useful to store plates and attach ticket rails and heat lamps. Wall-mounted shelves can house microwave ovens on the wall of the line or the set of spices and herbs in the prep area. A pass-through shelf is used for pick-up of orders when the kitchen is enclosed. Freestanding wire shelving (chrome plated and not stainless steel), comes in a variety of configurations and can have five adjustable shelves of depths from 12 inches to 24 inches. (Metro is the most popular brand name, and generic shelving is often referred to as "Metro shelving.") They are perfect to fit into any empty floor space to store almost anything. They are fitted to line the walls of storage rooms and walk-in refrigerators. For the latter application or to store wet dishes from the dish line, wire shelving can be polymer coated to prevent rusting.

## Pot Racks

Pot racks can be configured to hang from the ceiling or from pole-mounted shelves on a table. They are useful to store bulky stock pots and utensils, saving precious storage space on the floor or tables.

## Equipment Stands

Cooktops, charbroilers, and griddles often need an equipment stand as they are not freestanding with legs. At 24 inches in height, they allow the equipment to be on the level with tables and freestanding ranges and fryers. Mixer tables are a heavy-duty version of equipment stands, meant to hold up to strong vibrations and motions of powerful commercial mixers.

### Dish Tables

Dish tables connect to the dish machine to make a dish line. Dirty dishes enter on the "soil" dish table and exit on the "clean" dish table. Soil dish tables have a sink mounted into the table, in front of the dish machine, to be fitted with a garbage disposal and sprayer to remove waste from dirty plates. Dish tables are specified as either "right" or "left." When standing facing the dish machine, if the dirty dishes are coming in from the right and the sink is just to the right of the machine, it is a "right soil dish table." The clean dish table would be a "left clean dish table" in that instance. The opposite is true for dirty dishes coming in from the left when facing the machine. Corner dish tables are available when space is limited or design dictates this type of placement. There are undershelves and overshelves available to store racks that plates, utensils, and pots and pans are placed in to run through the dish machine, and to house chemicals. Dish tables come in a variety of lengths and accommodate racks that are about 24 inches square. The dirty dish table should hold at least two racks before the sink and two racks with clean dishes on the clean side, if space allows (room for three racks would be ideal).

### Bar Cocktail Unit

The cocktail unit or "jockey box" is designed to hold ice in an insulated bin. Size is rated by ice storage capacity and width, and is made of stainless steel, with a stainless "speed rail" mounted on the front to hold bottles of well or house liquors for fast access. There are single and double speed rails, and speed rails can be insulated, which makes them much quieter to use. A cocktail unit needs to be plumbed into a drain and can be freestanding or a drop-in model. If you are using a soda gun or a carbonator, you will need a cocktail unit that has a cold plate in the bottom. A cold plate is a temperature exchanger composed of a covered, self-contained line of aluminum or stainless tubing that snakes along the bottom of the ice bin in seven to ten loops (circuits). The more circuits you have the colder the soda or seltzer, and the more effervescent it will be.

**Major equipment:**

❑ Charbroiler
❑ Overhead broiler, finishing oven, or hotel broiler
❑ Griddle
❑ Range (with oven) or cooktop
❑ Fryer
❑ Steam table
❑ Ovens
    ❑ Deck oven
    ❑ Pizza oven
❑ Convection oven
❑ Cook and hold oven
❑ Combi oven
❑ Smoker
❑ Holding or heated cabinet/proofer
❑ Exhaust or vent hood with fire-suppression system

**Refrigeration (refrigerator, freezer, or a combination):**

❑ Reach-in refrigeration
❑ Under-counter or worktop refrigeration
❑ Walk-in refrigeration
❑ Ice machine with ice bin
    ❑ Cuber
    ❑ Flaker

**Countertop equipment:**

❑ Food processor
❑ Immersion blender
❑ Blender
❑ Mixer
❑ Slicer
❑ Scales/balances
❑ Juicer

**Dish machines and equipment:**

❑ Undercounter
❑ Freestanding
    ❑ High temp or low temp
    ❑ In-line or corner
❑ Prerinse sprayer
❑ Garbage disposal
❑ Water heater

**Wait station equipment:**

- ❏ Coffee machine
- ❏ Tea brewer

**Bar equipment:**

- ❏ Backbar cooler/backbar refrigerated storage unit
- ❏ Bottle cooler
- ❏ Draft beer cooler/keg cooler
- ❏ Glass chiller or mug freezer
- ❏ Soda gun
- ❏ Carbonator
- ❏ Under-counter glass washer
- ❏ In-sink, manual glass washer
- ❏ Blender
- ❏ Wine bottle cooler
- ❏ Frozen beverage dispenser
- ❏ Espresso machine
- ❏ Bar cocktail unit ("jockey box")
- ❏ Bar sink with drainboards
- ❏ Bar blender station
- ❏ Bar stepped or staircase liquor bottle shelving and display lighting

**Stainless steel:**

- ❏ Sinks
  - ❏ Three-compartment sink
  - ❏ Prep sink
  - ❏ Hand sinks
- ❏ Tables
- ❏ Shelving
- ❏ Pot racks
- ❏ Equipment stands
- ❏ Dish tables with drainboard

### Bar Sink with Drainboards

A bar sink should either be a triple or quadruple sink setup, and the drainboards should be as wide as possible so that you have the maximum amount of space for soiled and clean glasses on opposite sides. Opt for the tallest backsplash possible. If you have a four-sink model, you can use the first sink as a dump sink for debris from dirty glasses. The submersible glass washer goes in the second sink, along with low-suds glass soap. The third sink is for rinsing, the fourth for sanitizing. Washed glasses should air-dry on the drainboard adjacent to the fourth sink. With three-sink units, a separate sink is required for dumping dirty glassware. If you have an under-counter glass-washing machine, you typically are not required to have a bar sink, but the drainboards come in handy for staging glassware and you have a back-up if your machine breaks down. A bar sink needs both hot and cold water connections, as well as a drain connection. Optionally, a bar sink can have either speed rails or towel racks mounted along the front.

### Bar Blender Station

A blender station is a narrow (12- to 18-inch-wide) type of under-bar table that has a stepped-down shelf in front that holds one or two blenders. There is a hole on the backsplash of that shelf that allows the cords to be routed underneath, to keep them out of the way. Ideally there is a dump sink on the upper level, allowing you to rinse out the blender jars after blending a frozen cocktail. A blender station requires hot and cold water, a drain, and a duplex 110V GFCI outlet. Some local jurisdictions allow the blender station to also function as a hand sink. Check with local authorities to verify this.

### Bar Stepped or Staircase Liquor Bottle Shelving and Lighting

Most bars have a display backbar that shows customers which spirit labels they carry, usually on a stepped or staircase shelf system that is lighted from underneath. These can be built with basic carpentry skills or purchased in many different styles. Lighting is best from a slot running the length of each shelf, illuminating the bottles from below with flexible dual-white LED strips (that do not generate unwanted heat) set up on a dimmer. Fill light from above illuminates the bottle's label.

# 06

# Design Considerations

Given the restaurant's position on the site, there will usually be a best location for the entrance, which will dictate the FOH (front of house) position. First consider the size, dimensions, and shape of the allotted restaurant space. Usually there is an obvious natural or physical dividing line in any given restaurant space between potential FOH and BOH (back of house) areas. The standard formula for dividing a restaurant space between FOH and BOH is 60 percent for dining, including bar, restrooms, and service, and 40 percent for kitchen, storage, and office. Another way to consider layout and allotment is by square footage requirements. In the FOH, 5 percent of total seating must be wheelchair accessible. General seating requires about 15 square feet per person. A more formal restaurant's seating requires more, about 20 square feet per person. A one-hundred-seat casual dining restaurant requires a minimum of 1,500 square feet for dining, which comes to 2,500 square feet total restaurant space (1,500 square feet divided by 60 percent). Booths take up less floor space than tables, while counters use the most space. Seating guidelines will be discussed in detail later in this chapter. The design of the restaurant must comply with ADA (Americans with Disabilities Act) requirements, specifically parking, access to the restaurant and restroom facilities, doorways, and spacing between equipment. The design must provide access "with dignity." *Dignity* is a term used but not defined by the federal government. In essence, it means that one must avoid solutions that would embarrass disabled patrons, such as carrying them to their table rather than making the aisles wide enough for their wheelchairs, or having them sit in a special section of the restaurant to avoid costly modifications to make the main dining room accessible.

## FOH Entrance and Waiting Area

The entry area should be visually apparent from the street and parking lot, easily reachable from the parking area, handicapped accessible, well lit at night, spotlessly clean, and welcoming, with easily readable signage. New customers need to able to spot your entrance as they drive by on the road. The restaurant's hours and accepted credit card icons should be visible. Colorful landscaping, whether it is in planted beds or in pots, can greatly enhance the look of the entrance. It helps if you have a covered seating area outside so that customers can have a spot to convene before they enter the restaurant, or to wait while the cars are being retrieved before they leave. This is critical if the restaurant has valet parking.

There should be an ashtray outside so that there is a place to dispose of cigarettes, otherwise, they will be littering your landscape (ashtrays that include a garbage slot are preferred). Staff should sieve the sand frequently so it looks presentable. There should be a well-lit copy of the menu near the front door, so that customers can decide if they like the offerings and price range before they add to the crowd of diners waiting for a table inside. A weatherproof frame with a lockable glass door allows for frequent menu changes. Assume that anything outside that can be stolen will be stolen, including potted plants, ashtrays, tables, and chairs. Secure them accordingly.

Immediately inside the door is where the staff will greet customers and direct them to go to the bar or wait for a table, or to have guests pay as they leave. There is a fine balance between accommodating guests who are waiting when it is busy and having several empty benches to greet customers on less-than-busy nights. Psychologically, it is best if the entry looks bustling at all times; it promotes the image of popularity. Potted plants and artwork will enhance the look of the area. Having one of the speakers for the sound system, preferably with adjustable volume, mounted at the entry, will add to the atmosphere. In areas with a lot of rain or very cold winters, decisions need to be made concerning bulky coat and umbrella storage. Do diners drape coats over the backs of their chairs, use nearby racks or hooks, or is there a coat check room? Are there waterproof stands for dripping umbrellas? Whatever is decided, post discreet notices that the restaurant is not held legally responsible for any loss.

Essential at the waiting area is a host/hostess stand of some sort, to contain the telephone, POS (point-of-sale) system screen, a reservation book, wait list, business cards, toothpicks, mints, merchandise for sale, promotional items, and the like.

Depending on the business, there might be a need for a staging area for to-go or pick-up orders. In some family-style cafes the host/hostess stand also serves as a cashier's station, where customers pay out as they leave. In that case, make sure there is ample room for several customers to pay out while new arrivals are being seated or waiting to be seated. The area needs a clear view of the dining room, so that the host staff can see which tables are cleared and ready to be seated. If there is a bar, there should be a path for arriving or waiting customers to freely pass from the entry into the bar area.

There are some security concerns at the entry to be addressed, since there might be temporary periods when the host is absent from the area. Artwork should be secured to the walls, telephones positioned on a shelf under a counter, and throw rugs secured. It is beneficial to have a height scale on the door frame, so that a witness or a security camera can accurately estimate the height of a perpetrator. The scale can be incorporated as a design element of the door trim, so that it is less apparent. If there is a cash register at the entry, it should be lockable, firmly secured to the counter, and very rarely left alone. Having a concealed panic alert button at the entry is always a good idea. Any exit should be clearly marked with "exit" signage that illuminates if the power fails, and exit doors should never be locked from the inside.

## Dining Room Layout

Table size and spacing are major contributing factors in determining the likelihood that your guests will have a pleasant and comfortable dining experience. Tables that are too small, too crowded, or too closely spaced should be avoided. For a quick estimate, the industry standard for counters is 20 square feet per seat, tables at a formal or specialty restaurant is 20 square feet per seat, 15 square feet per seat for standard table service, 12 square feet for fast food, and 10 square feet for a booth. There are other factors to consider, such as menu and style of service, requiring additional space. Examples include pizza service to accommodate the pizza tray, additional glassware and tableware for fine dining, family-style service to house large platters and bowls, or a cafeteria with trays and many small dishes. The dining room design goal is to have seating and table space that accommodates the most people, without having a crowded room, and with smooth traffic flow. For a "four-top," start with 36-inch square tables for informal service and move up to 42-inch square in your design if more room is needed. A 48-inch square table is considered quite large for four.

## Seating Arrangement

Once the basic dining room footprint is finalized, get a blueprint of the space from your builder or architect, or measure it and draw it yourself, including all immovable features. With tracing paper or clear acetate, begin to roughly place the aisles and tables into the area. Factors to consider are flow, spacing, access for customers and staff, the price point of the menu, style of service, type of food, and the size of the groups of diners you most expect to have eating there. Also consider how the server's sections might be divided up so that it is easy to assign sections that ensure that each table in each section gets great service. Ultimately, a room's size, shape, and function will determine the layout of tables in a given room. Also consider that the local fire authority will probably assign a "maximum capacity" based on the room size, and in some jurisdictions, the number of parking spaces.

Diagonal arrangement of tables aligned corner to corner is the most efficient use of space. Starting the rows with corners of diagonally arranged four-tops directly off of a wall saves the most space (see Appendix D). Allow 18 inches from the edge of the table to the back of the chair for a seated person. Allow 24 inches between corners of diagonal tables for customer access with no aisle, and 30 inches between corners of diagonal tables for customer access with a narrow aisle. The accepted standard between squared tables is a space of 60 inches (5 feet) for chairs that are arranged back-to-back, which leaves a 26-inch service aisle. Between round tables, 54-inch spacing is required to provide for a minimal service aisle. Round tables can seat more than square, but they won't fit against a wall. Having two four-tops pulled together to seat a large party is more efficient than having a large dedicated round table that sits empty most of the time. Large round tables work best in large dining rooms, and can serve as focal points. In large restaurants there will usually be a group big enough to occupy a large round top, and it will sit idle for less time.

It is best to anchor a portion of the seating, where the table is set against an immovable object or wall, partition, screen, or curtain. It has been shown that diners spend more money when occupying anchored seating and stay longer after they finish their meal. Diners spend the most money per minute when occupying a booth, followed closely by tables in corners and along walls. The worst anchored seating is at a banquette, where half of the diners sit along a long couch, the banquette, which is lined with two-top tables. Banquettes are the darling of interior designers, but they have many negatives. They offer no privacy, every motion on the banquette is felt by all, servers have to reach across the table to service the seated guest, and it is difficult for the guest to sit at the banquette without disturbing neighboring tables.

Placing tables in what are normally undesirable locations (due to noise, crowding, smells, etc.) should be avoided whenever possible. At times they can be profitable, since guests often do not linger and turnover is high. Guests who are seated next to the restroom doors or entry to the kitchen might not be eager to return, however. But that might be the ideal spot for a family with noisy kids. Avoiding the placement of undesirable tables ensures a happier clientele. Isolating or grouping together families with small children is always appreciated by the majority of your guests.

The most profitable method of laying out tables is to mix anchored tables with floating tables (those in the middle of the dining space) in a configuration that enables them to be matched to accommodate different group sizes. A well-designed combination of table sizes can decrease the overall wait time for diners while maximizing capacity and profit. When designing the seating area, give priority to flow, and imagine how the diners and staff will move about the space. Have walkways that are wide enough. Main walkways should accommodate double-file spacing, 48 inches being ideal, while service pathways can be single-file with a 26-inch minimum path. If carts are involved with service or busing, pathway corners must not be too sharp or too narrow.

## Table Sizing and Finish

Table tops come in squares, rectangles, and rounds, in standard sizes (see Appendix D). The primary considerations for determining the size of the table top needed is what is being served to the customers, and how it is being served. You should list the planned tabletop items and think about the space required and the style of service offered. Options might include salt and pepper shakers, sugar packet caddy, napkin dispenser, bread bowl or cracker basket, sauces or condiments, candle, bud vase, oil and vinegar cruets, salad dressing caddy, baked potato toppings caddy, syrup or honey dispensers, butter pats, jellies and jams, pizza condiment shakers, water glass, wine glasses, and white wine bucket. Are condiments going to be on the table, or brought by the server when needed? It is easy to see how tabletop real estate rapidly gets consumed. Next determine the size of the serving plate or plates that will be used and consider the flatware and glassware as well (see Appendix F). It is recommended that a full-scale mock-up of the planned tabletop be made, using the exact products selected, so that you can judge if the table size is appropriate. It is often more crowded than originally thought.

The tabletop finish is determined by whether or not linens will cover the tables. If the finish of the tabletop is attractive enough, tablecloths should not be required. If tablecloths are not going to be used, make sure that the finish on the table is very durable. If tablecloths are required, and will always be used, it does not matter what the tabletop looks like; it could be unfinished particle board or plywood. Keep the cost of table linens in mind when considering table finish. Tablecloths are expensive at around $.65 to $.75 each. For a hundred-seat restaurant that fills its tables only once each day, the minimum cost of tablecloths is about $6,000 per year. The average is close to $15,000. Some restaurants put down a tablecloth and cover it with tempered glass, which is heavy and difficult to move when necessary. Another factor concerning tabletop material is whether or not the chairs will be stacked upside-down on the tables at the end of the shift so that the floor can be swept and mopped. If this is the case, tabletop pads can be purchased, which will keep a finished wooden tabletop from getting damaged during the stacking process.

## Table Bases

The tabletop is usually purchased separately from the base. See Appendix D for a breakdown on which tabletops will fit on table bases. Make sure that the height of the table and table base match the height of the seat of the chair. If the chairs have arms, the arms will have to fit under the table. Tables designed for dining should be 28 inches to 30 inches high (29 inches is standard) with chair seats 11 inches to 13 inches lower. The higher the tabletop, the more uncomfortable and formal the table feels. Allow a minimum of 24 inches of elbow width per person and a 12-inch to 15-inch depth from the edge of the table for comfortable seating.

Round table bases are designed to work with round tables, and square bases with square/rectangular tables. Round bases are easier to clean around, but do not allow chairs to push in fully; square bases are harder to clean around, but allow chairs to push in fully (three-legged bases should not be used with square or rectangular tabletops). It is best to talk to the table-base company representative prior to ordering to see what size screw or bolt will have to be used to secure the tabletops to the bases; penetrating the surface with a screw that is too long would be a terrible mistake. Table bases with adjustable, leveling feet are preferred, so that tables do not wobble. Above all, the tabletop must be level and stable when mounted to the base.

## Chairs

Restaurant chairs should be comfortable, durable, and easy to clean, especially if upholstered. Purchase the correct seat height to match the table, and if there are arms, make sure they will fit under the table. If chairs are to be stacked at the end of the shift, it would help if they are both lightweight and durable. It is preferable that the chairs have permanently attached glides on the bottom of the legs, so they do less damage to floors and are easy to slide in and out of the dining position by the guests. Chairs with fewer crevices will be easier to clean. From a design point of view, subtle patterns and muted colors are easier to incorporate into an overall interior design.

## Booths

A booth is generally between 46–48 inches in depth, spanning from the edge of the table at the aisle to the wall or space divider in back. A section of booths will begin on the left side with a single booth bench (a bench with a back fitted up against the wall or positioned in open space), with a table in the middle, and then a double booth bench with a common back between the benches. It serves as the bench seat for the table on the left side and a bench seat for the next table to its right. That pattern repeats until the completion of the run of booths, ending with another single bench on the right, with the back fitted up against the wall or positioned in open space. Booth tables are generally 30 inches wide, which produces a standard booth width of 72 inches, measured from seat back to seat back.

Corner booths can be round (known as a "3/4 circle full radius") or rectangular (known as a "3/4 circle standard"). If round, their standard diameter is 42 inches, and if square, their standard length and width is 42 inches. If pictured from above, a corner booth occupies a square measuring 88 inches on each side, with seat backs on the two aisle access points measuring 40 inches from wall to aisle. A U-shaped booth is larger than a conventional booth, using a table measuring 42 inches wide by 24 inches in depth; it will span 88 inches from seat back to seat back. Both corner booths and U-shaped booths will comfortably accommodate between 5 and 6 people.

## Floor Covering

There are several issues concerning floor covering, and several options. Carpet is attractive but it is hard to keep clean, and it is expensive. It deadens noise, helps to minimize dish breakage, and is comfortable to walk on. Stains and spills can be problematic with carpet, and uneven wear will be concentrated along walkways and access paths. Daily vacuuming and frequent cleaning will be necessary. Concrete, usually stained and patterned, is a popular treatment for remodels. It is impervious to stains as long as it is sealed, but is loud and reflective of noise. Anything falling on it will shatter, and it is hard on staff feet and joints. Vinyl, the least expensive floor treatment, is slightly better than concrete, but is still loud. Both concrete and vinyl are easy to clean. Wood is perhaps the most attractive option, lending the room warmth. It requires slightly more maintenance than vinyl and reflects about the same amount of noise. It is on par with carpet in terms of cost, but is much easier to keep clean and is easier on the feet.

## Lighting

Dining room lighting should be adjustable, so that light levels can be raised or lowered throughout the shift, as exterior light changes. It is best to accent main walkways, the area at the entrance, and the approach to the rest rooms. Broad overall lighting in the dining room is preferred, while many choose to use accent lighting over booths and tables. Accent lighting can be very dramatic and is a good, relatively low-cost option to augment interior design. It is preferable to incorporate ceiling fans into the lighting design, to help lower HVAC costs and move air faster when required. Use fluorescent bulbs rather than incandescent when you are not concerned about unflattering light quality. The trend today is toward extremely long-lasting and very low wattage LED lighting, so adopt LED bulbs when possible.

## Wait Station

The wait station is a beehive of activity, often with four or five servers and several bus persons trying to complete tasks simultaneously. The door needs to be wide enough for two servers to pass each other while carrying trays. It is a wet environment, so stainless surfaces and waterproof shelving are most desirable. Any non-stainless surfaces will eventually warp from moisture infiltration and have to be replaced. If it is not stainless, it should be aggressively caulked and sealed. Generally the station is divided into a wet side and a dry side, based on tasks.

Servers need a well-lit, flat working surface for totaling or paying out checks, figuring out separate checks or credit cards, counting change, and cashing out. A separate area is needed for assembling trays of tea, water, beverages, and coffee; rolling additional tableware setups; entering orders into the POS; and doing side work such as slicing lemons, stocking supplies, and such. Depending on the size of the waitstaff, a second POS entry screen might be required. Ideally the wait station lighting will be on a dimmer and dimly lit during the shift, with focused task lighting over the work areas.

There are plumbing and drain connections for the coffee machine, the iced tea brewer (although these can both be manual models), and the ice bin/water glass filler unit. Refrigeration will be necessary for creamers, lemon wedges, milk, butter, garnishes, etc. It can be as simple as a dorm room refrigerator, a counter-top retailer, or a single-door refrigerator. If bottled sodas are dispensed from the wait station, then capacity will need to be increased. If sodas and beers are dispensed, consider a small horizontal bottle cooler. The coffeemaker, warmers, pots or airpots, and bean grinder will need a space, as will the iced tea brewer. Water pitchers, beverage glasses, and coffee cups are usually stored on cafeteria trays or in racks; they need a location convenient to the water, tea, and coffee. Silverware divider boxes, rolled set-ups, linens, and napkins should be convenient for the bus staff, which also needs bus tubs, usually kept on shelves or on a cart, and a sanitizing bucket. All paper goods used for to-go orders should be stored here so that servers can quickly package left-overs. For larger dining rooms, it is best to have a screened-from-view satellite bus station, where bus staff can store their sanitizing solution bucket, bus tubs and cart, and tableware setups. This enables faster response time to getting tables cleared and reset, shortening the wait, and increasing profits.

### Restrooms

Signage on the doors should clearly indicate the gender of the room. Avoid ambiguous names (foreign languages, cute symbols, or illustrations) so there is no question regarding which door to choose. Restrooms should be ADA (Americans with Disability Act) access-compliant, which affects door widths, object heights, and wheelchair turning radius. All surfaces must be sanitary, sealed, and easily cleanable. Floor drains are preferred but not required. A venting fan is required in most jurisdictions. Many restaurants also use auto-spray deodorizers. It is best to have duplicate dispensers for toilet paper, so the chance of running out during a shift is remote. The overall restroom design should incorporate a janitorial closet for cleaning supplies, plunger, mop and bucket, sanitizer, toilet brush, and glass cleaner if possible. Generally these items are required on very short or emergency notice, and hurrying through the dining room with a plunger in hand is unseemly. Women prefer large, well-lit mirrors and appreciate a nod toward design. Fresh flowers are always appreciated. If the restaurant has a septic tank, having a lined waste receptacle with a lid is necessary for feminine hygiene products. Wall-mounted changing stations are valued if the demographic includes families with babies and toddlers. Men tend to have much more utilitarian needs in their restroom.

## Bar

When considering front of house design, a basic decision must be made. Will the restaurant have a bar or not? A bar will add considerably to the overall sales of the restaurant, and alcohol sales are generally high-profit with low labor costs, the highest profit center of the business in most cases. Depending on the theme of the restaurant, the effect of a bar could be advantageous or detrimental to ambience. Most critics agree that the availability of drinks adds to the dining experience, but it might not be a good fit in the area, depending on local mores or expected demographics. If there will be a bar, the decision must be made on how much space will be dedicated to bar seating, unless it is to be a service bar with no seating. Will the bar serve only beer and wine, or will it serve cocktails as well? For beer and wine only, service staff can usually dispense the drinks with no formal bar involved. Serving liquor and cocktails normally involves a display of available bottles and a bartender on staff. Depending on the situation, a trusted staff member or manager can pour liquor chosen from a menu, and dispensed from a service bar.

Each state has its own requirements of alcohol service permits, and the costs to establish a bar vary widely from region to region. Generally, the majority of sales (greater than 51 percent) must be from food or the permit cannot be issued for a restaurant. If there will be a bar, be aware that there is often a lengthy process involved in securing the permit, with many steps and considerable funds involved. Do not wait until the last minute to procure the permit. In most areas there are firms that specialize in organizing and submitting the lengthy and complicated paperwork. Hiring one of these firms might prove worthwhile.

The restaurant bar serves purposes such as a drinking establishment for the neighborhood, as an area for dining customers to have a drink while waiting for a table or after dinner, and as a service bar for the customers in the dining room. Placement and shape of the bar, and traffic flow around the bar are crucial design considerations. In some states, such as Utah and Wyoming, state law dictates the placement of the bar. Most often, the bar will be ideally located near the entry, so that customers who are coming to the restaurant only for drinks or a snack or light meal do not walk through the dining room to access the bar or have to circulate through customers who are waiting for a table. It is also advisable for the bar to be located close to the restroom, with a clear path free from the dining room traffic. It is beneficial to separate bar customer flow from dining room customer flow whenever possible.

A successful bar design provides appropriate equipment and layout based on a particular space and operating style. Effective bar design is measured by functionality and efficiency, not capacity or quantity of equipment. Ergonomics are essential for the bartender, while comfort is critical for the guest. If you do not have a strong background in bar operation, develop plans using a restaurant or bar consultant, or spend time in different bars, observing and taking notes.

Linear bars are considered the most efficient design, allowing unobstructed views of bar patrons and requiring the least square footage to accommodate the same number of bar stools as other shapes. A linear bar is the easiest design for positioning workstations, service pickup to the dining room, and equipment. It has low impact on traffic flow and costs significantly less per square foot to build, and it can normally be worked by one bartender during non-rush hours. From a design viewpoint, it is the least interesting but the most functional format. A linear bar for a 3,000-square-foot, one-hundred-seat restaurant should be between 12 and 15 feet long, assuming a bar seating area with tables for about twenty guests.

The L-shaped bar is easy to incorporate into many floor plans, adapts well to equipment layout and positioning of workstations, and can often be worked by one bartender during non-peak hours. The one downfall of the L-shaped bar is limited visibility of patrons seated at the far end, which can create service delays. Oval and horseshoe-shape bars allow guests unobstructed views of the room, but have several limitations. They are challenging to fit equipment and inventory into, often wasting space at curves. Their lack of functional efficiency presents challenges for bartenders, requiring much more movement for attentive service. They also require more labor hours, since they are difficult for a single bartender to work during non-peak hours. They are dynamic from a design point of view, but are a much less efficient use of space. Curves placed in linear bars present similar problems to those found with ovals and horseshoes.

Tables in bar areas are designed to hold drinks, snacks, and bar food dishes, and are smaller than dining tables. Bar tables are 24-inch, 30-inch, or 36-inch rounds or squares; rounds work best in bars because they allow freer movement between tables. Stools and chairs that are "bar height" are 30 inches high, with tabletops that are 40 to 43 inches high. Stools and chairs that are "counter height" have seats that are 24 to 26 inches high with a tabletop that is 36 inches high. Allow 10 to 13 inches between the surface of the barstool seat and the bottom of the table. This will leave plenty of room for legs and allow for comfortable turning if you choose a swivel design. If the stools have arms, make sure they have ample clearance under the tabletops. For stools positioned along the bar countertop, allow 24 to 30 inches between the centers of each stool seat to provide adequate space for arms, elbows, food, and drinks. Barstools should match the overall decor, must be designed to fit the tables used, and must be comfortable for guests. Options include a stool with a back, backless, with arms, or swiveling; unupholstered, or covered with treated fabric, leather, or vinyl. Regardless of style, buy only commercial-grade stools that are made for constant use, and get stools with comfortable footrests. For areas meant to accommodate standing guests, allow a circular diameter of 1 foot 8 inches per person or approximately 3 square feet per standing guest. See Appendix D for a visual layout.

## Bar Design and Dimensions

The optimum width for the aisle between the back edge and front edge of the bar is 30 inches. This allows the 23-inch doors of the backbar coolers to open freely, while reducing one step from the bartender's motion to access the backbar counter. If the bar has multiple bartender stations, they should be identical to each other and be spaced 10 to 15 feet apart. Consider the ergonomics and reach of the bartender; display bottles should be reachable without using a stepstool, and all mixers should be within easy reach of each cocktail unit. The bar countertop should be 30 inches wide, with a 6-inch overhang on the bartender's side to conceal under-counter equipment and surfaces. Along the back edge of the countertop is a trough that is recessed to fit the dimensions of bar mats that are selected (standard size is 27 inches long x 3 1/4 inches deep x 5/8 inches high). The top of the installed mat should be flush with the surface of the bar so that the bottom of a glass cannot "catch" on the bar edge, causing a drink to spill. The countertop surface under the mats needs to be epoxy-sealed, or have a stainless steel insert; it will stay wet throughout each shift. The countertop can be made of any material, but customers prefer warm materials (woods like oak, cherry, or mahogany) with rounded corners that are comfortable to lean on or drape arms upon. On the customer side of the countertop there needs to be adequate space for customers' knees when they are seated, and a footrail is necessary for comfort.

Bar equipment has electrical, plumbing, and drain requirements. Research the specifications for each piece of equipment. All plugs in the bar should be GFCI outlets for worker safety in moist environments. As with any restaurant workstation, there can never be enough electrical outlets. The cocktail unit, bar sink, glass washer, hand sink, blender station sink, beer tower, and ice machine (if positioned at the bar) all need a drain. The soda gun, various sinks, and glass washer need a water source. If the bar has an espresso machine, it will need a filtered water source, a flat surface, and 220V power. Note that not every bar will have all of these pieces of equipment.

There are specialized lighting needs in the bar. Attached under the overhang countertop on the bartender's side there should be dimmable LED strip lighting to illuminate the work surfaces. There are often muted spotlights illuminating the countertop at each barstool position. Illuminating the bottle display on the backbar is normally done from underneath with recessed LED strip lights on dimmers, or with recessed spots from above, or both. As in the dining room, overall floor illumination should be amended with ceiling fans, to increase air movement when required. If the bar allows smoking, a smoke extractor will make the space more comfortable for nonsmokers; in some jurisdictions they are required. In more and more locales smoking is not permitted in restaurants and bars.

### Backbar

The backbar wall needs a mirror so that the bartender can keep an eye on customers at the bar while his back is turned away from them and guests seated at the bar can view the activity behind them. It often needs to be tilted slightly to set the viewing angle for best vision by seated customers. From a design point of view, the mirror makes the room look larger and makes bottle selection look bigger. Refrigeration is positioned along the backbar. Make sure that all plug cords for equipment used on the backbar are long enough to be plugged in before the equipment is pushed into place. Ice machines are usually installed in the kitchen due to their heat and noise output, and are accessed when needed with ice buckets. The width of the backbar countertop is usually keyed to the depth of the refrigeration underneath. Make sure it has enough depth to store glasses and display bottles, but is still reachable by the staff. Glasses can be stacked upside down on poly mesh liner along the front edge of the backbar countertop, or on tempered glass shelves along the back wall. Bottles are normally placed on narrow stair-stepped shelves (illuminated through a cut-out slot with LED strip lighting), or on tempered glass shelves, to make bottles visible by patrons when selecting their order. Bars with limited choices might use a liquor menu instead. For displayed liquor bottles, consider a roll-down lockable cage, tambour doors, video monitoring, or some other means of security during hours when the bar is closed. In the backbar as in the kitchen, there can never be too much storage space.

## Under Bar

For multiple bartenders, the bartender-server pickup station should have a POS screen for each without sharing. The lead bartender station should have a phone tied into the restaurant's system. The lead station also needs a secure but accessible spot for a cash box or register for patrons paying out, storage for miscellaneous items, setups and plates for diners at the bar, and backup pouring supplies. One option for extra storage might be overhead, lockable cabinet storage in an over-bar soffit suspended from the ceiling. Some locales no longer permit storage of upside-down stemware from hanging racks. Be sure to verify this with the local health department before committing to this method, and have an alternative location for accessible stemware storage. If stemware is hung from the soffit, make sure that bartenders will not hit their heads on it, and that everyone can reach it.

It is difficult to keep a bar clean. Cleanup is easier with custom-fabricated or modular bar equipment that provides a continuous work surface. The fewer seams and gaps there are in equipment, the cleaner it will be. All equipment, fillers, and furniture should be hard-surfaced, sealed, and caulked (as always, stainless steel is preferred). Use the highest backsplashes that will fit the design and budget. Provide covered bases off of the floor, large enough to enclose soda and beer lines, cord sets, electric wiring, and plumbing, so that they cannot collect soil and are easier to keep clean.

A cocktail unit ("jockey box") is the insulated box that holds the ice for the bartender and the front-mounted speed rails that hold the "well" liquor bottles conveniently located for rapid access. "Well" liquor is the group of spirits that are used to make drinks when the brand is not specified by the guest ("scotch and soda"). "Call" liquors are specifically requested brands ("Glenfiddich and soda").

There are speed rail inserts that fit over the ice that hold mixers and juices near the sides of the bin so that they stay chilled. If the bar will have a soda gun or a carbonator, the bottom of the ice bin will require a cold plate, which is a tubular heat exchanger used to rapidly chill carbonated beverages. The more tubes the cold plate has, the faster it will chill the liquid, and the more gas bubbles it will retain. If there is a soda gun, there must be a storage area for bag-in-box syrups (which can be remotely located). Make sure this area is well-sealed and easy to clean. The gun should be mounted on or just below the edge of the countertop, just left of the mixing station, for use with the left hand, while pouring and shaking with the right.

The bar sink should have the widest drain boards that will fit the plan. Many bartenders like to use these drain boards for stacked clean glass storage during the shift. The simplest washing system is a three-compartment sink, composed of a dump sink to empty used glassware, a submersible motorized brush glass washer with low-suds soap, and a sanitizing rinse sink. For higher volume bars an automatic glass washer is appropriate. Some jurisdictions don't require a triple bar sink if there is an NSF-approved glass machine. Regardless, the sinks are convenient if the automatic machine breaks down, and with either method, chemicals will need a convenient storage space. There are specialized blender stations for bar blenders that have a utility sink and a gooseneck faucet for dumping and rinsing the blender. In some locales, the bar sink or the blender station utility sink can be used for a hand sink, if it has hand soap and towels furnished. Some municipalities do not require a hand sink in the bar if you use a powered brush glass washer, or if no food is being prepared behind the bar. Be sure to confirm the local requirements for bar hand sinks and triple bar sinks before the bar and plumbing plans are finalized. Do not forget a convenient location for a lined waste receptacle, accessible by the bartender, the bar back (the bartender's assistant), and the server. It is best that the receptacle be removable for safe dumping, since it can potentially contain broken glass.

### Server Pickup Station

Do not place bar stools too close to the server pickup station. Servers need ample landing area for service trays, especially if food is also being served in the bar. The servers need their own POS screens. If bar glasses are to be returned to the bar for washing, an area easily reachable by the bartender should be designated as a space for soiled glassware, along with a receptacle for empty beer and wine bottles. Servers need adequate counter space for chilled condiment and garnish trays, as well as 12- x 18-inch cocktail drain mats. It is preferable for the server to have access to the interior of the bar to help with glassware, grab a wine bottle, replenish garnishes from the backbar cooler, and such without disturbing the bartender. The servers have their own storage needs, so plan accordingly.

## BOH Design and Layout

The style of restaurant is a factor in determining the overall BOH space allotment. Fast food, or the purchasing of already-prepared product, requires the least BOH space, while general food preparation with full service requires approximately 5 square feet of kitchen space per dining room seat (500 square feet minimum for a hundred-seat restaurant or up to 1,200 square feet using the formula of 40 percent allocation of a total of 3,000 square feet). Formal dining with a large staff, more preparation, and more product storage, could easily require twice that amount. Before deciding on the kitchen space allotment, most experienced restaurateurs will advise that regardless of its size, the kitchen area can never be big enough and that any restaurant can never have too much refrigerated storage or dry storage space. In addition to refrigerated and dry goods storage, cookware and utensils; linens and tableware; beer, wine, and alcohol; paper goods; and cleaners all require separate space. If at all possible, allow for future growth, and be creative in utilizing any oddly shaped or hard-to-access areas.

Consider electrical, gas, and water requirements for each piece of equipment and the building's utility service capacities, as well as the location of those utilities. For example, if the piece of equipment needs a drain, is one available close enough to where the piece is positioned, or will it require a jackhammer or concrete saw to alter the drain location? Utility retrofits can be very expensive, and surprises at installation translate to costly time setbacks. It is best to formulate a utility requirement list for all of the equipment, noting electrical requirements (voltage, phase, frequency/hertz, amperage, plug type), gas requirements (supply psi minimum, inlet size), BTU ratings, and water (filtered and not) and drain needs (supply psi range, inlet size and location, outlet size and location).

All of this information is available on the specifications sheet of each piece of equipment. The architect or designer will need all dimensions for every piece of equipment. Contractors will need to know all utility requirements in their particular field so that total load requirements can be determined and adequate service can be provided where it is required.

Equipment_____

Dimensions:
    Length
    Width
    Height, including legs or casters/wheels, for proper height
    Door clearances:
        Will it fit into the kitchen?
        Do equipment doors have unobstructed clearance to open?
        Hinges on correct side for staff access? Reversible? Specify before ordering?
Electrical:
    Voltage
    Phase (single-phase or three-phase)
    Amperage
    Plug type
    GFCI circuit required?
Gas:
    Natural gas or propane
    BTU rating
    Inlet diameter required
    Minimum psi
    Does equipment require a flexible connection?
    Spacing requirements of equipment from flammable equipment, materials, and/or walls
Plumbing:
    Is water required? If so, both hot and cold?
    Inlet and outlet diameter dimensions
    Position and dimension of drains
    Is filtered water required?
    Backflow prevention requirements?
Venting:
    Is a vent required?
    Type I or Type II?
    Fire suppression required?
    Does equipment require separate/isolated venting?

Ideally the entire restaurant should be on one level. In high-density cities it might be necessary to design vertical use of a space in order to utilize every square inch. This could require the kitchen to be on another level. If so, fast, efficient, and safe passage of food (and staff) from the kitchen to the dining room, adequate access for food deliveries, and easy access for waste disposal are all required. If the kitchen is on another level, the restaurant will require an elevator, stairs, dumbwaiter, sidewalk ground-level elevator with delivery chute, and such to both access the kitchen and to get food to the customers. Make sure that these comply with local codes and have adequate capacities to handle the job. The service staff must be able to safely and quickly get the food to customers, get dirty dishes to the dishwasher, and the kitchen will require frequent product deliveries.

When considering the BOH design, look at each section in detail—the cooking line, food preparation area, dish washing, and office.

## Cooking Line

The cooking line will have a hot side and a cold side. The hot side is for the preparation of all hot dishes and contains the "pass" or pass-through space, where hot dishes are picked up by the service staff. On the hot side, try to make the area as compact and efficient as possible. This reduces unnecessary movement by cooking staff and the number of cooks required, and also limits the size of the exhaust hood, which can be a very expensive piece of equipment. It also concentrates the hot area so that it has less impact on ambient air quality and the overall HVAC, while making the heated cooking area cheaper and more efficient to cool. The exhaust hood will work best if it penetrates an outside wall and vents into open space. For that reason, cooking lines are often aligned against (or close to) an exterior wall. The exhaust hood/fire suppression system needs to overhang cooking equipment on both sides by 8 inches, and must be welded and not riveted. Wood-fired heat sources often require a separate exhaust hood. Fryers need to be 18 inches from any combustible surfaces and are often placed at the end of the cooking line.

The cold side of the line, or pantry as it is known, involves cold appetizers and soups, salads, and desserts, and it needs to be convenient and accessible for servers picking up food at the pass. It is best to isolate the cold side from any heat sources if possible, so that the refrigeration has to work less. Both hot and cold sides need direct, immediate access to refrigerated storage, either under counter or adjacent to the work stations. Being able to just turn around to reach the other side of the line is ideal for the cooking line, but there must be adequate room for workers to pass each other while behind the line and for under-counter doors to open.

## Food-Preparation Area

The food-preparation area, or prep area, includes preparation of all of the food, including baking and pastries and/or pasta making, as well as storage for dry goods, refrigerated food storage, and a walk-in cooler (if included). The prep area should be isolated from the cooking line and the dish line if possible. The back door should connect to the bulk storage area, which should connect to the prep area. In tight quarters, the food preparation might have to be done on the cooking line prior to service. Baking or pasta making requires enough space for relatively large equipment (ovens and large-capacity mixers), tray racks and proofing racks, and large tables for working dough. Storage by the prep area also includes a temporary delivery and check-in area with a well-lighted table to set boxes on for product inspection, and an accessible scale for confirming shipment weights. The back door needs to have a ramp, or be easily accessible by delivery hand trucks. The back door has obvious security concerns, so it needs to be well lit, have a buzzer or doorbell, and have a security window that provides open views of the immediate area.

## Dish Line

The dish line includes temporary and permanent storage of dish racks and wares, as well as a staging area for dirty bus tubs. In many jurisdictions, a three-compartment sink is required even if the restaurant also has a dish machine. This sink is then used for bulky pot and pan washing, or all dishwashing if there is no dish machine. The dish line needs to be accessible by bus persons from the dining room, transporting bus tubs of dirty dishes to the back, and taking clean glasses and tableware back to the front. The dishwasher needs to be able to stack clean dishes and get plates and cooking pans and utensils back to the cooking line and the cooking line needs to easily access the dish line to bring dirty skillets and utensils for cleaning.

## Office Area

The last elements of the kitchen design are the office, staff restroom and lockers, and janitorial closet, which often requires a separate mop sink. The office area is used for ordering, accounting, storage of files and invoices, private meetings with salespeople and staff, and, occasionally, money storage in a floor safe. It is best if the office has a lockable steel door with a security window offering a clear view of the kitchen so that managers can observe staff while inside. It is desirable to have an employee restroom, so that employees will not interfere with guests in the dining room restroom. In the kitchen, perhaps outside the restroom or near the office, there should be an employee area with employee lockers, time clock if using, and a bulletin board for posting schedules and other employee information and required state and federal posters. Janitorial staff needs a mop sink, a storage area for cleaning chemicals isolated from food storage, hangers for mops to dry, storage for brooms, vacuum, and sweeper, and the like.

All BOH workstations should be adaptable when more employees or larger production quantities are needed for peak volume. Employee ergonomics are a prime concern. Everything should easily be in reach at each workstation. Equipment doors and shelves need adequate clearance to open freely, and all doors must be hinged on the proper side for employee access. All existing and future electric equipment and appliances need adequate power supply and breakers. Areas that are used for portable appliances will benefit from having convenient power strips or hanging pigtail plugs when needed.

## Sanitation

The design and use of space must lend itself to methods that ensure sanitary conditions. Great care must be given to making all surfaces nonabsorbent and easily cleanable. Large equipment is best when mounted on casters, so it can be rolled out for thorough cleaning, otherwise it will need to be cleaned in place (CIP), and much care must be taken when this method is employed. If gas equipment is on casters, flexible gas supply hoses are a necessity. Ideally, the back wall behind the equipment line is lined with stainless steel. Tile surfaces with grout lines can be problematic. Floor drains are desirable, but not necessary. Floor surfaces should be nonslip and coped at wall joining for easy cleaning. Sharp corners collect dirt and should be avoided. Floor mats are bulky and get dirty during the shift, so it is beneficial to have an area where they can be scrubbed and hosed-off. This can be a shower stall–like area inside with pegs to hold mats, or an area outside. If mats are cleaned outside, the health department will require that the wash water enter a drain connected to the grease trap. It is easy to overlook, but adequate and safe access to the dumpster is required to dump waste during opening hours. The truck that empties the dumpster is very heavy. As it sits in place and bounces the dumpster up and down to empty it, the pavement or concrete pad in front of the dumpster will eventually degrade. Anticipate this damage by installing an extra-strong, reinforced pad if possible.

## BOH Plumbing and Lighting

Hand sinks are required to be "conveniently accessible" to each workstation. This is often open to local health department interpretation. Adequate hand-wash facilities are required, but it is less expensive to get by with as few as possible to satisfy the spirit of the law and still provide for public health. Change existing plumbing as little as needed, as it is one of the more expensive alterations. It is economical for the plan to adapt to existing plumbing. Some specialized equipment will need separate and filtered water, such as a steamer, and pot-filling faucets behind a range aid in filling large stock pots without lugging them from a remote sink. The ice machine, usually housed at the entrance to the kitchen, will also need separate filtered water. The dish machine will need a hot water supply and drain. There should be a hot water bib for a hose to spray down the floors at the end of the evening. The hot water heater should be located out of drafts and pathways, in a safe and vented location with good accessibility for repair and maintenance, close to the areas that require hot water. All hot water lines should be insulated to lessen demand and operating costs. Air gaps and back-flow preventers are required in all plumbing lines. Consult local codes for specific design requirements.

Kitchen lighting needs to be bright, especially over all workstations. Bright light helps keep the kitchen clean, reduces accidents and sloppy work habits, and helps staff see the food better. Fluorescent tubes are the standard as they are cool, efficient, easy to change, long-lived, and don't cast shadows. Fluorescent tubes should be encased within removable plastic shields for safety. Consider task lighting in the prep area over equipment such as mixers or ovens, as well as over large work tables. There should be an emergency lighting system that activates during power loss, as working around knives, flames, and heat when it suddenly goes dark is never safe. The walk-in cooler normally has a fluorescent bulb enclosed inside a removable glass dome protected by a cage. Newer models have sensors that turn the light off when the walk-in cooler is vacant. The back door needs to be very well lit for security, both inside and out. Just as fluorescent bulbs have replaced tungsten, LED lighting will eventually replace fluorescent.

## Scale Drawing for a Restaurant Kitchen

A separate sheet contains the list of equipment (numbers) and counters/stands (letters). Included are examples of the system.

1. Eagle Charbroiler, 36-inch, lava rock
2. Vulcan gas griddle, 48-inch
3. True Chef Base drawered refer, 79-inch
4. Vulcan Challenger XL gas convection range, 6 open burners, x2
5. Wolf 36-inch salamander
6. Vulcan 40# Fryer x2
7. Bakers Pride counter oven, brick lined

8. Vollrath counter rotisserie
9. Traulsen 2-door refer x2
10. Amana 2,200W microwave
11. True 44-inch pizza box
12. True worktop refer, 93-inch with drawers
13. Duke electric steam table, 3 bin
14. True worktop freezer, 27-inch
15. Hatco Glo Ray warmer
16. Hatco Glo Ray heated shelf
17. Wyott overhead warmer

A. Advance Tabco stainless steel table, premium, 8' x 30", galvanized legs and undershelf, 5" backsplash—x2

B. Advance Tabco stainless steel table, premium, 8' x 36", galvanized legs and undershelf, 5" backsplash—x2

C. Advance Tabco stainless steel sink, hand, 9" wide x 9" front-to-back x 5" deep

D. Advance Tabco stainless steel sink, 3-compartment with left and right-hand drainboards, 24" front-to-back x 18" wide compartment x 14" deep, 1" high splash

E. Advance Tabco stainless steel shelf, microwave, 24" x 2'

F. Advance Tabco stainless steel work table, 12" x 18" (filler)

G. Advance Tabco stainless steel stand, countertop cooking equipment, 84" x 30", 24" high

H. Advance Tabco stainless steel shelf, pass-through, 18" x 120"

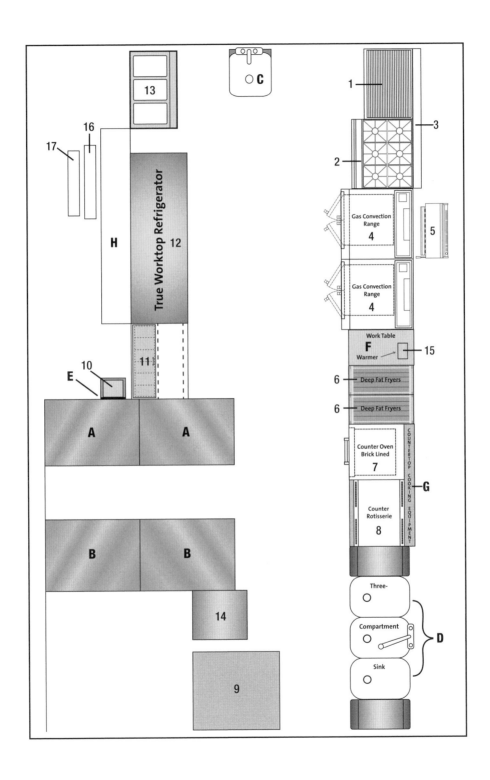

13

C

1

3

16

2

17

Gas Convection Range

4

5

H

True Worktop Refrigerator

12

Gas Convection Range

4

Work Table

F

Warmer

15

11

6    Deep Fat Fryers

E

10

6    Deep Fat Fryers

A

A

Counter Oven
Brick Lined

7

COUNTERTOP COOKING EQUIPMENT

B

B

Counter
Rotisserie

8

G

14

Three-

9

Compartment

D

Sink

## Ventilation and Exhaust

The exhaust hood blower needs either an outside wall or free access straight-up so that it can vent heat and smoke with the fewest turns and angles. Exhaust hoods are a necessary evil, and not the least bit popular with upstairs or downwind neighbors. The purpose of the exhaust or ventilation system is to evacuate air contaminated with heat, steam, smoke, grease, fumes, and particulates, as well as to provide immediate fire suppression to the cooking equipment. It is desirable to have a make-up air system as part of the hood to balance the volume of air being removed. Exhaust hood construction and installation require coordination between a sheet-metal fabricator, fire specialist, electrician, and your HVAC contractor. Most HVAC contractors have fabricators and fire-suppression companies that they work with on a regular basis.

Your exhaust hood contains removable metal filters that prevent much of the grease and particulates from exiting your exhaust blower. Channel, baffle, or mesh styles make up the low end, and are often acceptable, while the high end uses centrifugal fixed baffles and scrubbing systems. Filters need daily cleaning, while ductwork and fans need professional cleaning every 6 months at a minimum. Some cooking methods benefit from more frequent cleaning, such as barbecue and fried chicken restaurants, and those that primarily grill burgers and steaks.

## Equipment Placement

Once your equipment list is formulated and the demand for production or storage capacity of the equipment is determined, examine the planned installation area to verify that the equipment will fit in the allotted kitchen layout. Make sure that large or bulky pieces will fit through door openings, and that there is adequate ceiling clearance. Allow for mandated distances between heated equipment and flammable surfaces, and required distances between fryers and open flames.

Make a scale drawing of the kitchen area and obtain dimensions of your equipment from the PDF files that can be downloaded from most Internet restaurant supply companies and from the specific manufacturers of the equipment. Cut out pieces of paper to represent each piece of equipment, tables, sinks, dish line, etc. You can slide these around on the floor plan for best fit. This will enable you to see where shelving can be placed to maximize storage without hindering flow.

# Getting Started

Regardless of the type of construction (turn-key, minor remodel, major remodel, or new construction) several things must be accomplished before getting started on the way to creating your restaurant. In addition to having selected your site and having a negotiated contract/lease, you need your financing in place, a working bank account, and your working concept. You have decided whether or not to sell alcohol (and begun the licensing if so) and your menu is fairly set. You have a general layout of what goes where, and you know the approximate number of seats and tables. You should have some insurance in place to cover pre-opening issues.

## Minor Remodels

If this project is turn-key, you shouldn't need an architect or contractor. This type of construction often doesn't require any permits from the city. A fresh coat of paint, a thorough cleaning, some new draperies, and other minor decor changes should suffice. Consider an interior decorator or designer to help if this is not something you are comfortable with. For a minor remodel you may be changing around some of the interior features to suit your needs, but you are not adding onto the structure or making any major structural changes. A local contractor may make things easier on you, having this person responsible for getting things done in an orderly way, or you may be able to coordinate any outside workers yourself. If you have the skills, you can save money by doing some of the basics yourself, such as painting or repairing drywall, and hiring out specialists for electrical, plumbing, and HVAC issues. For some of the construction you may need permits from the city. Typically if you move a sink, remove or alter a load-bearing wall, add new windows to a wall, alter the footprint of the space, upgrade electrical service, or change the roofline, however, you will need permits. You may not need a permit if you are replacing existing windows, resurfacing the roof, changing or adding floor covering (new carpet, change to wood slats), doing minor electrical work (replacing an outlet), or repairing plumbing (fixing a running commode). Check with the city if there is any question. Electricians and plumbers that you hire should know as well. Now is the time to begin the permitting process for the health department and fire department. You should have a target date for opening that should be realistic and work backward to create a timeline for the individual tasks that must be completed.

## Major Remodels and New Construction

For many a major remodel of a space or ground-up construction is most likely the way you will go. Take your time to find a qualified contractor and an architect who has experience in designing restaurants. Check out their work and don't be shy in asking tough questions. No matter whom you select as a contractor, you should be the overall construction supervisor; everyone should answer to you.

### Inspections

The general contractor will pull permits for the overall job. All trade subcontractors will pull permits for the work they are to accomplish, and will obtain city or county inspections at the end of their phase of the construction for final approval of their specific work. Prior to opening, usually several days or weeks prior to actual occupancy of the building, the city or county will inspect the restaurant to confirm that it meets all applicable codes in order to obtain the Certificate of Occupancy (COO). This will also include an inspection by the local fire authority. The local health department will do a final inspection before they issue a food handling permit. This will be required prior to any food storage, food handling, or cooking. In some jurisdictions, especially those using well water, the local water authority will also require a test of the water source to make sure that it is certified as safe for human consumption. An inspection is usually required as part of the alcoholic beverage permitting process. Do not wait until the last possible minute to get any final inspections signed off or you could get a surprise that radically postpones a planned opening date.

## Architects and Contractors

If this is a major remodel, such as a space that has never been a restaurant or is a slab in a strip center, you will need an architect to draw up plans for the construction personnel to follow. They will be able to accommodate ADA regulations for seating, entry and egress, and bathroom and workplace requirements. Being familiar with building codes, architects can specify grade of materials, identify all electrical and plumbing needs with proper specifications, lay out the kitchen and equipment for electrical, gas, venting, and drain needs, and lay out the bar. Construction permits will require detailed plans, including permits from the health and fire departments. These plans are what the construction crews will follow as well.

Once the plans are drawn, it's time to select a contractor to organize the various "subs" (sub-contractors such as roofers, sheetrockers, painters, etc.), see to it that the work is being done properly and to code, and that they are completing their tasks in the proper order and time frame. The contractor will see to all permits and coordinate with the architect and you. Selecting the right contractor is critical to the successful completion of your project. Give yourself up to 3 months to select the contractor who is right for your job. This time will be spent checking the credentials of prospective contractors and holding interviews.

Begin assembling a list of potential contractors by asking around. If you know of a newly completed construction project ask the owners about their selection of contractor and if they would recommend him. One good question to ask is if they would hire him again for a new project. Local trade unions can recommend reputable contractors and the Better Business Bureau may be helpful as well. Once you have several potential contractors, arrange to meet with their lead project managers to discuss your needs and answer your questions.

At this meeting you should request that the representative bring proof of up-to-date insurance and licenses. Workers' compensation insurance is a must for the contractor to have. Do not consider hiring any contractor without sufficient "workers' comp." This type of insurance will protect you from liability should anyone be injured during the hazardous process of construction. Check to see if the company is bonded and what type of license it holds. A certified contractor can do work in any state and is deemed competent by the Department of Business and Professional Regulation. A registered contractor has fulfilled competency requirements in certain jurisdictions only. Ask for references and check them judiciously. Be wary of contractors who pressure you into signing, require large sums up front, or do not have a physical address (a PO box only). Make sure the contractor has a sales tax ID number and a federal tax ID.

Your state may limit the amount requested by the contractor for down payment. Agree to make payment only as progress develops. Create a timeline for completion of major tasks and insert penalties for missing these deadlines. Request a quote for the project and not an estimate. Quotes are set prices and should itemize all costs including labor, materials, and subcontractors. An estimate is subject to change. If going this way, negotiate a percentage limit that the actual cost can go over. Check with local authorities as to whether there are limits to how much an estimate can overrun.

Be sure to have a contract drawn up that protects both parties. It should be concise and spell out in detail all of the work and outcomes expected, including completion dates. The contract should have a payment schedule based on completion of major tasks. There are always changes that need to be made on projects such as this, so spell out the consequences of "change orders," which require additional payments and may affect the timeline of completion. How disputes will be settled should be addressed in the contract as well.

### Site Plan and Layout

Regardless of the type of construction, there are several things to keep in mind for you or your contractor when starting construction or remodeling. You will need access to the kitchen (back) door by large trucks, and a ramp leading from the road or alley to the door base is useful. This area should be well lit and a doorbell should be conveniently located outside. Keep this door locked at all times and a sign posting the hours of delivery. Garbage trucks tend to tear up the area surrounding the dumpster, so it is a good idea to have a reinforced concrete pad for the dumpster to sit on. With ground-up construction you have some flexibility as to how the restaurant is oriented on the lot. Keep in mind prevailing winds, both from a comfort standpoint (the wind blowing directly into the front door should be avoided) and the potentially unpleasant smells from your dumpster wafting across the entrance. You may want to shield the view of the dumpster from customers' sight using some sort of fencing or enclosure.

#### Parking

Parking can be an issue regardless of the type of construction. For new construction on a lot, hopefully the lot is large enough to accommodate off-street parking (a private parking lot). Each parking space requires 300 to 350 square feet, including access lanes and landscaping. Check with the city about "impervious ground cover," hard surfaces that encourage pollution runoff. There may be a requirement about the percentage of total area that must be unpaved to allow absorption of runoff. Your architect will know the number of spaces required for your facility, the number of handicap spaces, and the allowable impervious cover. If you are leasing a space that has off-street parking, make sure your lease addresses the maintenance of the parking lot. Repaving and resurfacing are done every 5 to 10 years. Restriping and painting the lot occurs more frequently, especially in harsh climates. Who is responsible for snow removal and minor repairs such as potholes and downed signs? The lot will need to be cleaned regularly. You will need insurance to cover parking issues.

### Signage

Signage is very important as it lets your customers know where you are. It should be easily readable from a distance and will need to conform to regional ordinances. A permit is usually required for your business sign.

### Exterior Wiring

Make sure the main electrical panel and water service outside can be locked to prevent vandalism, and keep exposed pipes and wires to a minimum, also to avoid vandals. Now is the time to bring in lines for Internet, satellite and cable TV service, and security surveillance. Make sure the exterior is well lit. Proper placement of outdoor light fixtures can enhance the look of your restaurant as well as prevent accidents and curb theft and vandalism.

# 08

# Suppliers and Purveyors

At this point in time the restaurant should have a fairly complete menu, with established recipes for each dish and drink. Using the menu and the recipes, a master list of ingredients should be assembled, ending up with a list of every grocery item used to produce each recipe and drink, as well as incidentals to operate the restaurant (paper goods, cleaning and sanitizing supplies, etc.). Recipes also indicate the quantities of each ingredient so that basic par levels (amounts needed on hand at any moment) and preliminary stock lists can be developed.

## Food Purveyors

When costing the menu (earlier in the development process), it was necessary to get ingredient prices from one or two wholesale food companies to compute food cost and the menu price needed for profitability. The sales reps of those companies, and all other potential local, regional, and national supply purveyors, should be given the lists you create from the recipes so they can provide bids. Once bids are obtained they can be evaluated to see who offers the best prices and service. When considering suppliers, request samples and do comparative tastings (this is very important). Evaluate not only the quality and price of the product, but issues such as delivery schedule, billing requirements, and response time. If a company can only deliver once a week, or will not break cases into smaller portions, it could present product storage problems between deliveries. A company that is offering 30-day net billing is preferable to one that requires C.O.D payment. If a product needs to be returned or an emergency resupply is needed, will the sales rep guarantee a "hot-shot" (bringing what is needed immediately)? Is there a local warehouse or is their inventory many miles away? If dealing with a particular company is a constant hassle, no matter how good their prices, it might not be worth the savings. When placing orders with food purveyors you will most likely be given a computer printout of all the items they carry, and most of the broadline suppliers have websites that you will be given access to (a password), in order to electronically place your order or to search for a particular item.

Suppliers deliver all of the raw materials you will need to produce the food, offer good service, and maintain a clean, sanitary establishment. Developing positive relationships with them will go a long way when emergencies develop, and you should feel they want to provide that extra step to ensure your continuous operation.

## National Suppliers

Suppliers such as Sysco, LaBatt, US Foodservice, and PFG are what are called broadline distributors, meaning they carry a very wide range of products required by restaurants and bars. These companies control about 40 percent of the nation's food service business. They want to be your purveyor for everything except alcoholic beverages. The balance is controlled by many smaller companies that often focus on a regional or local market, on a particular type of product (produce, seafood, meat, import foods, etc.), or focus on supplying a particular style of restaurant (Asian, Italian, franchise, etc.). Depending on the state's alcoholic beverage laws, some regional food distributors might also distribute beer or wine (Ben E. Keith Inc. in Texas, for example). Most restaurants purchase from a mix of broadline, local or regional, and specialty distributors, receiving product on a daily, weekly, or even monthly schedule.

General groceries are often purchased from the dominant broadline distributor in the area, whether that might be a national or regional distributor. Although the broadline companies will almost always have product lines of meats, fish, poultry, dairy, and produce, it is for these products especially that many operators choose local or regional companies, often enabling the restaurant to "buy local," or at least regionally. With specialty products such as seafood, meats, poultry, dairy, and produce, the local or regional supplier will often have a fresher selection, in several price categories, and a greater variety from which to choose, since these companies focus on their specialty. Produce deliveries are often daily, with dairy, meat, poultry, and seafood often occurring twice weekly. Local suppliers tend to be more accommodating, providing much better service. Be especially careful to keep up-to-date on payment of invoices with local companies, since they have a tighter profit margin and goodwill is important. Regardless of the purveyor, always check prices frequently and monitor the quality of the product from suppliers to "keep them honest." Some broadline distributors require a minimum order for delivery. Be sure to check the amount required.

### Specialty Suppliers

These suppliers often deal in focused product lines, such as Middle Eastern, pizza or Italian, Asian, Latino, "import," cheese, and so on, and tend to be regional. They will often offer high-quality products and product lines unavailable elsewhere. Since they are focused on a particular food aspect, their prices tend to be very competitive. For remotely located restaurants with no local or regional access to a specialty supplier, almost any product can now be purchased online and delivered to your door.

### Wholesale Clubs

Some restaurant owners purchase goods from wholesale membership clubs such as Costco and Sam's Club, finding their prices very competitive and/or quality exceptionally high for certain items. Owners with very limited product requirements might purchase all of their goods from these clubs, as some large national suppliers will require a minimum purchase for delivery. A yearly membership must be purchased and you must go to the location, pull your own order, and deliver the goods to your restaurant. Alcoholic beverages cannot legally be purchased from these clubs and then resold.

### Local Suppliers

Whenever possible, use local suppliers for your needs. It creates goodwill in the community and financially supports small businesses. In addition, produce grown locally will be freshest and of higher quality than items shipped across the country by train or truck. Developing a rapport with local growers can get you custom-grown and exotic items not available from national suppliers and unique to your restaurant. Locally manufactured items avoid shipping costs and local suppliers have inventory to ship immediately, often received on the same day. Whether it be equipment, produce, meat, fish, or services, local suppliers often go out of their way to please and ensure satisfaction with their product. Local suppliers mean convenience for you and special attention to your needs.

Baked goods and desserts are two items that many smaller restaurants lack the man hours and space to produce, so they tend to purchase fresh from a local supplier, getting frequent and often daily deliveries. Local suppliers will often have products that one could not buy from a broadline supplier, in a wide range of categories, and can offer exclusive products unavailable to your area competitors. Broadline suppliers will have lines of frozen cakes and pastries, as well as bake-off cookies and doughs, but they will lack originality and exclusivity. You might have the same frozen cake or cheesecake that many other restaurants in the area have. One broadline product that restaurants might want to consider is bake-off or "bake-n-serve" breads, which come almost completely baked and frozen and ready to quickly finish in the oven. They offer fresh taste with the convenience of a frozen product. The negative aspect is that they take up considerable freezer storage space and can be expensive (but reduce labor, materials, and storage costs). Other time- and space-saving frozen products that restaurants often use are doughs of an almost endless variety. Using these as a base, an unlimited range of custom pastries and desserts can be baked in-house. Be wary of purchasing desserts from private citizens who produce desserts in their home (noninspected) kitchen.

## Bar Suppliers

After the repeal of Prohibition in 1933, regulation of the sales of spirits was controlled by individual states under federal guidelines. Suppliers of alcoholic beverages to restaurants will vary widely, depending on the laws of that state. Eighteen states, the so-called "control" or monopoly states, require liquor and wine to be purchased directly from state-controlled sellers (in some, the state owns the warehouse, while in others the warehouse is operated for the state).

All states control the sale of alcoholic beverages within their borders. "Control" states have a monopoly on the wholesaling or retailing of some or all categories of alcoholic beverages, with the percentage of alcohol often determining control, ranging widely between 3.2 percent and 21 percent alcohol by volume (ABV). The nine states that run liquor stores are Alabama, Idaho, Maryland (certain counties only), Mississippi, New Hampshire, North Carolina, Pennsylvania, Utah, and Virginia. The nine states that either permit privately owned stores to sell liquor for the state, or contract the management of stores to private companies for a sales commission are Iowa, Maine, Massachusetts, Michigan, Montana, Ohio, Oregon, Vermont, and West Virginia. Some individual cities or counties in Minnesota and South Dakota also control sales. Roughly one quarter of the United States lives under the control of monopoly states. The "three-tier" system—where retailers are only allowed to purchase alcohol products from wholesalers, who in turn are required to purchase their products from manufacturers—is the most prevalent distribution system in the United States.

Contact your state Alcoholic Beverage Control Board for the local rules on wholesale purchase, and to access a list of the available licensed wholesale distributors in your locale. Noncompliance will result in criminal penalty and fines.

## Restrictions On Liquor Sales

Thirty-three of the United States have laws that allow localities to prohibit the sale (and in some cases, consumption and possession) of liquor; these are called "dry" localities. Control can be based on city, precinct, or county. A "damp" county is one where there are cities or precincts within the county that allow local alcohol sales; "wet" refers to a locality where sales are allowed. Prohibition can include "liquor by the drink," aimed at outlawing bars serving mixed drinks. A common method around this exclusion is to call the bar a private club, selling memberships in order to serve mixed drinks to patrons.

General bar supplies can often be purchased from a spirits wholesaler or from a broadline distributor, while fruit and garnishes are purchased from the produce purveyor. Soft drinks or soda syrups are available from the local soft drink distributor. Generally there will be at least two competing distributors covering an area. Broadline distributors will often sell soft drinks and mixers as well, in a complete assortment. Bar paper goods, such as beverage napkins, straws, and tickets, are available from paper suppliers, and cleaning supplies from a local janitorial supply. These can also be purchased from a broadline distributor.

## Linen

Linen companies provide napkins, tablecloths, bar and grill cloths, aprons, chefs' and cooks' pants, coats, hats, uniforms, and carpeted mats. They generally inventory and resupply twice a week, based on par levels set up by management. Soiled linens are usually kept outside in a lockable shed, called a "soil house." Be sure to get quotes from all local linen companies. Some companies charge a flat delivery rate, while others charge by a percentage of the total bill. Some companies charge for loss or damage by auditing the bags and doing individual counts, while others charge a flat percentage for loss. Linen napkins are usually rented by the hundred count bundle, usually around $.07 to $.10 each. There are paper napkins available that are almost indistinguishable from cloth. Kitchen or bar towels are in bundles of fifty count, and are about $.10 to $.15 each.

Tablecloths are a big expense, at around $.65 to $.75 each. Some restaurants place an underlay tablecloth on the bottom and then have a contrasting overlay tablecloth offset on the top, using two tablecloths per table. Restaurants generally replace the overlay tablecloth after each set of diners, so the cost added per month can be substantial. Restaurants should avoid using tablecloths whenever possible. Add in aprons, cooks' shirts, carpeted mats, and soil houses to hold the soil bags, and linens can get to be a major expense. Remember that anything a restaurant can do to control expenses puts more money in your pocket.

## Paper Goods

Paper goods are distributed by regional paper specialty companies, and by broadline, regional, and local food distributors. Typical products used by restaurants are napkins, napkin rings, beverage napkins, coasters, toilet paper, paper towels, C-fold or roll dispenser towels, plastic film and aluminum foil, straws, ticket books, notepads, parchment baking paper, bags and boxes, and to-go containers. Most paper products can be personalized with the restaurant logo. Be sure to compare prices, see if the vendor is willing to split cases (paper goods eat up a lot of storage space), and note their frequency of delivery.

## Chemicals

Chemicals for cleaning and sanitizing are available from most broadline, regional, and local food distributors. Local custodial or janitorial supply companies will also carry these products. Depending on sales volume, they might not deliver. All chemicals for cleaning and sanitizing are required to be kept in a separate storage area, so that they cannot contaminate any foodstuffs.

## Chemicals and Cleaning Supplies Checklist

- ❏ Sanitizing, all-purpose soap
- ❏ Silverware presoak solution
- ❏ Abrasive powder scrubber
- ❏ Degreaser
- ❏ Heavy-duty oven grill cleaner
- ❏ Liquid griddle cleaner
- ❏ Deep-fryer cleaning powder
- ❏ Stainless steel cleaner/polish
- ❏ Glass-window cleaner (or vinegar)
- ❏ Bleach
- ❏ De-limer, de-scaler for coffee/tea machines
- ❏ Drain opener or enzymatic drain maintainer
- ❏ Deodorizer, vomit-spill absorber
- ❏ Glycerin hand soap (for all dispensers)
- ❏ Hand sanitizer for kitchen
- ❏ Toilet bowl cleaner
- ❏ Urinal cakes
- ❏ Air freshener/deodorizer to fit timed restroom dispensers
- ❏ Furniture polish
- ❏ Soap and sanitizer for dishwasher machines
- ❏ Food-grade lubricant for kitchen machinery
- ❏ Low-suds glass soap
- ❏ Glass sanitizer/spot rinse
- ❏ Fly traps

- ❏ Sponges
- ❏ Scrub sponges
- ❏ Scrub pads
- ❏ Stainless steel scrubbers
- ❏ Spray bottles, 1 quart
- ❏ 12-inch to 18-inch hand squeegee
- ❏ Rectangular grill brush (wood handle, stiff wire bristles)

- ❏ Toilet brush
- ❏ Toilet plunger

## Service Suppliers

There are many services that a restaurateur might choose to employ, depending on need, cash flow, labor costs, and management free time. Some of these tasks can be done by staff, while others require specialized skill sets or equipment. Some are unnecessary for every business while others are critical to the success or safety of every restaurant.

### Accounting

A bookkeeper or accountant is useful for preparing sales deposits; paying invoices; reconciling the bank accounts; consolidating all of the daily entries into weekly and monthly summary reports; computing payroll and applicable taxes and preparing the payroll checks; generating the monthly, quarterly, and annual P&L statements; and generating your state sales tax, alcoholic beverage commission tax, and federal quarterly tax reports and payments. Generally a bookkeeper is less expensive than an accountant; an accountant deals with tax issues, budgeting, and financial projections, and not day-to-day finances. If you do not employ an outside service to perform these duties, you or some trusted and knowledgeable staff member will have to and it is a time-consuming process. When it comes to restaurant accounting, having a restaurant computer is a must, and having a POS system can prove invaluable. Depending on the sophistication of the setup, many of the required accounting summaries will be created by the POS system. When selecting a bookkeeper or accountant, diligently check out references from other restaurants they might be servicing as restaurant accounting requires a rather specialized skill set. Ideally, the owner or manager and the bookkeeper should have a set time to meet weekly, whether it is in person or over the phone, and no other restaurant business should interfere with that time. Finally, the owner should be capable of reviewing all financial statements and possess basic accounting knowledge to understand the reports generated.

### Armored Car

Armored car services can be hired to come to the restaurant at a set time in order to pick up the bank deposit and deliver the change order. They will work with your bank of choice. The alternative is for the restaurant to have a safe or other secure money storage area, and to make deposits and receive change orders directly at the bank. Obviously, the local crime rate statistics and staff safety should weigh heavily in this decision. If management decides to deliver deposits directly, change the pattern and route frequently.

### Banking Services

Banks and credit unions provide services for restaurants such as providing business loans and offering operating accounts and savings, but only with a bank can you deposit money from sales, provide change for the cash drawers, and participate in credit card sales process. Accepting credit cards is considered essential in today's restaurant environment. "Cash-only" purchases are considered an imposition on the guest and limit potential sales. Installation of an ATM machine can help with cash-only purchases. Restaurants may impose a minimum amount requirement for use of a credit card.

### Credit Card Processing Services

Accepting credit cards is a must for every restaurant and you will need a processor to do this. You should shop around for the best deal, including overall charges and services offered. Your merchant service agreement should spell out all fees and services, and should address things like dispute resolution, 24/7 access to a customer service representative, fee increases (and decreases), and security of data.

First decide the types of services you will need from your provider, including site swiping, mobile processing from cell phones or laptops, gift cards, and check verification (to accept personal checks). If a full-service restaurant rather than fast food, you will need to be able to accept tips, combine bar and dining tabs, accept multiple credit cards for a single bill, and be assured that their system works with your POS system (see next page). Lately some restaurants are having their servers swipe cards at the dining table using a remote, wireless reader. If accepting debit cards, you may need a PIN pad. When ready to sign up with a credit card provider, have the following available: legal business name and tax identification number; bank account details, including routing numbers and a sample canceled check; proof of ownership of the business (your DBA).

Statements from the processor can be confusing and difficult to understand, particularly the breakdown of the various charges. These should be spelled out clearly in the agreement you must sign. Do they charge a setup fee? (You shouldn't have to pay for this, and it is negotiable.) Be sure any surcharges are clearly spelled out and are acceptable and reasonable. Card-processing fees are based on three components: a fee to the card company (Visa, etc.), usually a flat rate for every transaction, called the "interchange fee"; a percentage charged by the card company (the ABVF), based on the amount being charged; and processing and service fees charged to you by your credit card processor to route money to your account. As an example let's say you own an upscale burger and sandwich shop and your average charge is $14. The interchange rate is set at $.04 and a percentage of 1.6 percent ABVF. That comes to about 2.2 percent of the $14 charge. The processing fee is 0.75 percent and $.20 per transaction, adding an additional 2.2 percent, which comes to an overall charge of 4.4 percent. When the $14 charge is credited to your account, $.61 to $.62 will be deducted and your account will be credited with $13.39. Generally expect to be charged between 4 and 5 percent overall; 6 percent or more is high, and less than 3 percent is quite low. To keep costs down always swipe the card and do not manually punch in the numbers; how you enter data affects these fees. Also, if given an option of swiping the card as credit or debit, always select debit. Finally, each card determines its own fees, so a charge to Discover may have an overall percent fee much lower than American Express.

Be diligent in resolving your sales daily. Balance the POS batch reports with daily totals (the "Z out") to calculate the sum of all transactions. Compare this to the credit charge totals to verify your balance before submitting for funding. This will avoid corrections and the fees charged for them. Properly train your sales team to check signatures, check for expiry dates, and have them match credit card numbers on the card with printed receipts. Practice for the event of loss of power and POS systems going down by having carbon authorization slips handy and the voice authorization number for the processor available. Secure transactions are a must so be sure only the last four digits of the credit card are printed on receipts and be diligent to destroy any private information sensitive to theft.

## Carpet Cleaning

Cleaning intervals are determined by quality and type of carpet, stain treatments, customer volume, and appearance, with restaurants cleaning carpets as often as monthly. Cleaning companies typically operate overnight, after the restaurant closes, using high pH chemicals that remove grease effectively. After cleaning, the damp carpet must be dried, so fans are brought in. Always opt for stain treatment.

Restaurant staff or the cleaning company must remove all tables and chairs, and reset before opening the next day. Choose a company that comes highly recommended and that is insured and bonded.

## Coffee and Tea Service

Restaurants can buy coffee and tea brewing and dispensing equipment and then purchase their own coffee, tea, and filters, or they can hire a service that will supply all equipment and supplies and maintain and clean the equipment. Quality and taste are superior when restaurateurs buy their own fresh coffee beans and tea from local or online sources. Get multiple bids and taste the products to decide if a service can provide acceptable quality and provide immediate repair and resupply if needed.

## Cooking Grease Removal

Also known as "yellow grease," used frying oil quickly accumulates at a restaurant with a fryer. There are companies that purchase and haul off yellow grease, which is typically stored in a 50-gallon drum outside, provided by the rendering, environmental, or septic company. Be aware that grease theft is on the rise, stolen for biodiesel conversion. Insist that the company you select maintain a clean, lockable container, and that they offer a fair price. Some restaurants make deals with local environmentalists, who come by as required to pick up used fryer oil stored in the empty oil containers, to be converted privately into biodiesel.

## Custodial/Janitorial Services

Restaurants can choose to hire a local custodial firm to come in to clean the restaurant, hire a local individual to do likewise, or pay their own staff to perform those duties. This function is done before opening or after closing hours, so security and theft prevention is always a concern. A professional company will often do a better job but will cost more. Make sure that the company is insured and bonded. Get multiple bids and clarify exactly what services and supplies are to be provided. If individuals are hired, make sure that they are very highly recommended and trustworthy, and that your insurance will cover any loss from theft. If staff performs the service, management will usually need to be on-site to supervise. Whoever performs the task should formulate a detailed checklist to be followed with some duties listed as periodic or occasional.

## Dish Machine Maintenance and Chemicals

There are two national companies that provide dish machine maintenance and chemicals—Auto-Chlor and EcoLab (owned by Sysco Foods). These companies offer options such as allowing a restaurant to lease the equipment with full service and all chemicals provided, or just provide chemicals and/or service. Restaurants can purchase their own dish machines and chemicals as well. With this last option, it is critical that the manager keep up with regular recommended cleaning and maintenance of the machine.

If you choose to lease and have a company supply the machine and chemicals, they can bill by the number of racks washed or use a flat rate plus cost of chemicals used. It is essential to compare the cost of the two methods on an equal basis, based on a realistic estimate of your volume. Consider water and electrical usage, chemical usage, and the maximum number of racks per hour for each leased machine. A leasing company is obligated to repair their machine when it breaks down, even after hours or weekends. They also periodically upgrade equipment at no additional cost. If you purchase the machine you will pay for the repairs and parts, will need to have a repair service handy, and replace the machine after 7 to 10 years (or sooner). Chemicals generally cost more from a leasing company, but they also keep you stocked and they deliver. Leasing a machine often comes out to be a better deal over time, especially in areas with a less than ideal water source. Areas that have water with high mineral content will experience increased dish machine problems.

## Electrical

Every restaurant should have a reliable electrician they can call and get immediate service from when a problem develops (and it will, usually at an inopportune time). Be sure the electrician is licensed, bonded, and insured.

## Emergency Services

Know where the local late-hours emergency clinic or emergency room is located, and have EMS/EMT on speed-dial. Serious accidents can occur in a restaurant setting or a guest may become seriously ill (heart attack, anaphylactic shock) or fall, and rapid medical services will be needed. It is also a good idea to have the local police number available (usually 911) to be there quickly should a tussle break out or if a theft occurs.

### Entertainment

Live entertainment can be a draw for a restaurant, as long as the volume is moderated during dining hours. Local entertainers can have a following of supporters that can boost sales for the restaurant. Management needs to audition entertainers to ensure the quality of their performance. Specify who is responsible for equipment, such as microphones and amplifiers, and make sure that the outlets used can handle the electrical load. Be very specific about details of payment, especially if there is a cover charge involved or they solicit tips. Clarify if they want a guest list and the number of patrons on it. Specify if there is any discount for beverages or food consumed by the entertainer, and if there are any quantity limits imposed.

### Equipment Maintenance

It is beneficial to have a multitalented maintenance person who periodically maintains, adjusts, and repairs restaurant equipment. Well-maintained equipment performs as designed and breaks down less often. Duties might include calibration of ovens, cleaning out gas burner orifices, mineral build-up removal from steamers, and replacing refrigeration gaskets. They usually have a broad skill set, and are able to handle a multitude of tasks. They usually prefer a guaranteed interval between visits, coming periodically to complete a list of pending intermittent repairs, as well as regular periodic maintenance. Negotiate a fair rate and seek referrals from other area restaurants.

### Exterior Landscape and Irrigation

Proper maintenance of an existing landscape can greatly boost curb appeal. Regular mowing, weeding, trimming, switching out seasonal annuals, and replacing dead plants are all tasks that might be considered. Some companies in northern areas also do snow removal. Irrigation systems often need periodic adjustment and repair to water properly, so it is preferred if the landscape company can handle that task as well. The company should come by to perform their duties during non-peak dining hours and clean up when finished, hauling off any debris they create (do not allow disposal of debris in your dumpster). Get bids and referrals and decide on a reasonable price. If a contract is signed be sure it has a nonperformance clause and that you can reduce visits during dormant months. Your staff can also perform many of these duties if equipment is available and if so, do not store the gasoline supply near any flame sources and make sure it has adequate ventilation.

## Exterminator

Every restaurant needs periodic insecticide and/or rodenticide application by a professional exterminator trained to recognize problems such as rodent feces and urine trails, cockroach egg cases, and insect waste. A certified exterminator knows which insecticides can be safely used inside the restaurant, their proper application rates and methods, and the safe re-entry interval. Make sure the provider also has an aggressive fly-control program. Instruct staff to notify management immediately of any pest sightings. If customers spot a rodent or roach, it can quickly ruin business. Exterminators should be licensed and insured. Research the local companies carefully, check referrals, and choose a company that uses the least toxic chemicals. Anytime construction is done (especially during initial construction) all wall cavities should be pre-treated for pests before sealing.

## Fire Safety Inspections

The exhaust hood fire suppression system and all fire extinguishers will have inspection tags with expiration dates punched out on them. According to local fire codes, periodic inspections are required to make sure the extinguishers are sufficiently charged. Area fire extinguisher companies perform this service and keep the restaurant compliant. These same companies refill extinguishers that have been depleted through use. Fire safety companies also sell and maintain first-aid kits. It is less expensive to put together your own kit, focusing primarily on cuts and burns. See page 130 for a first-aid kit supply list.

### How to Assemble a First-Aid Kit

Every restaurant needs a first-aid kit, primarily to handle cuts, burns, and sprains. Your fire extinguisher company will want to supply you with a kit that will be full of many items that you will never use and it can be quite expensive. It is much cheaper to assemble the contents yourself. Keep all of the supplies organized in a clear plastic box with a fitted lid, prominently labeled "First Aid" on all sides and have the manager inventory the supplies biweekly. Keep the kit in a central location that everyone knows. A manager should fill out an accident report form every time the kit is used and should be trained in basic first aid and CPR.

## Contents of the Kit

- ❏ Sterile adhesive bandages—heavy-duty, waterproof, 1" x 3", 100 count
- ❏ Sterile gauze pads—assorted
- ❏ Waterproof tape—1" x 10 yards
- ❏ Butterfly wound closures—waterproof, medium, 3/8" x 1 13/16", 100 count
- ❏ Finger cots—large, latex, 100 count
- ❏ Finger splints—3.5" x 1.5", 3 count
- ❏ Hemostatic dressings—2" x 2", 10 pouches per box, 1 box (use for bad cuts only; quickly stops bleeding)
- ❏ Paper bandage tape—1" x 10 yards, 3 rolls
- ❏ Elastic bandage—4" x 15 yards, 2 rolls
- ❏ Hydrogen peroxide—1 bottle
- ❏ Triple antibiotic cream—1 tube
- ❏ Cortisone cream—1 tube
- ❏ Antiseptic/anesthetic spray—1 can
- ❏ Water Jel Burn Jel packets—6 each per box, 2 boxes
- ❏ Water Jel Burn Jel bandages—2" x 6" 2 pack, 3 count
- ❏ Burn cream—An excellent burn cream is made using zinc oxide ointment mixed half and half with 100 percent aloe vera gel just before application.
- ❏ Burn dressings—sterile, nonstick, assorted sizes
- ❏ Latex gloves—large, disposable (for handling wounds)
- ❏ Aspirin—325 mg, 500 count, 1 bottle
- ❏ Sterile saline solution—1 bottle (for eye and wound flushing)
- ❏ Cotton swabs—1 box
- ❏ Elastic rubber hose—36" section, for tourniquet
- ❏ "Blue ice" packs (save from food shipments or packaging, sanitize, store in freezer)

## Firewood and Chimney Cleaners

Restaurants with log fireplaces, or wood-burning ovens, grills, smokers, or barbecue pits need a steady supply of seasoned firewood, preferably slow-burning hardwood. A dry, secure storage space is required for the wood, and some should arrive already split, or in a range of diameters. The supplier should be willing to stack the wood at its destination. Chimneys and fireplace flues should be cleaned annually. Flues associated with the cooking of food over live coals or with smoke require more frequent cleaning; grease and creosote build up in the flue, creating a fire hazard.

## Floral

Restaurants that have floral arrangements or flowers on the tables in a bud vase can hire a local florist to deliver needed flowers. Often a tax number is all that is required to purchase flowers directly from the local wholesale floral supply, while some jurisdictions require a state floral license as well. Purchasing wholesale flowers will save a lot of money over time, even if the license is required and must be purchased. Basic floral arranging skills can be acquired from books, online sources, or from a local community college.

## Compressed Gases

Tanks of $CO_2$ may be required for keg beer or older soda systems, and liquid nitrogen might be required for restaurants doing molecular gastronomy or mixology. Local welding supply companies stock these gas cylinders in various sizes and will usually deliver. The beer or soda route delivery truck can also deliver cylinders of $CO_2$. Expect to be charged a deposit on cylinders unless you purchase your own. Store them in a safe place where they are vented if they leak. Cylinders should be attached to a sturdy wall with brackets made for this.

## Grease Trap and Drains

Use a local drain/rooter company that provides 24-hour, 7-days-a-week, 365-days-of-the-year service; at some point it will be necessary for them to come at a moment's notice, usually at the worst possible time of peak business hours. Know and mark where all of your plumbing cleanout locations are. The grease trap will need periodic pumping out, with the interval based on the size of the trap, the amount of grease going down the drain, and the amount of business. It is far more desirable to schedule the grease trap cleanout than discover it needs cleaning when all of your drains back up during a dinner shift. When scheduling, be advised that it is a foul-smelling process, best done when the restaurant is not open for business.

### Handyman

Every restaurant needs a reliable, competent handyman to perform tasks that the management does not have the skills or time to perform. This person should be able to handle a wide range of tasks, from minor electrical and plumbing to finish carpentry and painting. There might be a staff member or members who can handle this job in their free time.

### HVAC/Refrigeration Technician

A reputable HVAC and refrigeration technician who can quickly repair equipment and heating or air-conditioning systems is an absolute necessity as the safety of food is in jeopardy. When food spoils because a refrigeration compressor fails or a relay burns out it has to be thrown out or customers could get ill. The comfort of the restaurant's guests is dependent on the heating or air-conditioning. When the kitchen fills with smoke because a drive belt breaks on the exhaust hood fan, the cooking line cannot produce food. Ultimately, breakdowns cost money. Obtain referrals from other restaurants if possible. Having the technician do periodic inspections is well worth the money to avert serious problems.

### Ice Machine Maintenance

Ice machines need periodic maintenance and cleaning to operate at their peak. The technical manual will have detailed information on maintenance schedules and they should be followed, performed either by staff or a qualified technician. Cleaning, sanitizing, and demineralization of the machines and changing the water filters is essential (filtering the supply water is always recommended). Plan ahead for a cleaning session and stockpile ice in storage bins in the bar and wait station (and insulated coolers), or schedule a delivery when the ice bin will need to be emptied and sanitized. If the ice machine is leased, the leasing company will perform these maintenance and repair tasks at their expense, even on weekends and holidays. When you own the ice machine all repairs and parts are your responsibility.

### Ice

Local ice companies can deliver cube or block ice on a regular or emergency basis (called a "hot shot"). Restaurants that do catering often employ their services as well. Ice companies are set up for emergencies and generally have very short response times.

### Insurance

Your best choice for insurance is with a local agent underwriter who can physically visit the restaurant, assess your needs, and make specific recommendations for coverage. A local agent will know the area's risks and regional rates, and can respond much faster should an unfortunate event occur. Ask around at several noncompeting restaurants and see who they use, and how they would rate their agent's service. Do online searches to see if there might be a local company that specializes in food service or restaurant coverage. Get multiple bids so that you can compare rates, and be aware of additional coverage that you may not necessarily need. Ask questions and make sure you get solid answers. Know the procedure for reporting a claim, and confirm that you can get 24/7 emergency claim service and resolution should it be necessary. Quick response time can be critical with business disasters like flooding, fires, or weather damage. Keep your agent apprised of any upgrades that might require additional or expanded coverage.

Keep a file of all accident reports, no matter how minor, and never throw them away. It is important to fully document all on-the-job injuries, with statements from any witnesses; expensive, after-the-fact claims can materialize from disgruntled employees. Know the local emergency medical clinic. Your staff will more than likely be utilizing their services. If a customer ever has an accident at your restaurant, seek immediate treatment that fully satisfies the customer, and get statements for the accident report from as many witnesses as possible. If your insurance agent cannot provide you with accident report forms, they are available online.

### Interior Landscape

Interior landscape companies lease interior plants appropriate for the conditions inside the restaurant, for a monthly fee. They come by during slack business hours to water, fertilize, polish the leaves, and assess and treat the plants for insect pests. Get bids from several companies and ask them to bring samples by, to see how they look in place. Make sure that they will use safe pesticides that do not emit strong odors and that the plants selected are not toxic to children.

### Internet Services

You will need an Internet provider, often a cable company that has specific rates and services for commercial establishments. Monthly or annual fees are paid to a web hosting company, and an annual fee is paid to register the website name. Restaurants often hire a local web designer to put up and maintain their web page and/or Facebook page. Web designers usually charge a one-time fee for setup. Establish a deadline with your designer for posting of the site. Facebook updates and tweets on Twitter are normally done by management or a trusted staff member. The restaurant must first secure a website name that is not already taken. Web pages should be straightforward, easy to read, and fast-loading; large amounts of animation and/or music slow the loading of a web page. Design the page to allow copy and pasting of vital information. Post the menu, hours, location (with a linked map), what credit cards are allowed, good media reviews, and any access issues. Some restaurants prefer to not list their prices online, but it is usually better to have your guests informed rather than surprised or disappointed.

### Parking Services

Parking services can be divided into four categories—valet parking, lot sweepers, striping companies, and towing companies. Valet parking is generally for restaurants that have inadequate parking capacity. They lease parking space from nearby businesses, and hire a company (or use restaurant staff) to shuttle guests' vehicles to and from a nearby lot. Many restaurants prefer to hire a company to provide this service, in order to avoid insurance and liability issues, such as collision and theft. Some guests resent valet parking, feeling that it adds cost to the dining experience; many simply do not trust valet parkers with their vehicles or with valuables that might be left inside the car. Unless there is no alternative, avoid valet parking. Hire only insured and bonded companies with good referrals, and monitor their performance constantly. You should know that federal law dictates that handicapped guests be allowed to park their own cars in handicapped spaces provided.

Lot sweepers are contracted to periodically sweep the parking lot clean, usually performing the task after hours or overnight. Staff using a power leaf blower can usually accomplish the same task. Striping companies are hired periodically to repaint the stripes in a parking lot and make minor repairs like resealing, patching potholes, or replacing concrete car stops.

Towing companies are hired to remove nonguest vehicles from what are often limited spaces. Make sure that well-lighted, highly visible warning signs are posted, alerting potential violators that they will be towed, with the name and contact information of the towing company, and that the restaurant will not be held liable for any theft from a vehicle in the lot. Incorrectly towing a guest's vehicle by an overzealous tow truck can create problems for the restaurant.

## Plumbing

Every restaurant needs a talented on-call plumber that can provide fast, 24-hour, 7-days-a-week, 365-days-of-the-year service. According to Murphy's Law, any plumbing problems will develop at the worst possible time.

## POS (Point of Sale) System Provider

Be careful and negotiate the amount you agree to pay the POS provider for setup, installation, training, troubleshooting, and programming, as these are separate charges from the hardware (monitors, computer, cash drawers, touch screens, printers, etc.). Also compare post-installation support and warranties. There are many systems and providers available, so ask local restaurants about the system they use and their satisfaction with hardware, software, and service from the providers they selected. Use the Internet for comparisons and get quotes from several companies once you have narrowed your needs. The most popular POS system providers include Micros, Aloha, AccuPOS, POS Nation, and Restaurant Manager POS. Each has advantages and disadvantages, depending on your specific application. Get bids and compare hardware, software, and service provided by each. Select a company that can help you expand as needed, starting with a modest system that provides the essentials and does not pressure you into purchasing all the "bells and whistles" that can be part of these highly complex (and expensive) systems. Look for the amount of support provided in getting your system up and running and through training and opening day.

## Pressure Washing

A restaurant might want to periodically hire a local company to pressure wash areas like the entry sidewalk or siding. Pressure washer compressors can also be rented, with staff doing the work.

## Recorded Music

Restaurants under 3,750 square feet (including patios) are exempt from music licensing fees if they play *only* radio and television music. Restaurants over 3,750 square feet are exempt from music licensing fees if they play *only* radio and television music, and if there are no more than four TVs that do not exceed 55 inches diagonally, with only one per room, with no more than a total of six speakers, and no cover charge is involved. To play live or recorded music (including CDs, MP3s, DVDs, tapes, DJs, live, karaoke, etc.) inside a restaurant larger than 3,750 square feet (including patios) you must have a license, obtained from four agencies that license the access rights of their member musicians: BMI, ASCAP, SESAC, and Sound Exchange. Unless it is determined that the music played is solely from one of the associations, you must pay for licensing from all four (although many register with BMI and ASCAP only, especially for older music). Restaurants that do not pay the licensing fee may eventually be visited by a "spy" who will come in and check the place out and discover there is no license, which could result in an expensive lawsuit for theft of services. Alternatives include satellite systems like Muzak and XM for Business, where the restaurant picks a theme from a list of musical genres and is not allowed any customizing. Licensing fees to the agencies are included in your monthly bill. Jukeboxes must be leased from licensed companies. These companies are also paying the agency license fees.

For a restaurant's sound system, use high-quality speakers that do not distort, in multiple locations that evenly cover the dining room, with controls that enable adjustment of volume, balance, and tone. Cheap or inadequate speakers create distortion that adds to the din of the room. Management should control what gets played and at what volume; staff tends to select inappropriate tunes, played too loudly.

## Restaurant Equipment and Supply

Regional and local restaurant supply companies will sell any equipment, smallwares, and supplies needed by a restaurant. Broadline food companies, such as Sysco, also deal in certain equipment and supplies. Operators should also consider online suppliers such as bigtray.com, centralrestaurant.com, katom.com, and instawares.com. These companies offer very competitive pricing, since much of their product is drop-shipped and not warehoused, with free shipping if the invoice is over a set amount. Some do not charge sales tax, but you may be responsible for the tax in your state. To procure something needed immediately, or in small quantities, the local supplier is your best alternative.

Many local and regional suppliers also offer used or reconditioned equipment, which can save up to about 40 percent in purchase price. As with all sales of anything used, buyer beware. It is recommended that a restaurant never purchase used refrigeration unless absolutely necessary; compressors and condensers have limited lives, and are expensive to replace.

## Security

Security can be divided into three categories—alarm companies, locksmiths, and security guards or bouncers. Alarm companies install and repair alarm systems that notify the local authorities or the monitoring alarm company (and occasionally management) during a break-in. The system can incorporate movement sensors, window and door sensors, glass-breaking sensors, pressure sensors under carpets, heat and smoke detectors, air gas detectors, video capture, automatic dialers (to police or the alarm company), panic buttons, flashing lights, and/or exterior sirens. They often require a separate, dedicated phone line. Reveal the security keypad code on a strictly need-to-know basis, and change when necessary. Be warned that false alarms, when police come out to investigate for no reason, are often billed to the restaurant, so make sure that the alarm company fine tunes the system to prevent such occurrences. Alarm or security companies occasionally provide a drive-by service, where a marked security vehicle repeatedly cruises by during the night or does external checks. The company will provide prominent signage that informs potential burglars that the building is protected.

Locksmiths are hired to install and repair locks and deadbolts. They can also rekey existing locks by changing or altering the tumblers. After the finish of construction, where the builders have been given keys, it is recommended that a restaurant rekey all of the locks. Keys should only be provided to management staff who are opening or closing the restaurant. Keys should be marked to prevent an employee from getting copies made at a local vendor.

Security guards or bouncers are normally only hired by restaurants with a very active scene, often one that is very crowded at night, when guests might be rowdy or intoxicated, or restaurants located in what might be considered questionable, dangerous, or "seedy" neighborhoods. Some very busy restaurants might hire security to direct traffic in large, busy parking lots, or to halt busy street traffic to allow guests to exit a parking lot. Security guards are often off-duty law enforcement officers who are moonlighting. Bouncers are normally provided by a security company, which should have its own liability insurance. Closely monitor bouncers to make sure they do not overreact to a given situation, creating potential publicity or liability problems. Bouncers working the door, who might exclude certain guests, should be informed of all discrimination laws and should have a well-defined idea of the criteria. Signage needs to be posted informing guests of all exclusion criteria (dress codes, no large parties, no singles, etc.). Bouncers should not be armed.

### Sign Company

Business signs often need preapproval from a municipal inspector, verifying that they comply with local codes. Sign companies design, build, and repair signs of all types, mounted on buildings or freestanding, lighted or not. Get bids and referrals, and look at examples of the company's work. Make sure the sign is visible and prominent, but more importantly, done in a font and a color that is easily readable from a distance. Restaurants and food trailers frequently select signage that is artistic but is virtually unreadable. Often it is impossible to tell what the business is. If you have decided on a logo for the restaurant, this is a great option but again make sure it is easily readable.

### Taxi

Many restaurants establish cooperative deals with a well-respected taxi company in town so that the restaurant gets fast, priority response to a call for a guest that might have had a little bit too much to drink or for guests staying in local hotels. Never allow inebriated guests to drive, even if the restaurant has to pay for the cab. It will be much cheaper than a lawsuit, and the guest will thank you the next day.

### Vent or Exhaust Hood and Deep Cleaning

Exhaust hoods, ductwork, and fans suffer from grease and particulate buildup and need periodic cleaning to prevent fires. The frequency of the cleaning is determined by sales volume, the angle and length of the ductwork, employee cleaning schedules, and the type of food being cooked. Restaurants that do a great deal of frying, wok cooking, griddle cooking, wood grilling, barbecuing, or smoking require more frequent cleaning of the vents and hood. Cleaning every 3 to 6 months is common; some jurisdictions set guidelines for the cleaning interim. The process is normally done overnight or on a day the restaurant is closed. Fire-retardant chemicals can be applied after the cleaning process. All kitchens need a periodic steam cleaning, sometimes called a "deep clean," where the equipment is moved out from the walls and all surfaces (and sometimes equipment) are steam cleaned. As with the vent hood system, the type of restaurant and the sales volume affect this cleaning interim. Get referrals for the company doing the cleaning, and make sure it is insured and bonded.

## Waste Removal

Local waste removal companies provide a dumpster of variable size (in cubic yards), which is emptied at negotiated intervals, and is based on the garbage output of the restaurant. The larger the dumpster is, and the more frequently it is emptied, the more it will cost per month. When selecting a location for the dumpster, consider prevailing winds; neighboring businesses or houses find it easy to complain about bad dumpster odors. The garbage truck will rock the dumpster up and down when emptying it, causing the truck's wheels to put great stress on the pavement underneath. If possible, reinforce the concrete pad or pavement to handle the extra weight and repeated stress. Many restaurants keep their dumpsters locked to prevent people from throwing their household garbage in the restaurant dumpster. Make sure that the cap on the drain at the bottom of the dumpster is secured; otherwise, liquids will drain out and pollute the immediate area. Insist that waste companies switch out the dumpster when it gets too soiled or odorous.

## Water Purification

In some areas, water purification is required to reduce salts, chemicals, off tastes, or minerals from the local water source. Water softeners that greatly improve the taste of water can be installed. In especially bad situations, a reverse-osmosis and/or deionization system can be installed. There is usually a local or regional water quality company that will service and maintain leased or purchased systems. Simple systems can be maintained by the restaurant operator.

## Window Washing

Depending on the number and size of the windows, especially if they are above the ground floor, a restaurant might choose to hire a window washing contractor. Window washers can clean exterior and interior windows. This task is often overlooked by restaurants, but the fees are nominal and the results are well worth it. Sparkling windows say much about the cleanliness of the interior and boost the look of the exterior. Providers generally set up a schedule and clean windows during slack business hours.

Accountant _____

Armored car _____

Banking _____

Credit card processing _____

Carpet cleaners _____

Coffee/tea _____

Cooking grease removal _____

Custodial or janitorial services _____

Dish machine maintenance _____

Electrician _____

Emergency services _____

Entertainment _____

Equipment maintenance _____

Exterior landscaper and irrigation _____

Exterminator _____

Fire safety inspections _____

Firewood and chimney cleaners _____

Florist _____

Compressed gas suppliers _____

Grease trap and drain cleaners _____

Handyman _____

HVAC/refrigeration technician _____

Ice-machine maintenance _____

Ice delivery _____

Insurance agent _____

Interior landscaper _____

Parking services _____

Plumber _____

POS (point of sale) system provider _____

Pressure washing _____

Recorded music _____

Restaurant equipment and supply _____

Security _____

Sign company _____

Internet services _____

Taxi _____

Vent or exhaust hood and deep cleaning _____

Waste removal _____

Water purification _____

Window washers _____

# 09

# Staffing

By now you should prepare to staff your restaurant. The hiring process can take weeks, followed by weeks of training, before opening. It may surprise you to realize how many employees you will need, and it is important to know the various positions they will fill and the factors that dictate how many are needed to fill those positions. The style of restaurant is one factor, as fine dining and casual dining require a cadre of servers, bus persons, and a full kitchen staff. An extensive menu influences the BOH in the number of prep cooks needed and the number of line cooks. More supervision is needed and tight controls over inventory, ordering, and par levels are a must. A large restaurant will need more servers and bus persons to handle the number of tables. Meals of the day, regardless of restaurant size, require more personnel. If open for breakfast, lunch, and dinner, more servers, prep cooks, line cooks, dishwashers, and supervisors are needed. A busy, modest-size restaurant of one hundred seats that serves lunch and dinner with the same menu (with specials added to enhance dinner offerings) and has a full-service bar will need more than twenty-five employees for the entire day (as many as thirty). Remember that overtime is costly and should be avoided, and so the same twenty-five employees cannot work every shift of every day. Using servers as example, the one-hundred-seat restaurant has twenty-five (four-top) tables and will be divided into four to five sections of five to six tables per section. You will need at least four servers for lunch and five servers for dinner and those nine server servers cannot fill all shifts for a week's operation. Most servers pick up four or five shifts per week, so to fill the week and have some backup employees to fill in for absences, you may need a minimum of twelve qualified servers, and overall up to forty-five to fifty employees. A profitable restaurant keeps labor costs under 35 percent of gross sales, with management making up about 10 percent of that figure.

The key to employees is that they be qualified for their positions, and it is not that easy to hire the large crew needed to staff a busy restaurant. Poor service and bad food are not the recipe for success. The hiring process may be frustrating, but take your time to hire the very best you can. Training can go a long way toward making up for experience and this, too, shouldn't be rushed. Until you open your doors to customers, money is going in one direction only . . . out from your account, and the pressure to open as soon as possible must be balanced by being ready to open. Resist cutting training time short to open and generate income; you only have one chance to get it right and word of mouth is strongest at opening. Having an ongoing policy of training for the future, by promoting and moving up from within, is important to maintain a pool of qualified workers. Attentive, hard-working bus persons should be encouraged to seek server positions, as they work carefully with your best servers. Prep cooks can be trained to be line cooks and dish persons can be trained to be prep cooks. The executive chef should have a policy of training and cross-training in place from day one for the BOH, as should the FOH manager.

Employees need to know what the policies are with regard to behavior, dress and grooming code, how and when they get paid, meals and discounts, how to handle absences, tipping, your policy on drugs and the like. The more you spell out to them in black and white, the fewer problems you will have down the road, and when problems do occur, you can be consistent with everyone. Carefully craft a policy manual and go over it with your employees when you have your first meeting with them after hiring is complete. Every position in your restaurant must have a job description written for it, explaining the qualifications, experience desired, duties, hours, and responsibilities and tasks to be performed (see example for FOH manager on page 148).

Now comes the really hard question. What position will you fill in your restaurant? Ideally, you are a talented cook and will head the kitchen as executive chef/kitchen manager. Being in this position allows for maximum control of quality and consistency. If you are the chef then you cannot quit and leave the restaurant in the worst of situations—no one can duplicate the food as you

## Employee Policy Manual Checklist

Use this checklist to formulate policies and create a custom handbook for orientation.

- ❏ Employee benefits—food discounts, employee meals, alcohol discounts and limits

- ❏ Vacation policy—eligibility requirements, length and accrual

- ❏ Insurance policy—workers' compensation coverage

- ❏ Unemployment and firing policy—probationary period, fireable offenses, firing procedure and number of warnings required

- ❏ Dress and grooming policy

- ❏ Professional conduct

- ❏ Coworker relations

- ❏ Absence policy—schedule rules, planned absence/what to do if you need to miss a shift, unplanned absence/sickness, covering a shift unexpectedly

- ❏ Pay policies—timecard/POS procedures, pay for mandatory meetings, training pay, overtime, how to enter different pay codes for different jobs

- ❏ Tip policy—tip pool and who is covered, charge-card tip procedure and dispersal, tax reporting

- ❏ Alcohol and drug policy—abuse while at work, sales or distribution

- ❏ Theft—policy on cash overage/underage, theft of money or goods, misappropriation of funds, credit-card abuse, theft of intellectual property (methods, recipes, menu, systems)

- ❏ Dating policy—inter-staff, customers

- ❏ Electronic media—cellphone use during work/texting, abuse of the restaurant/office computer

- ❏ Social media abuse—Facebook, Twitter, blogs (posting negative comments)

have been preparing it. Many restaurants have to close their doors when they lose their chefs as no one else can do what they do in the kitchen. If you do not cook, will you be the FOH manager? Are you willing to be there 12 to 14 hours per day, every day, regardless of the position(s) you assume? Once you've made this decision, the first hires must be the head chef/kitchen manager and the FOH manager (unless you will be assuming this role), so they can be involved in the hiring and training of the staff.

## Payroll Taxes

Payroll taxes are the state and federal taxes that you, as an employer, are required to withhold and/or pay on behalf of your employees. You are required to withhold state and federal income taxes as well as Social Security and Medicare taxes from your employees' wages. You are also required to pay a matching amount of Social Security and Medicare taxes for your employees and to pay state and federal unemployment tax.

As stated, Social Security and Medicare taxes, also known as FICA taxes, must be withheld from your employees' wages. As an employer, you must also pay a matching amount of FICA taxes for your employees. Currently the Social Security tax rate is 6.2 percent. You are required to withhold 6.2 percent of an employee's wages for Social Security taxes and to pay a matching amount in Social Security taxes until the employee reaches the wage base for the year. The wage base for Social Security tax is projected to be $110,100 for the year 2013 (and $128,400 in 2016). Once that amount is earned, neither the employee nor employer owes any additional Social Security tax.

The Medicare tax rate is 2.9 percent for the employee and the employer. You will withhold 1.45 percent of an employee's wages and pay a matching amount for Medicare tax. There is no wage base for the Medicare portion of the FICA tax. Both the employer and the employee continue to pay Medicare tax, no matter how much is earned.

Calculating what you owe in state unemployment taxes is simply a matter of multiplying the wages you pay each of your employees by your tax rate. However, every state limits the tax you must pay with respect to any one employee by specifying a maximum wage amount to which the tax applies. Once an employee's wages for the calendar year exceed that maximum amount, your state tax liability with respect to that employee ends.

## Staffing—FOH

Your FOH personnel are the face of your restaurant. Your guests interact almost exclusively with them, so they represent you. Keep this in mind when hiring for the FOH. It is not always easy to hire a complete crew in a short amount of time. You may be frustrated enough to hope that you can train some of the less desirable applicants in order to fill your personnel quota. It is difficult to find qualified employees in any profession, but take your time and hire only those you would want to serve your best friends or relatives. You only get one chance to make a good impression.

### Scheduling Basics

The best staff members should be scheduled to work the busiest shifts. You will want them to deal with the majority of your guests, and the best FOH employees will want to work the busiest shifts and make the most money in tips. Make sure that management retains final approval on any schedule substitutions initiated by an employee, as the substitute may not be able to handle a busy, rigorous shift. Workers sixteen years of age and older have no restrictions on when they can work, but those fourteen and fifteen have limitations placed on the maximum number of hours during a school day and during a school week, and the hours they may work (generally, 7 a.m. to 7 p.m.).

Split shifts (consecutive shifts on the same day) are legal, but the "off" time between the two portions of the shift must be in control of the worker. Employees who are "on call" must be paid if they are required to stay at the place of work, or if they have no control of their free time while "on call" (they must remain close to work or they cannot drink alcohol, for example). When employees are required to attend a meeting or training session, they must be paid for that time. Hourly employees who work over 40 hours a week or more than 8 hours a day must be paid overtime.

### Wages

The majority of FOH employees are tipped employees, and therefore are usually paid a lower hourly rate. The Fair Labor Standards Act (FLSA) sets a federal minimum wage of $7.25 per hour effective July 24, 2009, for covered, nonexempt employees (which was still in effect at time of publication). An employer of a tipped employee is only required to pay $2.13 an hour in direct wages if that amount plus the tips received equals at least the federal minimum wage, the employee retains all tips, and the employee customarily and regularly receives more than $30 a month in tips. If an employee's tips combined with the employer's direct wages of at least $2.13 an hour do not equal the federal minimum hourly wage, the employer must make up the difference. The difference between the reduced hourly rate and the normal rate is called the "tip credit." Different states have different rates for tipped employees, and federal law dictates that if federal and state rates differ, the employee gets paid the higher rate.

### Tip Pools

Many states allow employers to require tip pooling, where all employees subject to the pool have to chip in a portion of their tips, which are then divided among the group of employee participants. An employee can't be required to pay more into the pool than is "customary and reasonable," and the employee must be able to keep at least the full minimum wage. Only employees who regularly receive tips can participate in the pool; they can't be required to share their tips with employees who don't usually receive their own tips from customers, like dishwashers or cooks. No employers are allowed to participate in the pool; in some states managers and supervisors are excluded as well. In many restaurants the "to-go" tip jar funds are used to provide a bonus to kitchen and/or host employees (since the host often takes the order and the kitchen packs it to-go), or to pay for a seasonal employee party.

### The Tip

When bills are paid by credit card, some states allow the employer to subtract a proportionate amount of the designated tip to cover its expenses for the credit card processing fee. Other states say that the restaurant must give the employee the full tip amount indicated by the customer and pay the processing fee itself. When there is a mandatory service charge added to a bill, say for a large group or the use of a room, management is not required by federal law or most states to pass that money on to the employees working that table or event. Many employers give at least part of these service charges to employees, but that's the employer's prerogative—employees have no legal claim to that money. Several states, however, require the restaurant to inform the customer of who receives that service charge and what portion of it the restaurant receives.

### Positions

Here are the various positions that make up the FOH. They must work as a team as well as be proficient in their respective jobs. Keep this in mind when setting up training sessions. The FOH manager is the key position, so be especially selective when hiring for this position.

**FOH Manager**

In many smaller restaurants the FOH manager is also the owner. If not, then this manager handles all business matters not performed by the owner, often handling overall restaurant management duties as well as front of the house duties, and delegates any duties only to trusted, responsible employees. The manager is responsible for interviewing, hiring/firing, training, supervising, and scheduling all FOH employees. The manager resolves any employee disputes. He or she monitors the paperwork status on all FOH employee files to ensure they are up to date and compliant. He or she coordinates with the chef or BOH manager on menu specials and changes and communicates same to the servers. He or she handles all FOH ordering, pricing, and inventory, and supervises restaurant bookkeeping. If the bookkeeper prepares the bank deposit, the manager should review it. The manager is responsible for the counting and reconciling of the cash drawer(s) at both opening and closing, and reviews daily tickets and tapes for errors. He or she reviews all FOH-related figures on accounting and P&L statements and formulates strategies to adjust any problem numbers.

The manager supervises the bar manager, and has secondary input and final approval with any spirits salespeople, and approves any new spirits on menu. He or she selects the music and/or the TV channel, and monitors the volume through each shift. He or she monitors and adjusts ambient temperature, ceiling fans, fireplace, and lighting during the shift.

One of his or her most important functions is to be the management "face" of the restaurant, circulating through the dining room, bar, and entry to check on customer satisfaction, schmooze with regulars and VIPs, and effectively handle all complaints concerning product and service. He or she serves as a secondary quality control supervisor on all food coming out of the kitchen and spirits coming from the bar, and communicates and coordinates with the kitchen and bar on any food or drink compliments or complaints. He or she makes sure that the website and Facebook pages are posted and up to date, and monitors online reviews for issues that need addressing. The manager also has input on all advertising and marketing planning and execution. The manager must be certified with a local alcohol beverage awareness program and with the local health department.

## Job Description

Oversee final construction and completion of FOH; oversee and enforce health department code compliance; manage and control FOH waste; manage and control FOH inventory; establish checklists and training manuals for FOH operations and employees; schedule all FOH employees, meet labor budget; supervise FOH employees—emphasize safety, cleanliness, and security; train and hire new employees—server, bus, host/hostess, bar; establish and oversee FOH cleaning schedules; oversee bar operations; oversee bar and FOH equipment maintenance and cleaning; coordinate with BOH/kitchen; perform other reasonable duties as required

## Position Requirements

Possess excellent organizational and customer service skills, have basic computer skills and be familiar with POS systems. Strong communication and leadership skills are a must.

Able to function under limited supervision, knowledgeable of food and beverage products, preparations, and presentations. Flexible work schedule (58 hours per week standard)

Understand budgetary and labor goals and work to promote revenue and control costs.

## Advertisement

_____ is looking to hire its front of house (FOH) manager. Applicants should have a minimum of 3 years' experience as FOH manager for large, busy restaurants cooking scratch-based foods, with a very stable work history. Formal hospitality/restaurant schooling is desirable. Job skills include being bilingual, computer literate, an effective communicator, and food manager certified by the state. Strong leadership skills are a must. Experience as a bartender and server is desirable. Salary is commensurate with experience and education. References are required. Contact _____.

## Bar Manager

In all but large restaurants, the bar manager is usually the lead bartender, and regularly serves as the secondary FOH manager or supervisor in the manager's absence. He or she conducts the initial interview and input on bar hires/fires and is responsible for scheduling, training, and supervision of bar employees, as well as resolving any bar staff disputes. The bar manager has primary input on spirits decisions and drink menu development, and is the primary interface with spirits salespeople. He or she is the principal for developing all bar marketing programs, with the approval of the manager. He or she handles bar ordering and inventory, and is responsible for bar cash drawers and reviews all bar tickets and tapes at the end of the shift. The bar manager often supervises and secures dining room cash drawer consolidation at the end of the shift as well. He or she resolves any bar complaints and deals with any difficult or inebriated customers. The bar manager is knowledgeable about all alcoholic beverage laws and is certified with a local alcohol beverage awareness program and with the local health department.

## Bartender

The bartender's primary function is to make drinks for bar and dining room customers and to serve any food items to patrons seated at the bar. He or she has secondary supervision responsibility of bar servers and the barback, and FOH employees if no other management staff are available. The bartender is responsible for the bar's common cash drawer integrity and bar ticket and tape consolidation at the end of the shift. He or she should assist the bar manager with bar ordering and inventory. The bartender's side work includes stocking the bar with product and supplies and producing mixing supplies, such as juices, mixers, tinctures, and syrups. He or she cleans the bar at the end of the shift and stocks bottle goods for the next shift. The bartender should be certified by the local alcohol beverage awareness program and the local health department.

## Bar Servers

Bar servers provide spirits service to bar customers and waiting customers (and often seated diners in the dining room). He or she also serves bar food and bar diners, and in the process, interacts with the kitchen. He or she is responsible for individual cash drawer integrity and ticket consolidation. The server should alert the bar or FOH manager of any compliments, problems, or complaints (or the BOH manager regarding any food served in the bar). The server performs all side work before and after the shift, such as garnishes and supplies. He or she buses and cleans tables in the bar and retrieves empty cocktail glasses from the dining room or entry during the shift; at the end of the shift the server cleans the cocktail serving station. All bar servers are required to be certified by the local alcohol beverage awareness program and the local health department.

### Barback

The barback assists the bartenders in any requested tasks during the shift and is scheduled to work in the busiest bars at the busiest times. He or she washes all bar glasses and runs any dish bus tubs from the bar to the kitchen, and resupplies glassware and dishes from the kitchen. In some bars he or she might help with dispensing frozen cocktails from the machine, or pull draft beers as necessary. During the shift he or she replenishes ice, retrieves any needed spirits from the supply area, and hooks up replacements for empty kegs or soda syrups. The barback assists the bartender in stocking any mixing ingredients or supplies, the juicing of fruits, etc., and helps to restock the beer cooler and soda supplies. He or she buses the bar top and barback, sweeps and mops the bar walkway, washes floor mats, and helps in overall bar cleaning. The barback must be certified by the local alcohol beverage awareness program and the local health department.

### Food Servers

Food servers, or waitpersons, provide the primary interaction with dining customers, serving food and drinks, while directly interacting with kitchen line staff (and often the bar). They are the owner's ambassadors to the customer, and can have a great impact on the public's perception of the restaurant's quality and ambience. They must alert the FOH manager of any customer complaints, apprise the BOH manager of any customer compliments or complaints, and resolve any customer problems. Servers should keep host staff apprised of any soon to be vacated tables and work with host staff and the FOH manager in planning and securing adjoining tables for large parties. Servers must stay informed of the quantity of limited menu items available, daily specials, and items that are temporarily sold out ("86"). Servers are responsible for their own individual cash drawer integrity and ticket consolidation. They provide secondary spirits service and primary wine service. Servers provide secondary busing of tables and setting of tables, and have secondary responsibility of running dirty dishes to the back and clean dishes to the front. They perform all opening and closing side work in the wait station and for the tabletop such as roll setups, inspection for cleanliness of glassware and tableware, making tea and coffee, refilling salt and pepper shakers, and so forth. Servers must be certified by the local alcohol beverage awareness program and local health department.

## Bus Persons

The primary responsibility of bus staff is busing (clearing, cleaning, and resetting) tables, and must immediately alert servers of any customer requests or complaints. They keep host staff apprised of cleaned tables ready to be seated. In some restaurants, busers help with re-filling drinks or bread service on the floor. Bus persons have the primary responsibility of running dirty dishes to the back and clean dishes to the front. They also restock tabletop supplies (salt and pepper, sugar packets, napkin dispensers, etc.) while cleaning the tables. During the shift, busers stock ice, linen, and other supplies in the wait station. They often fill water glasses and replenish coffee and tea during the shift. Busers rotate and restock bread or tortilla chips in wait station warmers. During the shift they provide interim sweeping of floors, mopping, and trash removal as necessary. They are responsible for checking restroom cleanliness and integrity periodically during the shift (use a checklist and signature sheet) and clean when necessary. Busers must be certified by the local health department, and if they have any involvement with spirits, they must be certified with a local alcohol awareness program.

## Host Staff

Hostesses and hosts greet and welcome arriving guests, communicate with and thank guests who are leaving. They answer the phone, take reservations, book future parties, and deal with late parties or no-shows on the reservation list. In some smaller restaurants the host staff also serves as the primary cashier. If so, they are responsible for the integrity of the common cash drawer and ticket consolidation at the end of shift. They must alert the FOH manager of the length of the waiting list, of any customer compliments, problems, or complaints (while avoiding confrontation), or of any pending large parties. They must communicate with servers and busers regarding tables about to clear. It is essential that customers be given accurate estimates of waiting times. Host staff should assist customers in procuring spirits from bar servers (and should also be certified in alcohol beverage awareness if of age and serving alcohol). In some restaurants, host staff takes and enters tickets for to-go orders, and assists in paying out to-go customers (many restaurants have the bartender or an available server pay out to-go customers from their cash drawers).

Host staff should freshen the water in any host station floral arrangements, and stock and resupply all host station supplies, such as toothpicks, mints, business cards, and to-go menus. They must prevent customers from entering or exiting the restaurant with any drinks (unless exiting with recorked bottles of wine is legal in the locale), and keep the host station, entry, and exterior area near the entry clean and neat. They will occasionally assist customers with calls for taxi service, "Tipsy Taxi," etc. Host staff should be certified by the local health department. In restaurants that do not require the host position, a standing sign should read "Seat yourself" or "Please wait to be seated" by a server.

### Janitorial

The janitorial staff or service generally comes in early or arrives late to clean the front of the restaurant during hours when no customers are present. They stack or move the chairs and then vacuum carpets and/or sweep floors and mop. The restrooms are thoroughly cleaned and restocked. Janitorial performs miscellaneous dusting and polishing, and cleans glass and mirrors. They pick up trash outside, and make sure that all interior FOH trash cans have been emptied. They move any FOH rubber floor mats from drying racks back into position; nonslip carpeted mats at the entry and the wait station are vacuumed, and switched out weekly by the linen company.

### Staffing—BOH

Keep in mind that one employee may perform the duties of more than one position, depending on the size of the restaurant, the expanse and complexity of the menu, and how busy the facility is when serving. As an example, the head or executive chef could also be the kitchen manager in a small restaurant, and might be one of the line cooks or expediter during service. Prep cooks are often the line cooks after prep duties. For very upscale restaurants, there may be specialized chefs who only do sauces. All BOH employees should be food handler–certified by the local health department. The kitchen manager and executive chef (and possibly the sous chef) should be food manager–certified. In addition to classes offered by the health department and by restaurant associations, online classes can fulfill these requirements.

## Positions

Here are the positions that make up BOH.

### Kitchen Manager

The kitchen manager is responsible for the business end of the BOH. This person will check in deliveries, submit invoices to the bookkeeper and track payments, call in orders for delivery, schedule BOH employees, maintain records, supervise employees, and be responsible for maintenance of equipment and repairs. It is the kitchen manger's responsibility to do food costing, filling in all master lists, and to regularly check the pricing of the menu relative to food cost. The kitchen manager may be called upon to lend a hand during busy prep loads or when shorthanded. This person is often the first person to arrive in the morning to open the kitchen for employees and early deliveries, and leaves just before the evening shift begins. The kitchen manager is responsible for making sure the BOH follows health department guidelines with regard to food storage, cleaning procedures, and structural features.

### Executive or Head Chef

The executive chef is responsible for the food end of the BOH and sets standards of quality for all goods ordered and the quality of all foods served. "Chef" is responsible for menu development, training the line cooks (and cross-training at multiple stations), and checking and writing recipes used. He or she sets par levels, which are the minimum amounts of everything needed on hand for the daily operation of the kitchen. Chef sets out the duties of the day for the prep cooks, listing the specific recipes and amounts to be prepared on that day's shift, and ensures the quality of their work. The executive chef is often the expediter (see page 155) during the evening shift, placing the final touch on every plate that leaves the kitchen. The executive chef is responsible for seeing that all kitchen employees follow good health and cleanliness habits and follow proper food handling criteria according to the rules set out by the health department (see Appendix C). The executive chef may hold inspections of each cooking station on the line to ensure each has been properly stocked with food, cooking equipment, and utensils just before opening the doors to guests, and to inspect the grooming and attire of the cooks.

### Sous Chef

If a restaurant is large enough and its menu complex, a sous chef works under the executive chef (*sous* is French for "under") as his or her trusted assistant assuring that the orders of the day are carried out, working with the prep and line cooks, hands on. This person will be cooking on the line during important times of service, often as a "floater," helping wherever necessary to keep the kitchen running smoothly. The sous chef may be the main chef on the line, cooking most of the food, in a smaller restaurant kitchen. When the executive chef is absent, the sous chef is in charge of the kitchen and assumes those duties.

### Line Cooks

Line cooks are the heart of most restaurant kitchens; many have no formal training but years of experience. They can keep track of numerous orders at once and know exactly when to start an order, how to cook it the same every time, and get it out to the server when expected. The line has a variety of stations and some line cooks excel at just one station while others can work any position asked. It is good practice to have all line cooks be able to do at least two stations, both extremely well. In small operations there may only be two line cooks for all stations, and in larger operations a single cook for each station. The most basic stations are chargrill/griddle, fry, and sauté, each having its own skill set to produce quality food. The fry station is often combined with another for a line cook, as most restaurants do not have enough fried foods to justify it as a full time position (fried chicken and seafood restaurants can be exceptions). Italian restaurants are very popular and they will have a pasta station and possibly a pizza station as well. Large, busy restaurants may have a vegetable station for all side orders or a separate appetizer station. Line cooks are responsible for cleaning their station at shift's end, wiping down all stainless counters, cleaning their equipment, and sweeping around their station. Dirty mats are moved to a designated area for cleaning. They are also responsible for stocking their station with food at the beginning of the shift as well as having all utensils, plates, and condiments required for their station in place.

### Pantry

The pantry is part of the line, but since it deals with cold items such as salads and pastry and desserts, it is a specialty position separated from the hot cooking line. This person may also be the specialty baker producing desserts prior to the cooking shift. The person working pantry has a more artistic flair to his or her work, carefully arranging and garnishing the orders.

## Expediter

The expediter station, usually found in upscale or very busy restaurants, is responsible for coordinating all of the dishes being cooked to be completed at the proper time along with other dishes on a table's ticket. This person checks the stations to see if they are missing any orders and will request an "all day," meaning the total number of the same dishes being cooked at various stages of completion, matching all tickets in the kitchen at that time. (The expediter may count six salmon dishes on a total of nine tickets presently in the kitchen and expects the "all day" to be six salmon.) The expediter often does the final plate check and assures that the rims of plates and bowls are spotless, and may apply the final garnish to the plate. He or she also ensures efficient pickup of completed orders, making sure cooked dishes are not sitting under heat lamps waiting to be picked up, and that all dishes for a table are picked up by the proper server. The expediter is often the executive chef, but can be the owner or a manager. It may be a part-time position, only working at the busiest times of a shift or when the kitchen is backed up and the food is not coming out as quickly as needed ("in the weeds").

## Baker

Some restaurants do all of their own baking, supplying table breads, sandwich loaves, pastry for menu items (puff pastry and short doughs for potpies or "en croute" as examples), and all desserts. This is a highly skilled position and is not easily filled in more remote and less populated regions of the country. Bakers usually start their day at 3 to 4 a.m., so that fresh baked goods are ready for the first shift of the day, especially if breakfast is served.

## Pastry Chef

In truly upscale restaurants, a pastry chef creates magnificent desserts with intricate garnishes and stunning presentation and works next to the pantry station, in a dedicated space.

## Prep Cooks

Prep cooks turn raw materials into usable products for the cooking line. They are responsible for breaking down vegetables for salads, and making stocks and basic sauces ("mother sauces"). They clean and portion fish and seafood, trim and portion meats, make pastas and pizza doughs, clean and trim vegetables for side dishes, and cook casseroles and other complete dishes such as stews for the holding cabinet or steam table. Prep cooks ensure that par levels are met for everything the executive chef has indicated. The more that can be done at the prep table, the easier it is for the line cooks to get high-quality food out of the kitchen fast and at the correct temperature and degree of doneness. Prep cooks are usually the first to work in the morning and clean up and leave before the evening shift arrives. Extremely busy restaurants may have an evening prep cook available for emergencies, such as running out of fish fillets or needing vegetables prepared.

### Dishwasher

Often treated as the lowest of positions, the dishwasher is critical to the success of a kitchen's ability to run smoothly, and to keep the FOH stocked and able to perform efficiently.

In addition to cleaning the dirty dishes, glassware, and tableware, the dishwasher restocks the cooking line with its skillets, pans, and utensils throughout the shift. Clean dishes are placed back on the cooking line, flatware and glasses restocked in the wait station, and bar glassware replenished if the bar does not do its own cleaning. The dishwasher ferries garbage to the dumpster as it accumulates during a shift, and empties all waste containers at shift end. The final cleaning of the kitchen is also this person's responsibility, spraying down the floor at the end of the night, hosing down the kitchen mats, and returning all cleaned pots, pans, glassware, and tableware to their proper storage places. The wise restaurateur will treat the dishwasher with respect and pay a bit more than minimum to attract and keep diligent workers, and to pass this philosophy on to the kitchen crew.

## Hiring

Now that you have a list of all employees needed to run the restaurant, job descriptions for each position written, and a policy manual crafted, it's time to hire your staff and prepare for training. If all goes well, you are about 2 months away from opening. Where will you look and how will you get a large turnout for hiring qualified employees? In all but the largest of communities, word will get out among restaurant workers that a new restaurant is under construction. Have a banner printed and place it across the storefront that you will be "Hiring Soon." Set up a Facebook page and a website to refer prospective employees to go to read about positions available, the job descriptions and approximate timeline for opening, and put the website address and Facebook page on the banner. Have an application online they

❏ Application form

❏ Résumé or C.V.

❏ Notes from employment interview

❏ Notes from reference check

❏ Photo, stapled in the upper right-hand corner

❏ Contact numbers—personal, in case of emergency

❏ Commendations or warning letters

❏ Copy of Social Security card

❏ Form W-4: www.irs.gov/pub/irs-pdf/fw4.pdf

❏ Form I-9 (Employment Eligibility Verification), www.uscis.gov/files/form/i-9.pdf

❏ "Green card" resident alien card (if applicable)

❏ Acknowledgment of sexual orientation/racial/religious discrimination and harassment rules

❏ City, county, or state health department certification, copy on file

❏ Employee notification to employer of existing health problems

❏ Food handlers/managers training certificate, copy on file

❏ Alcoholic beverage commission training and certification, copy on file

❏ Restaurant training compliance

❏ Injury reports

can download and print out. Give them a contact e-mail address to send a copy of their résumé so you can start a file and begin evaluating the interest being generated. Other websites that feature employment opportunities, especially in the food service industry, should be contacted. Place an ad in the classifieds section of your local paper. A very effective means to getting the best employees is to eat out at restaurants and hand out business cards to those who catch your eye as being particularly good at their job. Unemployed workers are usually unemployed for a reason in the restaurant industry, and it is rarely due to downsizing and widespread layoffs, but could be due to a restaurant recently closing its doors; be careful.

Select a date or dates to have prospective employees come into the restaurant to fill out applications, obtain job descriptions, ask questions, and look over the restaurant. Be organized and have tables ready with application forms, pens, etc. Schedule your head chef/kitchen manager for interviewing the BOH prospectives and the FOH manager for the FOH prospectives after a review of the applications. Have interview forms printed so as to ask the same questions to each applicant for a specific position. Take a digital photo of each interviewee and attach it to his or her application (it's easier to remember a face than a name when going over dozens of applications). Don't be afraid to check references before interviewing (unless the applicant has stated not to contact current employer). Be on guard when an applicant does not want you to contact previous employers or with applicants having spotty work records (off for months at a time between jobs, inability to hold a job for a long period of time, or going from job to job in short periods).

**Training Overview**

Once your crew is assembled, all employees should have a thorough knowledge of their specific duties so they may practice them in a real-world setting and prove their knowledge to management. Every position should have a manual that provides the details of the job. The owner and management should agree on these details as they define the dining experience of your guests. Training should be broken down into three phases. The BOH needs the most practice, since the line and prep crew must learn the proper way to prepare everything and coordinate all dishes coming out at the same time for each ticket. The kitchen should have at least 1 week of training before the FOH begins to train. The FOH will need several days to learn the menu, adapt to your style of service, and learn the POS system. Finally, the FOH and BOH should have a day or two to work together to coordinate their roles in the overall process. Allow time for the appropriate employees to have health department training for food handlers and alcoholic beverage commission training on serving alcohol.

As to timing, training should not begin until the restaurant is complete. The kitchen must be ready for cooking and the dining area should have all tables and chairs in place. The POS system must be installed, programmed, and debugged. Only minor details of construction should remain to be done and none should interfere with your training schedule. You should have all of your licenses and final inspection by the health department. Once training begins, be prepared to open within 2 weeks or so. Remember that once you hire the staff, they expect to have a paying job. Required training sessions must be paid for at minimum wage rates or higher, but if there are delays that prevent you from opening after training has been complete, you cannot expect the staff to sit around waiting for you to open, as they are not making money.

The training offered in the next two sections is for just one meal of the day, most commonly dinner. If you are planning to serve lunch as well, will you have a separate menu or the same menu for both meals? If the menu is the same then train your lunch crew along with your dinner crew and have all of them share evening shifts for a week or so, opening for dinner only. After a week and everything is running smoothly, open for lunch (if lunch is expected to be have stronger sales, then first open for lunch). If your lunch menu is different from your dinner menu, you can train the lunch shift while dinner is being prepped and the dinner line is being set. Allow about 2 weeks of running smoothly for dinner before opening for lunch. Have the lunch crew train alongside the dinner crew before opening. If you are open for breakfast, you will need separate training for the kitchen, as this is a specialized type of cooking, and your experienced short order cooks shouldn't need much training except for procedures, POS, and where things go and are stored.

## Training—BOH

The heart of your restaurant is the BOH, where the food is prepared. Allow additional time for the BOH to get it right. Start BOH training at least 1 week before the FOH. Give them as much time as necessary to learn the proper way to prepare and cook every menu item, and to get the timing right in having multiple orders come out at the same time, in spite of differing cooking and prep times.

### Line and Prep Cooks

Training in the BOH should begin with the prep cooks. The line cooks cannot do their job until the prep crew knows what to do and can stock the kitchen with basics. However, the line can practice a lot without having to actually cook any food. While the prep cooks are running through the recipes for your sauces, stocks, dressings, etc. the line can work with index cards to learn where their prepped foods are stored in the walk-in and where to put their meat, fish, etc. on the line. You will need to make index cards with all of the things the line will need for opening a shift. For example, have cards with "8-ounce salmon fillet" written and placed where you will be storing them in the walk-in or fish box. The line cook will need a par level of fillets to start the shift and will go to the walk-in with the correct pan, take the correct number of fillet cards and put them where they should be stored on the line. Do the same for the entire menu and the line cooks can practice setting up the line without you having to purchase perishable goods. The cards can be used for breaking down the line as well. The leftover salmon fillets are placed in the proper storage container and if they need to be individually wrapped in plastic film or the container needs to be wrapped, the cooks can actually use the film for practice. They can use markers to date things as well.

The cards are useful to practice the cooking of orders too. Once the line has been stocked as it will be for a real shift, cooking the orders can be practiced with these same cards. The expediter can call out an order—"I need two salmon, a rib eye medium rare, two fried shrimp, a calamari appetizer, and one stuffed mushroom"—and the sauté cook can take the appropriate skillet or pan and set it on the cooktop, reach in the under counter refer for two salmon cards and place them into the pan(s). The grill man grabs a "rib eye" card from where he stores his steaks and places it on the charbroiler. This training method works well with a POS system also. In any case, timing can be learned and honed without cooking real food. This will save a good deal of money during the training phase of the cooking line.

Eventually every dish on the line will need to be cooked and the head chef should work one on one to demonstrate exactly how he expects each dish to be cooked and assembled. By hiring skilled personnel you should not be teaching them how to cook (you should have evaluated their ability to cook before hiring them), but rather how you want things done, such as the placement and arrangement of the food on the plate and the appropriate plate or platter.

### Prep Cooks

The prep cooks should be able to take your written recipes and get things started by assembling all of the ingredients, pans, and utensils. As they prepare an item the head chef should be looking over their shoulders and offer advice as required. Final adjustments to the recipe are done and everyone should taste the final product. Some instruction may need to be given, as it is possible that no one in the crew has made fresh pasta by hand or used an electric roller to make sheets of dough for lasagna, but you should have hired experienced personnel that can work off a recipe and produce a quality product. Obviously it is not always possible to hire the most experienced, so do be prepared to teach, if necessary, and allow for additional training in your timeline for opening.

You will need to decide on proper attire for the BOH. If you have an open ("show") kitchen, the line cooks must be particularly well dressed in a uniform of some kind. This can be anything from a logo T-shirt or polo to a chef's coat. The first two or three logo tops should be provided by you and then it is the responsibility of the employee to maintain and replace them as they wear. All should have the same head cover such as a baseball cap, beret, toque, or skull cap. If the kitchen is closed off from view, employees can either wear a "snap white" (a short-sleeved white shirt with snap closures) provided by the linen company and paid for by you, or a clean shirt provided by the employee. Dark pants or chef pants should be stipulated. For a show kitchen a chef pant would be most appropriate. All should wear bib aprons supplied by the linen company. Appropriate footwear is essential and an industrial, steel-toed shoe with nonslip, oil-proof sole is best. Clogs are quite trendy but are really not as safe. Sneakers, tennis shoes, and moccasins should not be allowed.

### Dish Personnel

Dish persons should not need much in the way of training, other than a brief familiarity with your machine and where to store clean items that come from the machine. They need to know where specific pans and utensils go on the line and in the prep area and where the garbage is tossed, where the mats are washed and the procedure for breaking down the kitchen at the end of the evening shift. Be sure to provide a rubber bib apron for the dishwasher, who usually will wear a T-shirt or polo from home.

### Training—FOH

Every position in the front of the house should have a manual, explaining the details of their position. The more detailed and clearly written the information is, the easier training becomes. The information packet should include details on restaurant rules and policies, the POS system, a menu and wine/beer list, table and section map, list of important contacts, etc. Employees should commit this information to memory before training begins. Do not be afraid to quiz them on the material.

## Servers

The first step in training servers is to go over and have them learn the complete, priced menu with accurate descriptions of the dishes and portion serving sizes. They should know the menu completely and should be tested repeatedly on content. The same holds true for the wine and beer lists. Beverage reps should provide full descriptions of all labels on the list, and just before opening they should provide tastings of the wines and train staff on proper wine service. New hires should be given this menu information to learn before they are formally trained.

The dining room should have all tables numbered and be divided into sections based on how many tables each server will cover. This number is loosely based on the targeted style of service; a more formal style of service will reduce the number of tables a server can cover, while a more casual style can increase that number. Management should have established a style that they feel comfortably fits the menu, price range, location, and ambience of the restaurant. The entire FOH staff needs to know all of the table numbers and sections.

The POS system needs to be fully programmed and ready for training so that servers can practice entering and closing out tickets. The company supplying the POS system generally provides a mentor for limited hands-on training. Servers and hosts/hostesses should be encouraged to come by on their own (at no cost to the restaurant) to practice on the POS machines until they feel comfortable with the system. If there is no POS system, the servers will need to know the proper menu codes and ticket order to use when writing tickets, and where the different copies of the ticket will end up. Servers need to know how a ticket is submitted to the kitchen and bar, how the order tracks along through the process as the item is prepared, and where and how the completed item is staged when it is ready to be loaded onto a tray and delivered to the table. Servers need to be trained on the routine for paying out a table and how to reconcile their tickets, their receipts, and their cash drawer at the end of the shift. They should receive training on recognizing counterfeit currency and the nuances of credit card security.

Servers need to be informed about proper grooming and the uniform or dress code that is expected of them. If there is a shirt with a logo required, the restaurant typically provides the first one or two shirts, and offers additional units for sale at cost. Suggested attire, such as "nice-looking jeans," black pants and white shirts, or khaki shorts do not have to be provided or paid for. Aprons are normally provided by the restaurant. Shoes should be closed-toe, comfortable for standing in for hours at a time, and slip-resistant. Servers are typically given a list of tools they are expected to have with them: pens, a small tablet or notebook, wine opener, small calculator, breath mints, stain pen, comb, etc. They need to learn the rules and policies of the restaurant that are specific to servers, as well as the general staff rules.

Now the servers are ready to practice on each other by breaking into groups, with one group representing customers seated at the tables and ordering off of the menu. The remaining group is the servers, taking practice orders and entering them into the POS system, or writing paper tickets. The group representing the customers is encouraged to order many items, as well as wine, beer, and cocktails (if there are alcoholic beverages), and to ask many questions. Complicated orders are encouraged, in order to familiarize the servers with all ordering options. After a period of time the roles are reversed, with the servers becoming the customers.

When the servers have completed their training with one another, the kitchen is brought into the process. Practice orders are submitted to the kitchen, while the kitchen uses note cards representing different dishes as they are prepared on the line and moved through the process. Faux orders are staged onto plates for servers to carry out to the "customers." The kitchen gets to practice receiving tickets, either on the POS or via paper tickets while they work on their timing. The servers get a feel for the timing of the ticket as it works its way through the kitchen and for orders coming out of the pass. Management should now assign side work tasks for both opening and closing servers, such as rolling setups, cutting lemon wedges, and making tea and coffee. Once the bugs are worked out and everything runs smoothly with this faux cross-training, the kitchen is ready to produce some real food, while the servers get the opportunity to wait on each other and taste many of the dishes of the menu (some of the more expensive items can be substituted with less costly ingredients: shrimp for lobster, or sirloin for rib eye, for example).

### Bus Persons

At this point the busers can be brought in to be trained. They need to know how to set up their station for clearing and sanitizing the tables, and when and where to run dirty dishes to the back and clean dishes back out to the front. They will learn the layout of the server's station and find out how to make coffee and tea, refill bread warmers, empty trash cans, etc.

### Host/Hostess

The hosts/hostesses also come in to train once there are run-throughs with customers. They should already know the tables and sections, and will have had enough practice with the POS to be able to recognize empty tables on the screen and deal with the reservation mode. Much of their training can take place on the job once they have mastered the telephone, limited POS functions, and a smile.

## Training—The Bar

Every position in the bar should have a manual explaining the details of the job. All bar employees must be certified by a local alcoholic beverage awareness program, and must be of legal age to serve alcohol.

### Bartenders

The bartender should be knowledgeable regarding all of the spirits labels served in the bar (liquors, liqueurs, cordials, schnapps, brandies, beers, and wines). He or she must also have a working knowledge of preparing both classic and contemporary cocktails, and be able to make certain mixers (syrups, tinctures, bitters, etc.) if the bar menu calls for it. The bartender should know the appropriate garnish for a particular drink. He or she needs to know the proper order in preparing drinks on the ticket, so that the least ice melts as possible. The bartender must be familiar with all of the dishes offered on the food menu, including descriptions, portion size, and any bar food or snack items. Bartenders must be able to use the POS system, and know all of the drink codes if paper tickets are used instead of a POS, or if the POS system fails. He or she should be familiar with the cleaning and maintenance procedures for all equipment used in the bar, including the frozen drink machine, espresso machine, rotary glass washer or under-counter glass washer, blender, soda and beer systems, and refrigeration. The bartender will supervise and more than likely train the barback and the bar servers, so he or she will need to know all of the details of their positions as well.

Bartenders should know the table numbers and sections of not only the bar, but the dining room also. They need to be trained on the routine for paying out a customer (including to-go and waiting customer orders from the entry), how to reconcile the bar tickets and receipts, and the bar cash drawer at the end of the shift. They will need to know how to run a tab for a customer by holding the credit card and have a system in place to keep those cards secure, making sure that they go back to their rightful holders. Bartenders should receive training on recognizing counterfeit currency and the nuances of credit card security. The bartender is occasionally the on-scene management representative at the end of the shift, responsible for closing out and securing the dining room servers' cash drawers, so that procedure should be known as well.

He or she will need to learn the routine of setting up the bar, including juicing, mixer preparation, bulk cocktail mixing, proper restocking and product rotation, stocking ice, replacing and troubleshooting soda syrup containers or kegs, and stocking miscellaneous supplies such as linens, tickets, or POS tape. Bartenders need to learn the par levels for each ingredient, and coordinate with the kitchen on the ordering of supplies (produce, dairy, bar supplies, paper goods, etc.) and must be trained on how to properly count and extend bar inventory figures, as well as order spirits based on established par levels. If par levels have yet to be established, careful monitoring of the quantities of supplies will be necessary until par levels become apparent (with a new restaurant, pars are often based on an educated guess of how busy it will be). Bartenders should be familiar with the basics of reporting figures to the ABC (alcoholic beverage commission), even though that will probably be done by the bookkeeper. They will need to know the closing side work and cleaning routine also.

### Bar Servers

Bar servers need to know the menu details of the bar and the dining room, the POS and ticket procedure (including drink codes), and the tables and sections of the bar and dining room. They need to know that the position of chair number one at any table is the chair closest to the entry, and that the positions progress around clockwise; the number one position at the bar is the chair nearest the main cocktail station. They should be familiar with all of the labels carried at the bar, as well as classic and contemporary cocktails and all drink garnishes. They need to know the proper order of writing down drinks on a ticket, or entering drinks into the POS.

The server needs to know how to run a bar tab for a customer and how to pay out a bar tab. If bar servers have their own cash drawer, they need to know the procedure for closing out the cash drawer and reconciling tickets at the end of the shift. They should cash in their tips for larger bills, so that the restaurant bank will have small bills for the following day.

Bar servers need to know the setup and closing procedures, and all related side work involved, such as wiping every table and chair, cutting garnishes, setting up paper goods and straws, finding out about any specials, covering and dating all garnishes, and wiping down the server station and all trays.

For training the bar servers, the bartenders and bar servers can begin by calling out potential drink orders to each other, responding with the ingredients of each cocktail, the price, the proper glass it should be served in, and the proper garnish. Once this phase has been mastered, training can move on to practicing the same process using the POS system (if there is one). Servers can switch out practicing on each other by being bar waitress and bar customer, taking orders to be submitted to the bartender.

### Barback

The barback is considered a training position for bartender. All aspects that apply to the bartender's job will need to be learned by the barback, including the handling of money. The primary role of the barback is to keep the bar glasses washed, polished, and stacked; pull bottled beers and sodas as required for orders; make espresso coffee; dispense house wines; keep trash cans dumped; keep the area clean and spotless; have all supplies stocked, assist the bar servers in busing tables when they get behind; and help run food from the kitchen for customers sitting at the bar who are snacking or dining. The barback should jump in and help whenever the situation calls for it. He or she needs to know all of the tables and sections and all menu details.

As time goes on and the barback begins to learn the drinks, he or she can be expected to assist the bartender in dispensing frozen drinks or help with some of the more time-consuming drinks, under the direct supervision of the bartender. The role here is to relieve some of the burden of the bartender during peak periods.

At the end of the shift, the barback will need to learn the closing procedure—mopping the backbar walkway, hosing off the mats when necessary, general cleaning of the bar area, removing soiled linens, polishing stainless, cleaning out refrigerators, cleaning and flushing the espresso machine and margarita machine, and so on. Trash cans will always be emptied and allowed to air out at the end of each evening shift. After the beer and soda stock has been rotated to the front (so that oldest gets used first), some restocking of bottled beers and sodas might be required. The bartender might ask for the barback's help in doing counts and filling out the order sheets and prep sheets for the following shift. The barback should also be learning the spirits guidebook and wine lists, and be familiar with all of the supplies behind the bar.

## Getting Ready to Open

Now the servers are ready to practice on real customers. Recommended practice is to start small, with a small group of invited friends (about twenty at first), who come in during limited dining hours (anytime between 6 and 7 p.m.) to eat for free, selecting from a limited number of menu items. Have the bar serve several selections of reasonably priced wine and beer (complimentary) as well as a signature cocktail, should you be having one. The kitchen and FOH staffers get live-fire training for a few hours, and management is able to observe and evaluate to see where any system breakdowns occurred. After correcting for any weaknesses (taking a day or two to resolve), the number of diners and menu options increases (about fifty guests during a period from 6 to 8 p.m.). Again, evaluation of any negatives takes place and problems are rectified. Now it is time for live action, large-scale practice, using an invited guest list composed of friends, restaurant salespeople, prominent residents, etc. to fill the restaurant to maximum capacity. The staff gets tested and evaluated over a full shift and complete menu, and the guests fill out questionnaires. Again, management has the opportunity to evaluate interaction between the kitchen and servers, observe any problems, and solve them before the real opening of the restaurant. In order to defray some of the cost, have a cash bar offering your entire bar menu, which will bring the bar into final training mode.

Once you feel that the staff is sufficiently trained, the restaurant is ready to open. In most locales, a new restaurant generates considerable buzz around town and the restaurant's opening is eagerly anticipated. "Soft" or unannounced openings are preferred (no advertising . . . just open your doors for business). It gives the restaurant the option of opening when ready and closing for the night if things suddenly go badly. Save the advertised opening with the big banners and klieg lights for a few days (or a week) later, when the restaurant has all the systems running at 100 percent, confident that every guest will leave satisfied and happy, ready to spread the word about how great the restaurant is. Remember that you only get one chance to open and get it right, so take your time and get it right.

## Scheduling Considerations

With so many different styles of service, from walk-up ordering to formal service, and variety of meal combinations you may be offering—breakfast, lunch, and dinner; dinner only; lunch and dinner; breakfast and lunch—here is a typical schedule for a one-hundred-seat restaurant that serves lunch and dinner with different menus for each meal. Assume a busy Friday for both meals, serving lunch from 11 a.m. to 1:30 p.m. and dinner from 5:30 to 10 p.m., with no happy hour.

## BOH

- 7 to 8 a.m., kitchen manager (1 person) in to open
- 8 to 9 a.m., line crew (3–5 persons) in if they are doing prep work for the day; otherwise 10 a.m.
- 9 a.m., prep crew (3–5 persons) in
- Noon, dishwasher (1 person) in
- 1 to 2 p.m., head or executive chef (1 person) in
- 2 to 3 p.m., lunch line crew out
- 3 p.m., prep crew out
- 4 p.m., evening line crew (3–5 persons) in
- 4 to 5 p.m., kitchen manager out
- 6 p.m., day dishwasher out
- 6 p.m., evening dishwasher (1 or 2 persons) in
- 11 p.m., evening line crew out
- Midnight, everyone left leaves

## FOH

- 8 a.m., bookkeeper (1 person) in
- 10 a.m., bartender (1 person) in if using
- 10:30 a.m., servers (2 persons) bar server (1 person) in
- 10:45 a.m., host/hostess (1 person) in
- 11 a.m., servers (3 persons) in
- 11 a.m., bus person (1 person) in
- 1:30 to 2 p.m., opening servers, bar server, and host/hostess leave
- 1:45 p.m., bus person leaves
- 2:30 p.m., remaining servers leave
- 2:30 p.m., salaried FOH manager in
- 3 p.m., day bartender leaves
- 4:30 p.m., servers (2 persons), bartender (1 person), bar server (1 person) in
- 4:45 p.m., host/hostess (1 person) in

- 5 p.m., servers (3 persons) in
- 5:30 p.m., bus person (1 person), host/hostess (2 persons), bar server (1 person) in
- 6 p.m., bus person (1 person) and bartender (1 person) in
- 10:30 p.m., first bar server leaves
- 10:30 p.m., 1 bus person and 2 hosts/hostesses leave
- 11 p.m., 2 servers, 1 bartender, and 1 bar server leave
- 11 p.m., last host/hostess, last bus person, and 1 bartender leave
- 11:30 p.m., 3 servers and 1 bar server leave
- Midnight, head bartender and FOH manager leave

### Maintaining a Full Working Crew

Employees come and go. You can lose your best server with little notice or your grillman might walk out in a huff. As with a championship sports team, personnel must be ready to step in and fill the shoes of every employee. This is no easy task. As a stopgap measure, your managers must be able to do every job in the restaurant competently and be able to fill in should an emergency develop. The key to being prepared for replacing an employee is to have a dedicated policy of cross-training and of hiring from within. For the BOH your best line cook should be shown how to do food costing, place orders to purveyors, and be given additional responsibilities whenever possible. When dishwashing is slow, have the dishwasher slice rolls and learn basic prep. Every line cook should be trained to work at least two stations with high skill, and know how to step in for any line position. Employees should be encouraged to bring in prospective employees that they know are good workers in other restaurants or even in unrelated jobs. For the inexperienced, give them only a few shifts, at the slowest times, working closely with your best employees. A bus person can slowly learn the subtleties of good serving by being assigned to "shadow" your best servers. Eventually he or she can take the order for a table with the server carefully watching and critiquing his or her performance. As your better barback shows motivation and skill, assign him or her a slow night as bartender, with the bartender as barback. Additional compensation should be offered for your best employees to train personnel in this manner. All of your employees should know that you would rather hire them for a better position than go outside the restaurant. Encourage them to want to learn a new position. Supplemental income is a great motivator.

# 10

# Marketing: Bringing in Patrons

Wendy's recently spent $300 million advertising dollars. It is said that McDonald's will be spending in excess of $2 billion! You would think that everyone has heard of these fast-food restaurants and knows exactly what they serve and how their food tastes. The reality of business is that you must get your name out there and keep it out there. The public is easily distracted. Marketing is bringing in guests through your door, both regulars and new patrons. Regulars need to be reminded of why they like your place so much and to keep your name in their thoughts whenever they get hungry. New faces must be enticed into trying your restaurant. However, you don't want to attract people you know will not like your food. That's where demographics and a target audience come into play. Early on in your decision-making process you established your target audience and that is where to begin.

## Establishing Your Market

Whether your market is large or small, it is crucial that you do everything possible to build anticipation for the opening of your restaurant, while generating a "buzz." In the process, make sure that a realistic and firm opening date is given. An incorrect or changing opening date reflects poorly on your management skills. It is essential that the restaurant be tuned to its highest level and that the food and service are as good as possible before the doors open for the first time. You only get one chance to make a good first impression, and success or failure will be amplified by the word-of-mouth buzz that you have worked so hard to generate.

Throughout the development process you should cultivate an e-mail list of interested people who would like to hear about the opening and any associated events. Direct e-mail is an effective method of communicating information to the customer, and should be as personalized as possible. Never spam and never share or sell your list. Temporary signage, such as a large and highly visible banner, should be installed, posting the name and projected opening date, along with a tagline that describes the restaurant's concept in just a few words. Handbills should be printed that include the menu (or a shortened version), opening date, web and social media addresses, hours, and basic information about the restaurant. Servers and staff can distribute them to nearby offices and neighboring businesses, and they can be given to all salespeople who call on you. Have handouts available at the job site during the last phases of construction, and pass them out to friends and family to help distribute, giving them to anyone who shows interest. Do not allow anyone to post the handbills in an irresponsible or illegal manner.

Use social media to keep the public informed of how many days remain until opening. Notify any local media of the opening, especially any local food or social-events editors, and make sure they are invited to any pre-opening parties, run-throughs, or tastings. Invite as many influential locals as possible to any pre-opening events, including patrons of the arts, known bloggers, and "foodies." Have friends post on local review sites about the approaching opening, and how wonderful your food was at any pre-opening tasting events.

Several weeks after opening, when you feel you have all the problems worked out and your restaurant is running smoothly, you could have the official "Grand Opening." This event needs to be highly publicized to get maximum coverage in local media. Again, putting up a large banner, sending out e-mail invites, and posting on social media are essential and should target your audience. Targeted marketing is aimed at a specific market, matching your demographics selected, and works best and is most practical in larger cities. Target marketing might focus, for example, on college students, families, tourists, seniors, business professionals, or sportsmen. Nontargeted marketing takes a broad, less focused approach aimed at widespread appeal and is more effective in smaller locales.

Word-of-mouth marketing will build your base clientele. There is no cost and it is a strong motivator for people to try your food. But you must make your initial guests satisfied with service and have them love the food. If you open unprepared, word of mouth can destroy your reputation before you can get your business off the ground. A personal endorsement from a friend is more effective than an advertisement from someone you do not know.

## Traditional Advertising

Traditional methods of advertising include radio and TV, newspapers, and local and regional magazines. These methods can be effective, but can be expensive. TV ads reach the largest number of people per dollar spent, and the cost of the ads is based on the market share and size of the broadcast area. Radio has become much less influential with the advent of satellite subscription radio, which is commercial-free. Many are now getting their news from the Internet and not subscribing to daily papers, but the weekly food section is still a good place to consider placing an ad or coupon. Weekly papers, handed out free of charge at supermarkets, restaurants, and other high-traffic areas, are often entertainment-based, with columns dedicated to restaurant reviews, news, and announcements. They are wholly supported by advertising fees and this may be a good place to run your ad or coupon.

The best way to be noticed in these traditional media is for them to write about you in a feature, column, or story. There is no cost for this and it is even more effective than taking out advertisements. The question is how to get included. Sponsoring local events such as a 5K run supporting feeding the homeless, donating money to support local farmers' markets, or other related charitable, food-related events is an excellent way of being written about. If you have the resources, hiring a publicity firm specializing in restaurants and the food service industry is the way to go. These businesses focus on getting your name in the papers, having your restaurant mentioned in the most-read blogs, being reviewed in the most influential media, and generally creating and maintaining a buzz about your restaurant.

## Website

Having an up-to-date website is essential in today's market. It should include your address, operating hours, phone number, reservation policy, large-group policy, and your menu(s) with prices. Leaving off prices is not a good idea, as eventually your guests will find out what you charge and may be disappointed or caught short. It does not have to include much content other than these items. Linking to your Facebook page or other electronic media is also a good idea. Specials, discounts, happy hours, or special events should also be listed. You may want to encourage the reader to submit an e-mail address for future specials and discounts. This is an excellent way to build a database for e-mail marketing. If you decide to offer coupons, your website is the best place from which they can be printed. You may want to include a photo gallery of your dishes, links to

YouTube videos of your chef preparing dishes, a chef's blog, a recipe section, or links/quotes of particularly good reviews or press. Linking to Google Maps for an interactive way of finding you is useful.

Your website should be easy to read. Black on white is always the best choice for type and background. Keep animation and such to a minimum for fast loading of your site. Music is rarely appreciated, but if you feel it's necessary, make sure a mute icon is easy to find. The site should be easily navigable; it should not take much "hunting" to find the menu, hours of operation, and other basic information. There are excellent website creators who will design a first-class site, maintain it, and ensure exposure to the major search engines for a monthly fee. The cost is nominal and highly recommended. Be wary of a relative or friend who "knows computers" and will do it for free or for trade in food at your restaurant. You get what you pay for, and these cheap ways out rarely produce satisfying results.

## Search Engine Placement

You want search engines to see your website and post it early in a person's search. The more specific the key words typed in by the searcher and the closer it matches your website name and key words you provide (through meta tags when creating the site), the sooner it will appear in the results of the search. For example if someone types in "Italian food Chicago," you have little hope of being at the top of the search list without optimizing your site. If, on the other hand, one were to type in "Gianni's Trattoria in Chicago" (and that was your restaurant's name), you will probably be right up near the top of the search. The closer the name of your website to the search words, the higher up you will appear (GiannisTrattoria.com will appear earlier than Giannis.com or GiannisItalian.com). The more general the search words the more you need to get search engines to recognize you and post you higher up. Doing this is called "Search Engine Optimization" or SEO.

There are companies that specialize in SEO and can be worth the expense if you or a relative is an amateur computer person trying to do this yourself. Whether you pay to have it done or do it yourself, SEO requires several things from your site. They are looking for content and design of the site. They are looking for key-word density, where you supply key words (when creating your site) that you believe will be used by searchers to find you. Most importantly they are looking for relevance, which is determined by the number of links you have to other sites and the number of sites that are linked to yours.

Do not get too carried away with all of this, as you do not utilize a website as most retailers do. Most of the time the searcher knows your restaurant name and is looking for your menu, hours of operation, address or map, or a contact number. He or she will enter your restaurant's name and city in the search box and you will come up early in the search. Optimization would be necessary if you were a retailer of tractors and all that was entered into a search engine box was "John Deere tractors."

## Social Media

Participating in social media is an important way to publicize your restaurant and expose it to a large audience at no cost, other than the time involved. Social media such as Twitter and Facebook allow you to share specials, exclusive offers or discounts, menu updates, and comments with your followers. You can participate in the discussions about your restaurant and quickly gauge customers' reactions to new dishes. With any social media, regularly posting material is key.

- Twitter (www.twitter.com)—Use your restaurant's name as your user name, and write a short but compelling and descriptive 140-character bio. Use it daily to post tweets about the menu of the day, specials, contests, publicity, etc. Your followers can read and re-tweet your messages to a larger audience.
- Facebook (www.facebook.com)—Set up your page as a local business, as posting business information on a personal page can get you banned. Invite friends to "like" you, post status updates often, post photos of dishes from the menu, regular customers, the interior, parties held, etc. Smartphones allow you to make updates from your phone. Monitor the activity on your page frequently.

Keep your eyes on the social media that are set up to review and critique restaurants. This is an excellent way to see what the buzz is about your place. Yelp is a site where you can register and respond to reviews. Sign up at www.biz.yelp.com/support. Other sites to monitor to see how you are perceived include Chowhound (http://chowhound.chow.com/boards), Urban Spoon (www.urbanspoon.com), and Tripadvisor (www.tripadvisor.com/Restaurants).

## Marketing Examples

1. Coupons—Coupons can offer discounts on meals, two-for-one entrees, free dessert, beverages, etc. They can be posted in newspapers, on your website, via e-mail, on Facebook, etc. Be careful about offering deep discounts or two-for-one offers as the public will become "addicted" to these and will wait until you run a coupon again before returning.

2. Loyalty programs—Reward your frequent visitors with giveaways such as T-shirts, discount coupons, special desserts, etc. for a specific number of visits.

3. E-mail—Obtain e-mail addresses of your guests to offer direct perks to them. Announce special, seasonal menus, benefit dinners, cooking classes, holiday dinners (Thanksgiving, New Year's), and the like. Consider a monthly e-mail newsletter with a calendar of events.

4. Package deals—Through media or tent tops/flyers, alert the public of combined savings with a lunch or dinner special that includes a beverage and dessert, a four-course prix-fixe meal, a six-course tasting meal, and such.

5. Sports-oriented—Focus on local sporting teams and have a fan night with discounts. Hire a bus to take fans to the venue and let them park in your lot (linked to a meal purchase before or after the game). Financially sponsor a team and get billboard advertising credit.

6. Charity—Sponsor a sporting event (10K run, bike race) to benefit a local charity, especially one related to food, such as feeding the homeless. Donate food to feed volunteers at the MDA Telethon or a police/fire department fund-raiser. Offer a scholarship to a regional culinary arts program.

7. Seasonal events—Celebrate seasonal foods with a special menu featuring these items and associate with food festivals (maple syrup run, Oktoberfest, Mardi Gras, the opening of crab fishing season, etc.).

8. Cooking classes—These prove to be quite popular, teaching how to prepare some of the restaurant's favorites, illustrating techniques, bringing in celebrity chefs, cookbook signings, food pairings.

9. Special nights—Theme dinners can be offered that feature the wines of Spain, local cheese producers, or regional cuisine menus (Tuscany, Provence, Southwest, etc.)

10. Food contests—Sponsor a chili cook-off, a barbecue competition, a baking contest, or a competitive eating challenge.

# 11

# Up and Running—A Day in the Life of a Restaurant

Here is a typical day in the life of a one-hundred-seat, 3,000-square-foot restaurant that is open for lunch and dinner, with separate menus for each meal. It follows the scheduling guideline from chapter 9.

## BOH

The first person to arrive in the morning is usually the kitchen manager. Some purveyors have early deliveries and someone with check-signing clearance should be there to check in the merchandise. This person will also turn on the ovens and any other equipment needing to be on in the morning. The ice machine should be checked for a full bin of ice and the walk-in and refers/freezers should be checked for proper holding temperatures. The line should be checked for cleanliness and proper storage of foods in the line refers (to report any deficiencies to the head chef from the evening before). Par levels should be checked and a prep list made for the prep crew and lunch line crew. Any orders that are needed for next-day delivery should be noted and called in or listed for the evening call-in.

If the lunch line crew does some prep work, which is a good idea to get them a reasonable number of hours of work per day (otherwise they are only working the lunch line for four hours per day), they will check par levels for their station and get to work. Typical prep work for a line cook would be to make pizza dough for both day and night shifts if they are cooking on the pizza station. The pantry cook can "bust" cases of lettuce and make salads for both shifts and perform similar jobs. The prep crew comes in and starts on all of the prepared foods, based on a list given to them or the one they make if checking par levels in the walk-in and refers. Since the prep crew is responsible for most of the food being served, the kitchen manger should check their work throughout the morning.

By 10:30 a.m. the line crew should begin to set up their stations, stocking soups, hamburger patties, cold cuts, rolls, condiments, sauces, casseroles, and all things needed to cook off the lunch menu. Each station should be checked for the right amount of plates, bowls, cooking utensils, kitchen towels, and so forth. Their floor mats should be put down and their station should be ready for a brief inspection by the kitchen manager just before opening. When done, the kitchen manager will announce to the FOH that the line is ready to take orders.

When the restaurant is open for lunch, the line crew is busy filling orders. The kitchen manager may need to expedite orders at the busiest time to ensure smooth flow. The prep crew is busy preparing everything that is needed for the evening shift and next-day lunch as required. Dirty dishes are building up and the day dishwasher soon comes in to get them cleaned and restocked. If the kitchen is running short on anything before the dishwasher shows up, a bus person, the FOH manager, or the kitchen manager can step in for a brief time.

When lunch is over the line brings any dirty pans, skillets, and utensils to the dish line (they may be dropping off dirty pans to the dish line to be cleaned throughout the cooking period as well). Each station on the line is cleaned by the line crew. All equipment is wiped down and cleaned with appropriate cleaners and disinfectants, as are all counters. The area around their station is swept and garbage is removed to the dumpster. All leftovers are properly labeled and dated and placed either in the walk-in or in their line refers. They may be required to submit the number of items used and remaining for par levels to be adjusted for the next prep session.

The head/executive chef would come in as the lunch rush has died down or just ended. Paperwork would be done and any prep lists or purchase orders would be issued. A meeting with the kitchen manger to coordinate the day and night shifts' needs, improvements, etc. would be discussed. The chef would look over the POS printouts for the previous evening and make any adjustments to par levels, changes in offerings, price changes, and such. Par levels are double-checked for the evening shift and a brief meeting is held with the FOH manager in the late afternoon.

At the end of the prep shift, the prep crew cleans all surfaces—equipment, counters, and sinks. Everything is stored properly and labeled correctly, including date and employee who prepped the item. They may be asked to submit a report on all items done and their quantities. The prep area is swept and mats are brought to the area for cleaning by the dishwasher. The dishwasher mops the floor in the prep area, cleans the mats, and places them back on the floor where they belong before leaving at shift end.

The evening line crew comes in and begins to stock the line and address any prep they are assigned to do, such as making sauce mixes, garnishes, and sauté add-ins, filling soup wells and sauce wells, and stocking the steam table. The equipment, tools and plates are checked and readied for opening. The kitchen manager meets with the head chef for final instructions for the next day and coordinates any ordering that must be done at evening shift's end, and then leaves for the day. The head chef checks the line and readies for opening. Any specials are gone over with the line and FOH and a brief meeting with servers is held to go over the specials and anything that is in short supply or needs to be moved (too much salmon in the walk-in, for example). The day dishwasher checks out, having restocked everything that has been washed. The dish machine is wiped down, any chemicals refilled, and the drain boards wiped down. Any garbage is removed to the dumpster.

The evening line is opened and the FOH alerted. The evening dishwasher checks in. The chef "floats" to help where necessary and becomes expediter as the FOH fills the tables. Any menu items about to run out are announced to the servers as "asks" (they need to ask the kitchen if they have the particular item before entering it in and then telling the guest about availability) and when something is out it is called "86." Some kitchens have a board where they write specials, "asks," and "86" items so the server can check at will or send a bus person in to check the board. As the evening rush dies down, the chef might let one or two line cooks start to break down the line where applicable. When the last ticket has been filled the line is broken down and everything cleaned. Garbage is removed to the dumpster. Mats are brought to the designated area and floors are swept by each station cook. All food is properly stored, labeled, and dated. Line cooks leave. The chef checks that all line equipment is off and refers are properly closed. The dish line is cleaned, disinfected, and chemicals topped off. The dishwasher hoses/sprays down the floor and mops. The mats are cleaned and brought to the storage area for the evening. The dishwasher leaves and the chef calls in any essential deliveries for morning and then locks the back door, setting any BOH alarms and alerts the FOH manager that they are closed and locked for the evening.

Should you be open for breakfast, the short order cook(s) arrives at least 1 hour before opening to stock the line and do any prep (cook bacon, make cereals, etc.). Just before opening the line he or she should alert the servers of any breakfast specials. If the restaurant is very busy, a dishwasher should come in 30 minutes after opening. This person should help break down the line after breakfast and clean the pots and pans from the morning prep crew. If you have a baker and serve fresh baked goods for breakfast, this person should come in at least 3 hours before opening, maybe earlier. If you do not serve breakfast but do have a baker, this person can come in by 8 a.m.

## FOH

The bookkeeper arrives at 8 a.m. and, in the secured office, removes the sales receipts, credit card receipts, and cash of the previous day's sales from the floor safe. He or she consolidates the previous day's receipts (using POS data, or hard tickets matched with the kitchen's soft copies of the tickets). The bank deposit, including the previous day's charge card deposits, is prepared, and the change order required for cash drawer(s) and an additional change bank are figured. If it is on a Friday, or before a bank holiday, the change bank amounts are increased. Some restaurants have one cash drawer for the dining room and one for the bar, while others have a separate drawer for each server. The bookkeeper also deducts tip cash from credit card sales to be dispensed to the servers at some later point in time, dispensing the largest bills possible. Some restaurants dispense charge tips immediately, while others account for the interests paid to the credit card company, holding the charge tips for a few days longer.

The bookkeeper enters cumulative data for sales and alcohol taxes, and payroll data (hourly rate and employment taxes). At appropriate times, quarterly taxes, sales taxes, or alcohol taxes are paid. The bookkeeper sets up the cash drawer(s) for the next shift, makes the bank deposit, either using the services of an armored car service, or by taking it to the bank (the bookkeeper or the manager can take the deposit to bank). He or she "Z's," or totals out, all POS data and gets the system ready for the current sales day. If there is no POS system, the bookkeeper logs hard ticket sequential numbers for the current day. They might dispense COD payments to any deliveries that arrive and are approved by the kitchen or bar manager.

If there is no breakfast served, the janitorial crew arrives early morning to do a top-to-bottom cleaning of the entire restaurant, including the entry exterior, the grounds, and the parking lot. If breakfast is served, a bonded and insured janitorial company often comes in overnight to accomplish the same tasks.

Should you have one, the lunch bartender arrives to set up the bar, check prep and par lists for mixers (infusions, tinctures, syrups, etc.), bulk cocktails (batches of frozen margarita mix, for example), and juices, making any that are required. He or she stocks any bottles of spirits (beer, wine, liquor) that might be needed during the coming shift. The bartender also deals with any bar spirits and supply orders that arrive, making sure that product gets rotated, credits for bad wine are noted, and all empties (beer bottles, soda syrup canisters, empty kegs, etc.) are hauled away. The bartender counts the bar cash drawer just before opening and checks with the kitchen manager to see if there is any cooking alcohol that needs to be included in the next call-in order. The bar server arrives for the lunch shift, sets up the server station, prepares garnishes, and checks the bar floor and tables for cleanliness.

The opening dining room servers arrive to set up the wait station, check all tables in the dining room, roll flatware in napkins ("set ups"), and do other opening side work. They check any shift specials with the kitchen and the bar, and just before opening count their cash drawers. The servers arrive in two overlapping shifts, one that performs opening duties and handles the initial rush, while the second group deals with closing duties, wait-station clean up, and any late rush. The closing servers keep the kitchen constantly appraised of the status of any later orders that are yet to be submitted.

The host/hostess arrives to set up the entry area, making sure that all goods are stocked, flowers are fresh, and that the entry and exterior are clean and appealing. He or she checks the reservation book for any lunch bookings and informs waitstaff of any large parties or special-needs tables. During the shift the host/hostess greets and seats, keeps track of tables that are turning or ready to be seated, and thanks leaving customers. He or she will also be handling to-go orders and taking bookings for subsequent shifts over the phone. When business slows down the host/hostess is relieved of duties and the job is assumed by the bar server, with the assistance of dining room servers.

The lunch bus person arrives and sets up the busing materials, such as sanitizing buckets, bus carts, trays, or bus tubs, and tableware presoak buckets. He or she checks the restrooms before opening and monitors their condition throughout the shift. During the shift the bus person is busing and setting up tables, while running all dirty dishes back to the dishwasher, and clean dishes back to the front. When the dining room starts to clear, the bus person cleans the bus station and is relieved of duties, with the servers taking over the busing of any remaining tables.

The bar servers deal with any remaining customers while cleaning up their stations, and stocking supplies for the evening shift. The bartender cleans the bar and stocks all supplies for the evening shift. In many restaurants the lunch bartender serves as auxiliary floor manager, helping to close out and secure the bar and dining room servers' cash drawers.

The salaried FOH manager arrives at 2 or 3 p.m., making sure that all orders have arrived, all FOH staff show up for their evening shift, and that all equipment is in working order. He or she checks the reservation book for that night's bookings, and checks with the kitchen manager for any issues that need to be dealt with before the kitchen manager leaves for the day. The FOH manager reconciles the lunch receipts, sets up the change banks and the cash drawers for the evening shift, and "Z's" out the POS system for the evening shift. He or she surveys the cleanliness and orderliness of the entire FOH and corrects any problems.

The opening dining room servers arrive to set up the wait station, check the floor, and perform all opening side work. They meet with the kitchen manager or chef to get information on any specials or changes in that night's menu. Just before opening they verify their cash drawers. The lead bartender arrives to set up the bar, stock any needed spirits, and make any mixers that are required. The cash drawer is counted just before opening, and the servers are informed of any specials, shortages, or wine vintage changes that night. The opening bar server sets up the cocktail stations, and makes garnishes for the shift. He or she checks with the kitchen for any changes in bar food or the menu. The opening host/hostess arrives to set up the entry area, and review bookings for the evening, informing servers of any large parties or special customers.

The closing dining room servers arrive at opening, find out about any menu specials or changes, help with any opening tasks that are incomplete, and verify their cash drawers. The opening bus person arrives to set up the bus station (trays, carts, or bus tubs). He or she fills sanitizing buckets and tableware presoak buckets. Bus persons check the status of the restrooms and also meet with the hosts/hostesses to see what the reservation book shows for the evening. The hosts/hostesses set up the entry, check the reservation book, find out about any specials on the bar and food menus, and gets set for a big opening rush. The second bartender (or barback) arrives to set up the second pouring station and complete any opening bar tasks that are incomplete.

During the shift the servers and bus persons are keeping the FOH manager and hosts/hostesses informed of any tables that are going to turn so that the hosts/hostesses can plan on seating arrangements for any large parties that might need adjacent tables. All staff keeps the FOH manager informed of any complaints or compliments. The bus persons try to ensure a smooth flow of dirty dishes to the dishwashers so that there are no surges in workload, and regularly monitor the condition of the restrooms (with the help of the hostesses in the case of the women's restroom). Servers keep tea and coffee supplies replenished, and the bus persons keep bread or tortilla chips rotated and warmed. All servers are making sure to keep a smooth flow of totaling checks, presenting checks, and paying out tables. If that flow gets restricted, servers get overloaded, which directly transfers throughout the restaurant, slowing down the kitchen in the process. It is paramount to avoid overloading any position during the shift, or all will suffer.

As the shift nears end, servers are communicating with the kitchen about how many tickets are remaining to be turned in or cooked, and bus persons are keeping all dirty dishes transported to the dishwasher. The host/hostess will alert any server to any late-arriving tables. As soon as workload diminishes adequately, servers and bus persons begin their cleanup, and start any closing side work. Prep lists based on par levels are written down, so that the following shift knows what is needed to begin. When final orders are submitted the kitchen is notified.

The same holds true for the bar. The bartender completes order sheets for any supplies that need to be phone ordered for delivery for the following shift and alerts the kitchen manager or chef of any supplies that need to be ordered for the bar (produce, bottled or canned goods, paper supplies, etc.). Prep sheets for the following shift are filled out. Cleanup and breaking down commence, and all equipment is cleaned, with all mixing supplies covered and dated. Restocking and rotation of product for the following shift is completed.

Once their closing procedures are accomplished, all employees using a cash drawer reconcile their tickets and count their cash. Cash tips are totaled and removed from the total cash, leaving as many small bills in the cash drawer as possible. The goal is to leave the cash drawer as close to its original starting bank as possible, with mostly small bills. The tickets, credit card receipts, and cash matching the sales are bundled and handed over to the FOH manager for reconciliation. In some restaurants, the bar manager or lead bartender handles some of this responsibility.

The FOH manager gives final approval for any staff leaving, making sure that they have performed their tasks as required. The goal is always to release staff that are no longer needed so that labor costs are reduced with no sacrifice in the quality of service to the customer. Either the bus persons or servers remove all bags of dirty laundry and trash, anti-fatigue floor mats are taken to be hosed down, and bar and wait station floors are swept and mopped. Depending on the needs of the janitorial crew, all chairs and stools might be placed upside down on table tops, or otherwise relocated so that the floors can be thoroughly cleaned.

During late hours, constant attention is paid to security. Doors are kept locked when possible, and money is kept secured. All staff members are made aware of anyone who acts strangely or suspiciously. The kitchen door should be kept locked, and any employees reentering the restaurant through that entrance need to use a buzzer and be verified visibly before admittance. Any staff members leaving the building for their cars can be escorted if they want to be.

The FOH manager makes sure that all tasks are performed by staff, that all staff have signed out, the money is secured, the thermostats are moderated, the lights are turned off, all access points are locked and secured, the building is empty (including checking the restrooms), and the alarm system is armed before leaving.

If the restaurant serves breakfast, two servers should be in 1 hour before opening to do side work, including making lots of coffee, filling syrup dispensers and creamers, softening butter, and stocking jellies. Many coffee cups or mugs should be on hand along with spoons. If a host/hostess is used ("Please Seat Yourself" signs may be an option), this person should be in just before opening to check the entry, newspapers, etc. Two additional servers (if needed) would come in at opening and finish any side work. A bus person would also come in at opening and get right on setting up the bus station. Cleaning tables is very important during breakfast as sticky syrups and jellies and greasy butter residues are prevalent.

At some point a transition from breakfast to lunch must occur and a manager should be on shift in time to "Z" or total out the POS system between breakfast and lunch. Servers would generally need to close out their breakfast tickets. They might close out their cash drawers, or management might choose to combine breakfast and lunch if servers were doing a combined shift. The host and bus staff might also work straight through from breakfast to lunch.

After 18 months it should be fairly clear how your restaurant is doing. Basically there are three outcomes—you have a smash hit; you are paying your bills but not pocketing much in the way of profits; you are hemorrhaging money and will lose everything, including your life savings and home, very soon. Each of these scenarios has a follow-up to it and requires some tough decisions.

## Things Are Going Well

If your restaurant is successful as planned you should consider how to make it even better. If you do not want to expand your present space, you should be striving to improve service, the menu, and the quality of food. No matter how smoothly things are running, there are always places for improvement. However, do not fix what is not broken and do not change for the sake of change. Take a hard look at your menu and the POS printouts as to the best and poorest sellers. Are there patterns? If you have very strong sales of fish and seafood, consider adding several more choices to your menu. Notice trends in dining and see if it would be wise to include "locally grown," "hormone-free," "organic," and other high-quality ingredients into your recipes and on your menu. Basically you are not looking to increase your workload. Instead you want to appreciate the success you have, ensure its continued success, find others to replace you in boring and repetitive tasks, and sit back and enjoy your life.

Can you enlarge or expand your present space? It is often the case that your kitchen can produce more food without expanding (by increasing the number of line and prep cooks, etc.) and without costly renovation. Can you build a patio adjoining the dining room or add a few more tables? You may want to invest in expanding your FOH and add a significant number of tables and a full bar with table seating if you do not already have this. If you started really small, can you afford to move into or build a larger facility that may double your seating (and sales)?

Often, successful restaurateurs find the need to open a second restaurant. For many the excitement is in the challenge of building and opening a successful business, and soon become bored with the routine of everyday tasks. They typically open a clone of their first restaurant in a different neighborhood of the town or city in which they are doing business. If this seems a reasonable venture, you will find it much easier than opening the first location. All of your menus and recipes are set, your purveyors know what you order, and you have trained personnel to do the menu and provide the service you require. You can bring some of your most experienced employees to help open the new location, you have your POS system debugged and your bookkeeping should be easy to implement. Be very careful if this is the path you choose. The last thing you want to do is to be in competition with yourself. You need an entirely new set of diners to fill this second space or you will be dividing your original clientele between two spaces, doubling your expenses without increasing your sales.

Instead of a clone of the first restaurant, you may want to consider a derivative of it. If you are already known for excellent seafood, a seafood restaurant may be just the thing. A more casual version of your first restaurant, such as a bistro or a diner, may be right. An upscale pizzeria may be just the thing if your first restaurant is Italian-themed and you had excellent pizza as appetizer or bar food. Try not to venture too far away from what made your first place successful. Food trucks and trailers are an excellent way to expand. They have low initial cost and are very popular. These small, mobile restaurants allow you to introduce new items to see how they sell (and then incorporate them into your "brick and mortar" restaurant), and they allow you to expand lunch or move into a profitable catering business.

Franchising is another way to clone your restaurant, but instead of you doing the work, you sell the concept to another person. There are several advantages to franchising. You "expand" with someone else's capital. The franchisee is responsible for hiring, leases, and operating expenses and assumes all of the risk in making it a successful venture. But your business needs to be "franchisable." Does your concept work beyond your neighborhood or are you filling a niche in your locale? Often you must have several restaurants running in different locations to prove the concept to investors. You must have something that is unique and that attracts the attention of the public and potential investors. Your concept must be streamlined and it should be easy to train inexperienced personnel. If you or your chefs are the only ones who can produce your food, franchising is not for you. Think "cookie-cutter" operation, where it is easy to hire workers to reproduce your concept and food. Regardless, there are state and federal regulations that apply to franchises and you are strongly urged to seek the advice of a franchise attorney before pursuing this avenue of expansion.

If you do not want to open a second restaurant, but still are looking for new ways of increasing sales and allaying boredom, consider marketing some of your products on a retail basis. Your own line of bottled sauces or other specialty foods may be just the thing to keep you occupied in a venture that is not particularly risky and doesn't require a large investment. Consider writing a cookbook about your restaurant (there are ghost writers available if you need help) or try getting involved in the food scene in your city or state. Radio spots, magazine and newspaper articles, and morning television are all within the realm of being a successful restaurateur.

## You Are Just Breaking Even—No Profit

If you are managing to keep your head above water and are paying all of your bills, but not seeing a profit, you must take a hard look at two factors most responsible for not meeting your goals—labor and food cost. If these are outside the guidelines of percent of sales, measures must be taken to bring them into line. Often the FOH is not a labor issue as most of your FOH employees work for tips and draw a minimum salary. If you have salaried FOH managers, be sure you are getting your money's worth and they are putting in the long hours required of them. They may have to do additional work to replace hourly employees' hours, such as bartend, work in the business office, host, and/or bus tables. Servers and bus persons may have to increase the amount of side work they do, relieving some of the trivial work done by the BOH. They may have to do more cleaning so as to save on external cleaning crews.

The BOH may be the best place to focus on labor (and food cost) issues. Can more prep be done in bulk? Can the kitchen manager do some of the prep work? If the dishwasher isn't busy, can he do some of the more mundane prep such as vegetable peeling, etc? Can you reduce the line crew and combine two stations? Sauté may be able to handle the grill or fryer at all but the busiest of times. Is the head chef really being used efficiently? If he or she is in the office much of the time, you have to find a way to get the chef into the kitchen and have more of the paperwork done by the bookkeeper and kitchen manager. He or she may have to expedite and cook at a line station at the same time. If you can cut labor costs by just 5 percent across the board, that would be a savings of $7,200 in a year, assuming monthly sales of $60,000.

Food cost can really eat into your profits. Waste must be kept under control, portion size must be strictly regulated, and theft held to a minimum. A key factor to food waste is the menu itself. Many restaurants that are not profitable have a menu that is too complicated with too many items. This plays havoc on perishable inventory. Every day you are gambling on who will order what item, and you must have some of everything that is offered on the menu prepped and in the walk-in. (Complicated menus also slow down service, cooking times, table turnover, food quality, and increase BOH labor.)

As an example of portion control, let's assume you hand form your hamburger patties at 4 ounces. Without an accurate scale used for every hamburger, you will never notice a half ounce overage by eye. If you sell 40 hamburgers for lunch every day, that comes to an overage of 325 pounds of hamburger meat per year. If you have a $2 profit per hamburger, that's a loss of $2,600. Cutting overage/waste by just 5 percent across the board could mean a savings of $11,000 per year on $60,000 in monthly gross sales. If your menu pricing is off by 5 percent (you should be selling the stuffed chicken breast dinner for $13.50 and you are charging $12.95), that would be $36,000 in lost profit over a one year period. To summarize: A 5 percent improvement in waste/overage loss, a 5 percent decrease in labor expense, and a 5 percent increase in menu adjustment comes to $54,200 in one year!

Be sure your purveyors are being kept honest by carefully checking in all supplies. Weigh and count everything, and carefully check all invoices. Don't be afraid to comparison shop with secondary purveyors and have your kitchen manager constantly check prices and do food costing more often. Inform your primary purveyors that you want to be alerted when any abrupt changes occur in regularly ordered goods. Produce prices can vary from day to day and can soar with inclement weather and delivery interruptions. A diner in a large city sold about one hundred hamburgers per day. No one noticed that tomato prices had skyrocketed. A quick calculation showed that a single slice of tomato went from $.09 cents to $.40 between daily invoices. That increased the food cost of this popular item by over 15 percent. Increase the number of inventories you do in the restaurant and make them as accurate as possible. Now imagine cutting theft by just a little bit. A closed-circuit camera system that oversees the kitchen and walk-in and the bar and bar area, can save thousands of dollars in stolen goods.

If you are running a tight ship and none of the above seems to be the problem, it is probably sales that are the cause of lack of profit. There are so many fixed costs in running a restaurant that if you do not bring in more customers, nothing will help. The same crew that cooks and serves one hundred dinners per night in a one-hundred-seat restaurant can easily serve two hundred. Why are customers not coming in? Is it the food quality/portion size/flavor profile? Is it the style of food or maybe the location? Is there too much competition for a limited pool of diners? Do people know that you exist?

Carefully analyze your menu to see which items are your best sellers and compare them to the number of poorly selling items. Also look at the distribution of items such as appetizers, soups, and desserts. Are people coming in and ordering an appetizer or two and a beverage? The appetizers portions may be too large and you are encouraging them to skip an entree. Are your appetizer prices too high? You may be encouraging your guests to skip this very profitable item. Are your dessert portions too large, pricy, or are the items too rich and filling to attract an impulse buy at meal's end? Consider offering free tastes of new items or of appetizers and desserts to stimulate interest in your menu. Develop a signature dish, at a reasonable price, that attracts "word of mouth" interest in the community. You do not have to be an authentic Spanish restaurant in order to serve spectacular paella, which has low food cost but a high buzz factor among diners everywhere.

Marketing is always a good place to start when trying to bring in more customers, although it can be expensive. Think of ways to get your name out without spending dollars on advertising. If you have a large parking lot, host a weekly farmers' market. That will get your name in the press as well as send a goodwill message to the public. It also implies that you use fresh, locally grown produce and support your community. Get involved in local charities, especially those that center on food, such as Meals on Wheels or food banks.

How about a family night? You could serve a special menu and set out large bowls of salad and vegetables and platters of meat for a reasonable price. If you have a bar, have you tried a happy hour with snacks from the kitchen? Maybe a trivia contest or some sort of lottery held on a typically slow night. Your servers can market the local office buildings and hand out business cards with discounts or freebies. This marketing technique works for lunch business and dinner as well. Be careful about falling into the "two-for one" trap, where the second dinner is free, using a coupon printed in the local paper. Diners get used to this and only go to your restaurant when there is a coupon to be clipped. If you want to give something away, make it a beverage, a modest appetizer, or a special dessert that has low food cost. Facebook and Twitter are ways to advertise without expense. You will develop a loyal following and can offer these customers instant specials not available to the general public. Diners can be alerted to new menu items, specials and special events on a moment's notice. It is an excellent way for your tasty food to be critiqued and viewed by many who enjoy surfing social media outlets. You can post your hours, contact information, and menus to be printed out.

More extreme measures may have to be taken to boost sales and profitability. If a cash infusion is required to redecorate or remodel, taking on investors may be the solution. Is the location keeping you back? You may need a financial boost to relocate to an area more applicable to your talents and menu offerings. Along with an investment in decor, a serious look at trimming and changing the menu may be in order. Costs may have to be trimmed "to the bone," but do not jeopardize the quality of the food. Skimping on portions, replacing butter with margarine, and so forth are not ways to hold on to your loyal customers or attract new clientele. A shake-up in management may be in order to bring new life and ideas to your business. A new chef with fresh ideas and more talent may be needed or a FOH manager that has more enthusiasm and experience. Bringing in an unbiased consultant to look over all aspects of your operation is a valuable way to evaluate from the outside. Look at your fixed costs and see if there are ways to negotiate a lower lease payment or refinance a high interest loan.

## Getting Out

Sometimes it is too late to save the restaurant. You have exhausted all of your assets and bankruptcy is looming. There are so many reasons for a restaurant to fail that this is not the time to ponder what happened, but to act swiftly to save what you can and get out, putting your life back in order. An open, operating restaurant, no matter how poorly it is doing, is easier to sell than one that is closed. There are always people looking for a "turn-key" operation and you can offer this to them if your restaurant is alive, thriving or not. Make sure the place is immaculately clean before showing it and fix as much broken equipment, tables, and chairs as is reasonable without spending too much. Estimate the worth of the business by first totaling the value of all of the equipment you own. Remember to value based on prices on the used market, and this market is flooded with used restaurant equipment. Since your restaurant has failed, there may not be much you can value on the business side of the sale. The purchaser will probably change the name, the concept, and the decor, so do not expect much worth here.

It may be time to just walk away and declare bankruptcy, which can provide protection from your creditors and save your home and personal effects. Consult attorneys who specialize in bankruptcy, as they know all of the ins and outs of this complicated aspect of the law. There may be several options available, from restructuring your debts to dissolving them completely. This is not a painless procedure that you should consider unless there are absolutely no other options. It can destroy your credit for 10 years, making it difficult to obtain personal credit or to invest in another business.

## Concluding Thoughts

If there were a magic formula for creating a successful restaurant, everyone who opened one would be a millionaire and there would be a zero percent failure rate. Usually the only guarantees are what will likely happen if you do not do things well. The best we can do is to do the best we can! Serve tasty food that is at the correct temperature and is delivered promptly to the guest. Run a spotlessly clean kitchen and serve wholesome food. Make guests feel welcome and comfortable with a courteous staff. Pick a location that is convenient and easily accessible from any direction. Know your market and target clientele. Price your menu and size your portions so that there is perceived value and offer dishes that guests will talk about to their friends. Adhere to good business practices and don't fall behind in your tax payments. Hire the most experienced and capable staff that you can and train them to work together efficiently and with pride in their work. Finally, everyone needs supervision, and you are their ultimate supervisor.

- ❏ Honest evaluation of your commitment to the project
- ❏ Honest evaluation of your financial ability to fund the project
- ❏ Select a style of service, concept, and size (seating, square footage) for the restaurant
- ❏ Decide if alcohol will be served and in which form—if yes, begin alcoholic beverage permit process
- ❏ Select a location
- ❏ Design the menu (evaluate skills required to cook it and the talent pool available)
- ❏ Price the menu
- ❏ Estimate monthly fixed costs
- ❏ Write recipes
- ❏ Select food purveyors to help in food costing your menu
- ❏ Create Inventory Master, Prep Master, and Menu (recipe) Cost lists
- ❏ Estimate startup costs based on type of construction selected (how much to borrow)
- ❏ Obtain EIN (employer identification number)
- ❏ Obtain State Sales Tax and Use permit (State Comptroller)
- ❏ Set up business organization (sole proprietor, LLC, etc.)

- ❏ Open bank accounts
- ❏ Write a business plan
- ❏ Secure finances
- ❏ Select architect and interior designer
- ❏ Select equipment needed (obtain PDF files on each piece of equipment for architect)
- ❏ Create floor plan, design, and blueprints with architect and interior designer
- ❏ Obtain health department approval of kitchen plans (and other agencies requiring)
- ❏ Select contractor
- ❏ Obtain insurance covering pre-opening and eventual opening
- ❏ Obtain all permits and licenses to begin construction
- ❏ Begin construction
- ❏ Order all equipment, smallwares, table service, etc. (specify/estimate delivery dates)
- ❏ Select all suppliers and purveyors of materials and services
- ❏ Finalize construction and hold all inspections and complete all licenses
- ❏ Hire BOH management—head chef and/or kitchen manager (depending on the positions you will assume)
- ❏ BOH management prepares all forms and lists—inventory, par levels, station prep, etc.
- ❏ Hire FOH manager (depending on the positions you will assume)
- ❏ Hire business office manager (depending on the positions you will assume)
- ❏ FOH management prepares all forms/lists—server checkout, work scheduling, end of shift, etc.
- ❏ Stock kitchen, bar, and wait station

- ❏ Prepare for hiring of all staff positions—salaries, manuals, policies, job descriptions
- ❏ Hire all staff positions
- ❏ Conduct training sessions
- ❏ Open doors

Notes _____

_____

_____

_____

_____

_____

_____

_____

_____

_____

_____

_____

_____

_____

# Appendix B: Useful Pre-Opening Checklists

## Inspections:
❑ Health _____
❑ Fire _____
❑ Building _____
❑ Electrical _____
❑ Plumbing _____

## Licenses and Permits:
❑ Health department _____
❑ Sales tax _____
❑ Alcohol _____
❑ Fire department _____

## Wiring:
❑ Computers _____
❑ POS system _____
❑ Telephone/intercom _____
❑ Music/PA _____
❑ Burglar/fire alarms _____
❑ Video surveillance/security _____

## Emergency:
❑ Lighting _____
❑ Sprinkler systems _____
❑ Smoke detectors _____
❑ Emergency exit signs _____
❑ Fire extinguishers _____

## Utilities/Services:

- ☐ Gas (deposit) _____
- ☐ Electric (deposit) _____
- ☐ Phone system (select, listings, also any advertisement in Yellow Pages) _____
- ☐ Water (check hardness/quality for post-treatment) _____
- ☐ Garbage/dumpster (select) _____
- ☐ Grease/grease trap _____
- ☐ Sewer _____

## Insurance:

- ☐ During construction _____
- ☐ Comprehensive for opening _____
- ☐ Workers' compensation _____

## Banking:

- ☐ Select bank _____
- ☐ Set up accounts (construction, payroll, BOH checking or credit card, lines of credit, deposit bags) _____
- ☐ Credit card service _____

## Design:

- ☐ Logo _____
- ☐ Signage _____
- ☐ Menus _____
- ☐ Business cards _____
- ☐ Stationery/letterhead _____

## Signage and Banners:

- ☐ Coming soon _____
- ☐ Opening date _____
- ☐ Now hiring _____
- ☐ Hours of operation _____
- ☐ No deliveries between . . . _____
- ☐ No smoking _____
- ☐ We accept . . . credit cards (no checks?) _____

- ❏ Restrooms _____
- ❏ Open/Closed _____
- ❏ Emergency exits _____
- ❏ This door open between . . . _____
- ❏ Ring bell for service _____
- ❏ Required signage from alcohol commission _____
- ❏ Firearms policy _____
- ❏ Immigration signage required to post _____
- ❏ OSHA _____
- ❏ Parking (handicap, reserved, valet) _____

## Parking:
- ❏ Lot paving/striping _____
- ❏ Valet (arrange for site, service) _____
- ❏ Handicap _____
- ❏ Lighting _____
- ❏ Security patrol _____

## Keys/Locks:
- ❏ Storage (bulk, liquor) _____
- ❏ Walk-in, refrigeration _____
- ❏ Offices _____
- ❏ Entrance and back door (pre- and post-construction) _____
- ❏ Rekey just before opening _____

## Pest Control:
- ❏ During construction (between walls, etc. while exposed) _____
- ❏ Pre-opening _____
- ❏ Regular visitations _____

## Computer Services:
- ❏ ISP _____
- ❏ E-mail _____
- ❏ Website _____

## Music:

- ❑ Equipment _____
- ❑ Satellite services _____
- ❑ Muzak _____
- ❑ ASCAP/BMI licenses _____

## Social Media:

- ❑ Facebook _____
- ❑ Twitter _____

## Landscaping/Plants:

- ❑ Exterior _____
- ❑ Interior _____
- ❑ Accent lighting _____

## For Opening Day:

- ❑ Final cleaning (windows, walkways, interior surfaces, bathrooms) _____
- ❑ Office products (pens, pads, flashlights, etc.) to all stations
  (host/hostess, bar, BOH, wait station) _____
- ❑ Cash for servers' banks, bar register _____

# Appendix C: Food Safety

As the owner of a restaurant you should be very concerned about preventing food-borne illness. We recommend that you take a course and be certified as a food manager. Local health departments and Internet sources can administer the exam. At least one person in the BOH should be certified, as should the FOH manager. Everyone who touches food in any way should take a short course to be food-handler certified.

Food-borne illness is most often the result of microbes, especially bacteria. Typically there are three ways for bacteria to enter your food.

1. It was in an ingredient purchased (salmonella in raw poultry).
2. It came from your employees due to poor hygiene (E-coli from feces).
3. It came from cross-contamination of food with unclean or infected surfaces, such as a cutting board used for cutting raw chicken, which was then used to cut raw vegetables.

Microorganisms are everywhere and proper temperature controls are essential to prevent outbreaks of food-borne illness. If food is cooked to the proper temperature, most issues of food-borne illness can be avoided. If foods are refrigerated and held at proper temperature, and foods are never held in the "danger zone," you are on your way to serving safe food.

- Danger zone: 41°F to 135°F (Any prepared food held in the danger zone for more than 4 hours should be discarded).
- Proper refrigeration temperature: 34°F to 40°F (use hanging interior thermometers in all refers and freezers)
- Chilling temperature (for raw meats): 33°F
- Freezer temperature: -10°F to 10°F

All foods should be cooked to an internal temperature within the range of 130°F to 190°F.

- Beef, lamb, and fish 145°F
- Pork 160°F
- Ground beef 160°F
- Egg dishes 160°F
- Poultry 165°F

Hold cooked foods at 135°F or higher, but do not serve these or any previously cooked food until serving portions are heated to 165°F for at least 15 seconds. Reheat previously cooked foods only once.

"Ready to eat" foods, such as chili sealed in plastic film on display to be microwaved, must be labeled if not sold within 24 hours of preparation. They can be held for 4 days at 45°F.

Most food-borne illness occurs due to improper cooling of hot foods. Never place hot food in a refrigerator or walk-in, as it could raise the internal temperature of the refer into the danger zone. Hot foods need to be cooled in two stages:

- Stage 1: 135°F to 70°F in 2 hours
- Stage 2: 70°F to 41°F in 4 hours

Some hints to achieve this include breaking into small portions; using shallow dishes and small containers; using an ice bath; stirring and rotating frequently; adding ice as an ingredient.

Potentially hazardous foods are high in protein, are moist and only slightly acidic. The list includes raw and cooked meats, poultry and seafood; milk and dairy; eggs and egg dishes; cooked vegetables; raw sprouts and soybeans; cut melons; cut leafy greens; cut tomatoes and preparations with cut tomatoes.

The acronym HACCP is a management system to ensure food safety wherever food is handled and processed. It stands for Hazard Analysis and Critical Control Points. Basically it is a way to follow the manufacture of any food item from receiving raw materials and ingredients to serving the prepared item, and to identify steps that could lead to food-borne illness and control them to prevent any outbreak. It is a good way for you to examine your operation and identify places to be particularly careful when handling food. Let's take selling a hamburger as an example. The first critical step would be the check-in of the ground beef to see if it was delivered at the proper temperature and with wholesomeness. The refer should be checked to see that the patties are being stored at the correct temperature and to check for expiration dates. The cook should be checked to see that he is following proper sanitary policy and is washing hands frequently and is disease-free. The meat should be cooked to an internal temperature of 160°F and the salad garnishes should have been washed and stored in the correct manner and at proper temperature. The server should be disease-free, groomed, and should not touch the food with his or her hands.

When storing foods in a walk-in or refer, there is a priority as to where different items should be stored. Raw meats, poultry, and fish should be on the bottom shelf and never above any other foods. Raw produce should be kept apart from cooked produce. All containers must be covered and labeled properly (item, date, operator). Dry goods must be separated from refrigerated foods and should be located where no splashing of liquid can contaminate. Dry storage should be held between 50°F and 70°F with adequate air circulation, and be pest-free. Dry goods must be 6 inches above the floor, as should the bottom shelves of the walk-in. Chemicals, such as cleaning agents and disinfectants, can never be stored near any foods and should have a separate storage room or area.

## Most Serious Pitfalls to Avoid

Health inspections are a serious matter. If there are too many violations over multiple inspections, you may be closed down temporarily or permanently. Minor infractions are noted and are expected to be corrected by the next inspection Major infractions are given a short timeline for correction or the restaurant risks being closed down. Here are some of the more serious violations noted by health inspectors.

1. Rodent and insect infestation
2. Improper temperatures for storing, holding, cooking, and serving food
3. Cross-contamination of raw meats with vegetables and cooked foods, improper storage of foods in refrigerators
4. Inadequate hand washing stations—no soap, towels, too few stations
5. Workers without health cards, without training certificates
6. Inadequate heating of dishwashing water, inadequate disinfecting of dishes

# Appendix D: Table Layout and Seating

How you arrange your dining area is critical to efficient service and guest comfort. Tables spaced too close together make guests uncomfortable, as they do not want to hear others' conversations or be overheard. They want a modicum of privacy when dining. There should be adequate room to slide chairs back when seating or standing. Servers need adequate space to move around the entire table and not be forced into reaching across a table to remove a plate or serve a dish. On the other hand, you want as many tables as can comfortably fit into your allotted dining space to make money. Below you will find guidelines to accommodate both server and guest and to maximize seating without your dining area appearing crowded. Generally upscale restaurants require more space (and larger tables) to satisfy their clientele.

## Table Spacing

Refer to the diagram on next page. In order to figure the spacing, and therefore the maximum number of seats in the dining area, there are some average space allotments you can use. Allow 18 inches for the seat to protrude from the table (1). Also allow a minimum of 18 inches from the seat back to a wall (2), in order for the guests to slide their chairs out and for space for a server to go behind. Adding these values, the table should be placed 3 feet (36 inches) from a wall (3), with this orientation. Allow 24 inches between tables (4), seatback to seatback. For a 36-inch square table, from the wall to the end of the second table (8) requires 15 1/2 linear feet

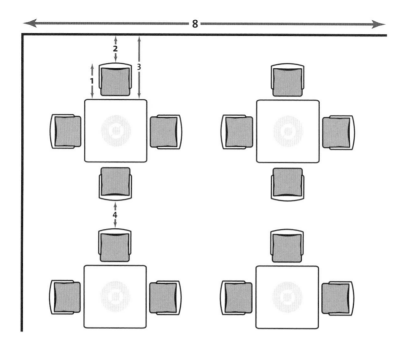

With diagonal orientation, more tables can be fit into a given space. From the corner of the table to the wall (5) requires 18 inches and spacing between tables is 24 inches (6). From the wall to the end of the second table (7), for the same 36-inch square table, requires only 12.7 feet and the tables are 18 inches closer to any wall.

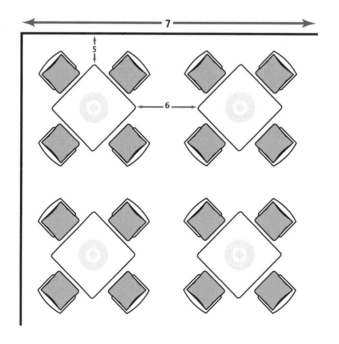

## Bar Measurements for Seating

| | |
|---|---|
| The height of the table from the floor (A) | 40–43 inches |
| The height of the stool from the floor (B) | 30 inches |
| The height of the stool to the table top (C) | 10–13 inches |
| The height of the bar counter to the floor (D) | 36 inches |
| The height of the stool to the floor (E) | 24–26 inches |
| The height of the stool to the bar counter (F) | 12–14 inches |
| Spacing of bar stools, center to center (G) | 24–36 inches |

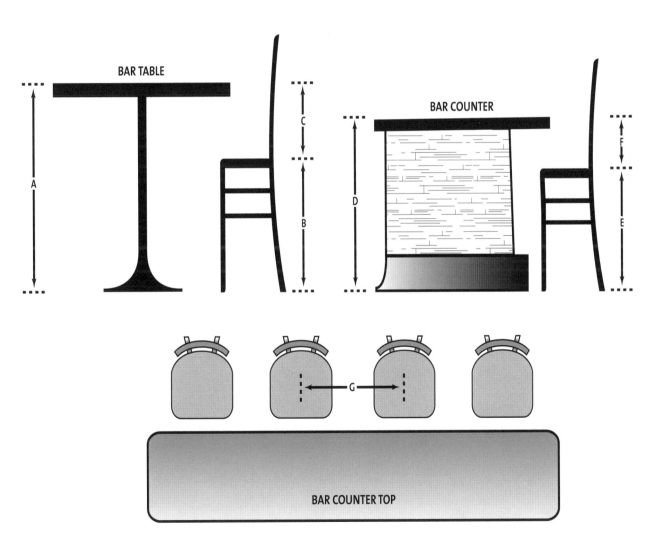

## Dining Room Measurements for Seating

| | |
|---|---|
| The height of the table from the floor (H) | 28–30 inches (29 inches is standard) |
| The height of the seat from the floor (I) | 16–18 inches |
| The height of the seat to the table top (J) | 12 inches |
| The distance from the center of the table (K) | 15–18 inches to the table edge |

## Seating

How you orient your tables can influence the seating capacity of your restaurant and the shape of tables can affect versatility in accommodating large parties. Two square or rectangular tables can be joined together for a large party; round tables cannot. Table size is often dictated by the type of food you offer and the level of service. A pizza takes up a lot of real estate on a table!

### Square Tables

Square tables are very versatile as they can be joined to accommodate as many in a party as required.

- 24 inches will seat 2 guests
- 30 inches will seat 2 to 4 guests and is best as a "three top" with one side against a wall

- 36 inches will seat 4 guests and is considered "standard"
- 42 inches will seat 4 guests very comfortably

## Rectangular Tables

- 24 x 30 inches will seat 2 guests and provides more room than a 24-inch square
- 24 x 42 inches will seat 4 guests, but a 36-inch square is more practical
- 24 x 48 inches will seat 4 guests, but a 36-inch square is more practical
- 30 x 42 inches will seat 4 guests, has a bit more space than a 36-inch square, but is less versatile
- 30 x 48 inches will seat 4 guests, is large, and is less versatile than a 36-inch square
- 30 x 72 inches will seat 8 guests, but a round table is more versatile

## Round Tables

- 24 inches will seat up to 4 guests very tightly
- 30 inches will seat up to 4 guests
- 36 inches will seat up to 4 guests very comfortably (a fifth guest can be fit in, if necessary)
- 42 inches will seat up to 6 guests tightly
- 48 inches will seat up to 6 guests
- 54 inches will seat up to 6 guests very comfortably (a seventh guest can be fit in, if necessary)
- 60 inches will seat up to 8 guests
- 72 inches will seat up to 10 guests

## Table Supports

It is critical that you select the correct base for your table. Cross-foot bases allow chairs to slide in completely to a square table, where a round base prevents this. The wrong size base may cause wobbling. Be aware of three-legged table bases, which should never be used on a square table. It makes it impossible to tuck in four chairs.

## Cross-Foot Table Base Standard Sizes:

- 22 x 22-inch table base will support tops up to 30 inches square or 30 inches diameter round
- 30 x 30-inch table base will support tops up to 42 inches square or 42 inches diameter round
- 36 x 36-inch table base will support tops up to 48 inches square or 54 inches diameter round
- 22 x 30-inch table base will support rectangular table tops up to 24 x 47 inches

## Round Table Base Standard Sizes:

- 18-inch round table base will support table tops up to 24-inch diameter
- 22-inch round table base will support table tops up to 36-inch diameter
- 30-inch round table base will support table tops up to 60-inch diameter
- 22-inch end bases are a versatile solution for supporting a variety of table-top shapes

# Appendix E: Smallwares

Below is a basic list of smallwares that are needed to operate a restaurant. It is a list to get you started, but specialty wares have not been included, such as for a pizzeria. Quantities have been left out as they depend on the style of cooking and the theme of your restaurant. Smallwares should be easily obtained locally from a restaurant supply company; order modestly to start and fill in additional amounts as needed.

## Kitchen:

- Sheet pans, heavy gauge, 24 x 16-inch, 12 x 16-inch
- Bun pan rack, full size, 20-pan capacity
- Pan grate/cooling rack, chrome, footed, full pan 24 x 16-inch, half pan 12 x 16-inch
- Baking pan, round, 9 x 2-inch
- Springform pan, heavy gauge, 10 x 3-inch
- Single open-top bread pan, 8 x 4 x 2 3/4-inch
- Pie pans, 18 gauge, 8 x 1-inch, 8 x 2-inch
- Fry basket, round, wire, 11 1/2-inch
- #1 can opener, table-edge mount
- Colander, heavy-duty aluminum, footed, 11 quarts
- China cap strainer, 12-inch
- Handled strainers, 10-inch medium mesh, 6-inch fine mesh
- Chef knife, 10-inch, plastic handle, everyday use
- Chef knife, serrated 7-inch or 8-inch, plastic handle, everyday use
- Chef knife, Santoku 7-inch or 8-inch, plastic handle, everyday use
- Butcher knife, 10-inch, plastic handle, everyday use

- Slicer, roast, 12-inch or 14-inch, scalloped
- Boner, flexible 6-inch (meat)
- Boner/fish-fillet knife, flexible, 7-inch, narrow
- Bread knife, 9-inch, scalloped, offset
- Cheese knife, 8–10-inch, with holes in blade
- Paring knife, 4-inch, plastic handle, everyday use
- Serrated utility/paring knife, 5-inch, plastic handle, everyday use
- Oyster knife, 2 3/4-inch
- Heavy utility cleaver, 7-inch
- Sandwich spreader, 7 1/4 x 1 1/4-inch, stainless steel
- Kitchen knife rack, magnetic, wall mount, stainless steel with front skirt, 12 x 12-inch
- Sharpening steel
- Pot fork, 10-inch
- Carving fork, 6-inch
- Cutting boards, poly, white, assorted sizes and colors
- Cutting board rack, heavy wire frame, 6 boards per rack, vertical storage
- Dishers, #40, #24, #16, #8
- Aluminum scoops, 24 ounces, 12 ounces, 6 ounces
- Ice scoop, 58 to 64 ounces, aluminum
- Dough scraper, 6 x 3-inch, stainless steel, plastic handle
- Dredger (shaker), 10 ounces, stainless steel, without handle
- Food storage boxes with lids, polycarbonate, square, clear, 2 quarts, 4 quarts, 8 quarts, 12 quarts, 22 quarts, 17 gallons
- Fry pans, nonstick, first quality, 10-inch, 12-inch, 14-inch
- Curved saucepans, stainless steel, 1 quart, 2 quarts, 3 quarts
- Sauce pan, straight-sided, aluminum, 4 1/2 quarts, 6 1/2 quarts
- Stockpots, heavyweight aluminum, 12 quarts, 20 quarts
- Stockpot, heavyweight stainless steel, 40 quarts
- Roasting pan, heavy-duty, aluminum, 18 x 24 x 4 1/2-inch, strapped
- Funnels, plastic, 4 ounces, 8 ounces, 16 ounces, 32 ounces
- Box grater, stainless steel, heavy-duty, 9-inch, 4-sided
- Rubber spatulas, high-temperature 13 1/2-inch, 16 1/2-inch
- Rubber spatulas/scrapers, 9-inch, 13-inch
- Kitchen shears

- Ladles, stainless steel, 1 piece, 1/2 ounce, 1 ounce, 1 1/2 ounces, 2 ounces, 3 ounces, 4 ounces, 8 ounces
- Flat-bottom ladle, stainless steel, 1 piece, 4 ounces
- Transfer ladle, stainless steel, 1 piece, 32 ounces
- Mallet/tenderizer, 2 3/4 x 2 3/4 x 3-inch cast-aluminum head, wood handle
- Mandoline, stainless steel
- Measuring cups, dry, heavy-duty aluminum, 1 cup, 2 cups, 4 cups, 8 cups, 16 cups
- Measuring cups, liquid, graduated measure, polycarbonate, 16 ounces, 32 ounces, 64 ounces, 1 gallon
- Measuring spoons, stainless steel, includes 1/2 tablespoon
- Measuring spoons, stainless steel, odd sizes: pinch, 2/3 teaspoon, 3/4 teaspoon, 1 1/2 teaspoons, 2 teaspoons
- Mixing bowls, stainless steel, heavyweight, 1 quart, 2 quarts, 4 quarts, 8 quarts, 16 quarts
- Disposable pastry bags, box, 18-inch
- Pastry tubes, star tip, stainless steel, sizes 0–9
- Decorating tube set, 26 pieces, standard coupling
- Cake decorating comb with 3 decorating edges, triangular, aluminum
- Dough divider, stainless steel blade, 4 1/2-inch
- Pastry brush, 2-inch width
- Basting brush, boar bristles, 4-inch
- Pie markers, aluminum, 6 cut, 8 cut
- Pizza cutter/wheel
- Rolling pin, maple, 15-inch, ball bearing
- Wire skimmer, 6 3/4-inch square, fine
- Serving spoon, slotted, heavy-duty 18/8 stainless steel, 11-inch, 15-inch
- Ingredient bin, mobile, 37-gallon, 2-piece, sliding lid
- Thermometer, pocket, digital, 1-degree accuracy, waterproof
- Meat thermometer, dual-face dial, dishwasher safe
- Oven thermometer, dial, 200–550°F range, stainless steel
- Candy/deep-fry thermometer, 2 1/4-inch dial, 12-inch stem
- Refrigerator/freezer thermometer, -40–80°F
- Triple-alert timer, with clock, LCD display
- Peppermill, stainless steel, 10-inch

- Oil can, spouted, stainless steel
- Tongs, coiled spring, heavy-duty, stainless steel, 9 1/2 -inch, 16-inch, 12-inch
- Fish turner, stainless steel, 6 1/2 x 3-inch, slotted
- Turner, perforated, 8 x 3-inch, offset blade
- Turner, solid, 8 x 3-inch, stainless steel blade
- Hamburger turner, 4 x 3-inch, stainless steel offset blade
- French whips, heavy-duty stainless steel, 12-inch, 24-inch
- Piano whip, stainless steel, 8-inch
- Portion scale, 16 ounces, in 1/4-ounce increments
- Squeeze bottle dispensers, clear, 12 ounces, 24 ounces
- Cut-resistant gloves
- Wire mesh
- Disposable gloves, box, vinyl, powdered, 5 mil, beaded cuff, small, medium, large
- Skewers, stainless steel
- Oval griddle
- Pumice stone, with handle
- Grill weight, 2-pound, cast-iron steak weight, wood handle
- Small can opener
- Bottle opener
- Film/foil dispenser
- 5-gallon pail opener
- Waste container, without lid, round, 32-gallon
- Waste container, untouchable, half round, 21-gallon
- Waste container dolly, 32-gallon
- Cart, utility, 2-shelf, plastic

## Cleaning and Janitorial:

- Warehouse broom, heavy-duty, padded handle
- Scrub broom, stiff bristles, 36-inch width
- Broom and mop rack, wall-mounted
- Dish apron, rubber-coated, with pocket
- Dish gloves, vinyl, medium, large
- Flatware washing basket, no handles, half size, 8 compartments

- Dustpan, upright
- Mop head, swinger loop wet mop, large, 1-inch headband
- Mop handle, hardwood
- Mop bucket
- Mop wringer
- Chlorine test strips
- Scrub brush, short handle
- Scrub brush, long handle
- Spray bottle, 1-quart trigger sprayer, refillable

## Wait Station and Bus:

- Bus tubs, 7-inch depth
- Bus tub lids
- Sweeper, Hoky
- Cutlery box, 4 rounded compartments
- Food-serving tray, cork-lined, oval, 23 x 28-inch
- Food-serving tray, cork-lined, oval, 19 x 24-inch
- Food-serving trays, cork-lined, round, 11-inch, 16-inch diameter
- Tray stand, 38 inches tall, mahogany or walnut, nylon straps
- Servers for tea, stackable teapot, 18/8 stainless steel, 20 ounces
- Pitcher, 60 ounces, clear plastic
- Pepper refiller, 1/2 gallon, plastic
- Salt refiller, 1/2 gallon, plastic
- Table levelers
- Table crumber with pocket clip
- Toothpick dispenser

## Bar:

- Poly cutting boards, with mesh shelf liner underneath, 12 x 16-inch; 6 x 10-inch
- Bar drink mats, 24 x 3-inch, rubber, for length of the bar
- Cocktail drain mat, 24 x 24-inch
- Trash can, half-moon or slim rectangular, 22 gallons

- Shaker glasses, 16 ounces, heavy
- Shaker tins, stainless steel, 28 ounces, heavy (or Parisian-style cocktail shakers with lid and built-in strainer)
- Jiggers, 2-sided, stainless steel, 1 1/4 and 1 1/2 ounces; 1 and 2 ounces
- Cocktail strainers, stainless steel, 4-prong
- Strainer, stainless steel, mint julep
- Muddler, stainless steel or wood
- Cocktail stir spoons, twisted handle, 10 to 12-inch
- Fine-mesh strainer, 6-inch
- Lemon zester, V-channel
- Vegetable peeler
- Ice scoops, stainless steel, 4 to 6 ounces
- Ice scoop, 60 ounce (for ice machine)
- Ice bucket, 5 gallons, with handle
- Ice chipper, 6-prong
- Paring knife, 3 1/2 to 4-inch
- Serrated utility knife, 4 to 5-inch
- Sharpening steel or stone
- Microplane grater, fine
- Peppermill
- Glass-edge rimmer
- Condiment holder, stainless steel, 4 compartments x 1 pint, with enclosed freezer pack chillers
- Bar caddies (Bevnap, Sipstir, and straw holder)
- Speed pourers, screened #220 liquor
- Wine openers with knife, waiter-style
- Wine chiller/buckets, floor stand or table models
- Manual vacuum pump with wine stoppers
- Champagne stoppers
- Cork retriever
- Wine funnel with fine screen
- Bottle/can opener, stainless steel
- Can opener with lid catch, locking, stainless steel
- Juice and mix containers, store-and-pour style, with extra tops, 1 quart
- Cream whipper, with nitrous mini-canisters

- Thermal airpot, stainless steel, for coffee
- Server trays, cork-lined, round, 12-inch, 16-inch
- Fire extinguisher
- Flashlight, LED, heavy-duty, rechargeable, 110V
- Push-style floor sweeper (for bar use only)
- Warehouse broom (for bar use only)
- Mop (for bar use only)
- Mop bucket (for bar use only)
- Squeegee, 12-inch
- Scrub sponges
- Spray bottles, 16 ounces, trigger-style

## For All Areas:

- Floor mats (different sizes, materials for each area—bar, cook line, dish, wait station)

# Appendix F: Glassware and Tableware

There are numerous styles of glassware, tableware, and flatware and each can be found in a broad range of prices. To some the very basic plate is fine, but an upscale restaurant may want its dinnerware to reflect the high quality and costing of its menu. A 10 1/2-inch round dinner plate can cost anywhere from $1.00 to over $100! Whatever you choose, be sure there is plenty of that brand and style available, as you will be replacing chipped plates, broken glasses, and twisted forks often.

## Bar

For bar use, tempered, heat-treated glass is preferred. The bottom of a bar glass should be sturdy and heavy enough to help hold the chill in the glass while reducing breakage. The simplest designs are often the best and most economical. The glass quantities should reflect the specialty of the bar. A specialty beer bar would need additional beer glasses, while a whiskey bar might need more rocks glasses. If a bar were to stock only five types of glasses, they would be rocks, highball, white wine, cocktail (martini), and beer pint. Quantities listed are for a full bar in a busy restaurant of one hundred seats.

- Shot or shooter, 1 1/2 to 2 ounces, 5 dozen (for straight-up shots of liquor)
- Highball, 9 to 11 ounces, 10 dozen (for highballs and mixed drinks)
- Rocks/"old fashioned," 5 to 6 ounces, 10 dozen (versatile, straight liquor, or cocktail over ice)
- Double rocks: 10 to 12 ounces, 8 dozen (some bars use double rocks in place of a highball)
- Collins, 10 to 14 ounces, 8 dozen (for plain sodas, cocktails with fruit juices and soda, tall highballs with soda, and mixed drinks)
- Cocktail (or "martini") glass: 6 ounces, 10 dozen (for strained cocktails; should have a stem)

- Cordial/pony, 2 to 4 ounces, 2 dozen (for straight-up cocktails, layered shots)
- Brandy snifter, 6 to 11 ounces, 3 dozen (bottom of the glass can be cupped so the hand warms the spirit)
- Red wine, 10 to 12 ounces, 12 dozen (broader and larger than white, beaded rim)
- White wine, 8 to 10 ounces, 12 dozen (used for sours or cocktails on the rocks, or as a water glass)
- Champagne flute/coupette, 8 ounces, 6 dozen (the flute is preferred for showcasing, extending life of the bubbles)
- Sherry, 2 to 4 ounces, 2 dozen (also used to serve aperitifs, liqueurs)
- Beer pint, 16 ounces, 12 dozen (can also be used for tea or water)
- Beer mug, 16 ounces, 12 dozen (less efficient to store or chill than a glass)
- Pilsner, 12 ounces, 12 dozen (the best glass for lagers and pilsners)
- Pitchers, 60 ounces, 3 dozen (if serving keg beers)
- Coffee mug, 12 to 16 ounces, 3 dozen (clear glass for coffee-based drinks)

## Table Glassware

- Water/tea glass, 16 to 20 ounces, 15 dozen
- Bud vase, 3 dozen
- Glass salad plate, 9-inch (if using), 6 dozen (see below)

## Tableware

Plate size offerings will vary among companies. Sizes below are approximate. Look for dishes that are chip-resistant (some companies will offer a chip warrantee). Styles include rimless, narrow, medium, and large rim. Look for plates and bowls that are designed to be low profile when stacked. Consider weight when selecting items, as this can place quite a strain on servers if extra-large and heavy dishes are chosen. Catalogs often provide the weight per case for each item. Make sure flatware is sturdy enough for everyday use and that fork tines will not bend easily. Loss of flatware often comes from inadvertently throwing away with table refuse. Consider a magnetic device used to catch flatware when emptying into a waste bin by the dish line.

- Plates, 6 1/2-inch, 8 dozen (bread)
- Plates, 9-inch, 10 dozen (salad/appetizer/dessert)
- Plates, 10 1/2-inch, 14 dozen (entree)
- Platters, 12 1/2 x 9-inch, 8 dozen (if menu is heavy on seafood/steak items)

- Rarebit/casseroles, 4 dozen
- Round soup bowls, 9-inch, 6 dozen
- Monkey dishes, 16 dozen (side dish/sauce on side)
- Bouillon, 6 dozen (cup of soup)
- Coffee cups/mugs, 6 to 12 ounces, 12 dozen (add saucer for cup)
- Hot water/teapots, stainless steel, 2 dozen
- Espresso cups, 3 ounces, 5 dozen (if serving espresso)
- Espresso saucers, 5 dozen (if serving espresso)
- Salt/pepper, 4 dozen
- Sugar, 4 dozen
- Dressing cruets, 1 dozen (typically for oil and vinegar)
- Creamers, 3 dozen (stainless steel or ceramic)
- Bread baskets, 3 dozen (if serving table bread)
- Dinner knives, 12 dozen
- Steak knives, 6 dozen (if specialty steak house, 12 dozen)
- Dinner forks, 12 dozen
- Salad/utility/dessert forks, 8 dozen
- Teaspoon/dessert spoons, 18 dozen
- Soup/table/bouillon spoons, 8 dozen
- Demitasse spoons, 5 dozen (if serving espresso)
- Iced tea spoons, 10 dozen

## Specialty Restaurants Require Additional Tableware

In addition to the basic tableware mentioned above, specialty restaurants require specialty tableware. If you specialize in seafood you may need utensils to crack a crab claw or dig out lobster meat. These items would not normally be stocked in the quantities as needed for a restaurant featuring seafood (but may have handy a few of these and other specialty items listed below, stored in the wait station).

### Pizza/Italian:

- Pasta bowls
- Parmesan/crushed pepper shakers
- Pizza pans to serve pizza
- Pizza stands for tables

**Steak House:**

- Steak platters
- Sizzle platters with wood base
- Baked potato fixing caddies

**Hamburger/Sandwich Shop:**

- Ketchup/mustard squeeze bottles
- Burger/fry/onion ring baskets

**Mexican/Tex-Mex:**

- Tortilla warmers
- Large platters (as entree plates)
- Fajita sizzlers/wood base/potholder handle
- Tortilla chip/tostada baskets
- Salsa bowls

**Breakfast:**

- Syrup dispensers
- Jelly caddies
- Butter service

**Asian:**

- Soy/fish sauce dispensers
- Ramekins for dipping sauces
- Soup servers, aluminum (center chimney for chafing dish fuel heat source)
- Asian-style soup spoons
- Chopsticks
- Dim sum steamers
- Small oval platters
- Condiment containers with lid and spoon
- Large bowls for noodles, curries, family soups
- Notched rice bowls with lid

# Index

MUA (make-up air) systems, 65,
   110
mug freezers, 78
multitasking, 2
music, 128, 136

**N**
names, business, 14
National Sanitation Foundation,
   49
newspaper ads, 172

**O**
offices, 105–106
"off site" liquor permits, 9
"on call" employees, 145
openings, 167, 171
organization skills, 2
outlets and plugs, 99
ovens, 56, 58, 61–62
overtime, 141

**P**
package deals, 174
pantry staff, 154
paper goods, 121
parking, 11, 44, 114–115, 134–135
partnerships, 41–42, 42–43
payroll taxes, 144
perceived value, 19
pest control, 129
PFG, 52, 117
pizza ovens, 61–62
plumbing, 103, 107, 135
Point of Sale (POS) system, 44–45,
   135, 162, 183
policy manuals, 142, 143
pop-up restaurants, 42
pot racks, 82
Preferred Lender Programs (PLPs),
   40

Prep Master List, 29–31
pressure washing, 135
price per person averages (PPAs),
   18, 23
pricing, 10, 13, 18–21
profits, 184–189
proofers, 63–64
propane, 13, 51
purveyors, food, 17–18, 116–117, 187

**R**
radio ads, 172
ranges, 57–59
recipes, 24–27
refrigeration, 54, 55, 65–70, 99,
   107, 132
remodel construction
   architects and contractors,
      112–114
   as construction type, 11
   expense estimates, 35–36,
      37–38, 39
   inspections, 112
   menu plans affecting, 16–17
   preparation, 111–112
   signage, 115
   site plan and layout, 114–115
restaurantandbakeryconsultants.
   com, 8
restaurant businesses, overview
   closing, 189–190
   rewards of, 3
   self-evaluation for, 1–3
   success *versus* failure, 2, 4, 34,
      184–190
restaurant concept and plan
   alcoholic beverage services,
      9–10
   formulation of, 7–9
   location, 10–14
   logos, 14

name selection, 14
resources for, 8
service style, 5–6
types of restaurants, 6–7
worksheets for, 15
restaurant design
   BOH (back of house), 102–110
   FOH (front of house), 88–102
   levels, 104
   overview, 87
restaurantowner.com, 8
restrooms, 95–96, 106
retail sales, 186
reviews, 174

**S**
safety. *See* health and safety;
   security
salamanders, 56
Sam's Club, 118
sanitation
   ashtrays, 88
   bar cleanliness, 100
   dumpsters, 106–107, 114
   pest control services, 129
   restaurant design and, 106–107
   supplies for, 121–122
   waste receptacles, 96, 101
   waste removal, 106–107, 139
scales, 72
scheduling, 145, 167–169
Search Engine Optimization
   (SEO), 173–174
seating arrangements, 90–91
second restaurants, 185
security, 88, 89, 115, 137–138, 183
security guards, 137–138
self-evaluations, 1–4, 8–9
self-service, 6
septic systems, 13
server pickup stations, 101–102

# About the Authors

**Arthur L. Meyer** is a successful restaurant and bakery consultant who has cooked professionally since 1963 in New York, San Francisco, San Antonio, and Austin. He has taught cooking internationally, is considered an expert on world cuisines, and has achieved Master status in baking. He opened a specialty bakery in 1983, which became the subject and name of his first cookbook, *Texas Tortes*. He also is the author of *Baking Across America* and coauthored *Appetizer Atlas*, which won Best in the World from Gourmand Cookbook Awards in 2003. *Appetizer Atlas* has been his best seller and is a mainstay in many professional kitchens. Recently released are Art's fourth book, *Corsican Cuisine*, and his fifth cookbook, *Danish Cooking and Baking Traditions*. His sixth book, *The Houston Chef's Table*, was published with Globe Pequot Press in the fall of 2012. Art's consulting website is RestaurantAndBakeryConsultants.com.

Self-taught chef **Jon M. Vann** grew up working in restaurant and hotel kitchens during high school and college (Chariot Inn, Holiday Inn, McDonald's, Westwood Country Club). Selected as one of the two principals on the corporate restaurant opening team, Vann opened Pelican's Wharf restaurants in Texas (Temple, College Station, Port Aransas, Victoria, McAllen) between 1976 and 1977. In late 1977 Vann opened the Pelican's Wharf in San Antonio and was offered the management position, where he stayed for 5 years. In 1982 Vann moved back to Austin to open and manage Clarksville Cafe, where he won numerous awards. Since 1998 Vann has been a food writer for the *Austin Chronicle*. Vann is the co-author of *The Appetizer Atlas* and currently does freelance food writing while working with Art Meyer as an associate in his restaurant consulting firm. He is currently working on a culinary tourism guide to Thailand as well as a book on modern mixology.